AN ILLUSTRATED HISTORY OF
NEEDLEWORK TOOLS

AN ILLUSTRATED HISTORY OF
NEEDLEWORK TOOLS

GAY ANN ROGERS

JOHN MURRAY

For Sylvia Scott

© Gay Ann Rogers 1983

First published 1983
by John Murray (Publishers) Ltd
50 Albemarle Street, London W1X 4BD

All USA sales enquiries
and orders for this book to
Needlework Unlimited, PO Box 181
Claremont, California 91711

Printed in the United States of America by
The Book Press, Inc., Brattleboro, Vermont

British Library Cataloguing in Publication Data

Rogers, Gay Ann
  Needlework tools.
  1. Needlework
  I. Title
  746.4   TT712
  ISBN 0–7195–4021–6

Frontispiece: *Mother-of-pearl and ormolu workbox
in shape of shell holds Palais Royal mother-of-pearl
needlework tools shown here in front of closed box.
French, c. 1800. 15.5cm wide.*

Contents

List of Photographs

7

List of Photographs

Preface

The history of needlework implements is inescapably linked with the history of needlework itself but whereas the latter is well documented, there is little background information available on needlework tools. It is only in recent years that they have begun to attract the attention they deserve.

Probably the first person to concern herself seriously with needlework implements and their history was Madame P. W. Cocheris, a Frenchwoman, married to a noted Paris archivist, who in 1886 published a book entitled *Histoires sérieuses sur une pointe d'aiguille*. No doubt owing to her husband's influence, Madame Cocheris' work is strong on the Middle Ages but her classical allusions and somewhat romantic approach are hardly to the modern taste. Nor does she appear to have made much impression on her contemporaries because her book was soon forgotten and lost almost without trace.

The next writer to concern herself with needlework implements was Gertrude Whiting, an American, who was a Fellow of the Metropolitan Museum of New York and the founder of the Needle and Bobbin Club. In 1928 she published a book entitled *Tools and Toys of Stitchery* which was reprinted a few years ago and is relatively well known. Gertrude Whiting's interest was that of a collector who had many friends who were also collectors and, independently of the Cocheris book which was apparently unknown to her, she amassed a diversity of information of her own. This she used as the basis for her book and thereby pioneered a more general interest in needlework tools.

And lastly came Sylvia Groves, an English lady and a talented writer who in 1966 published *The History of Needlework Tools and Accessories*. Not only is this well written but it also reflects the author's taste for scholarly research. Oddly enough she too appears to have been unaware of the Cocheris book but she did have the advantage of consulting that of Gertrude Whiting and was able therefore to present a more objective and historically accurate account of the subject. However, since Sylvia Groves wrote her book, the collecting of needlework tools has become increasingly popular, we have a new breed of collectors with a more modern approach and it is in this context that Gay Ann Rogers' book is to be welcomed.

Gay Ann Rogers belongs to a younger generation which draws its inspiration from the same traditions but grew up in different circumstances and later surroundings. For her the classical attractions and elegance of the eighteenth century stand removed from the industrial growth and exuberance of the Victorian era and she concentrates on the nineteenth century and its aftermath which she treats objectively and in detail. It requires imagination to project oneself into the past and she manages the transition admirably. For instance in an age when horse-drawn transportation has virtually vanished, it is not immediately obvious that the development of the railway steam engine in the 1840s would come to affect even needlework tools, though this is precisely what happened. She explains that as a consequence the yearly migration of large numbers to holiday resorts led to an enormous growth in the demand for needlework tool souvenirs. She also helps to explode some widely cherished myths such as that of the novel and contemporary nature of the plastics industry. It is not always realized that the plastics industry has its roots in the 1860s and that by 1885 many needlework tools, including thimbles, were made of plastic-like material.

Inevitably Gay Ann Rogers' researches led her to England and to that mecca for all small antiques collecting, the Portobello Road market. There she was able to find a wide selection of needlework implements which could be handled, discussed or bought according to taste. She also met experienced dealers and collectors and being a professional needlewoman with a trained mind and good powers of observation, she acquired valuable information. The result is a book which will appeal to collectors of needlework tools because it is modern, up-to-date, and corresponds to their needs. More importantly, as they will find, it also marks a considerable advance in our knowledge of the subject.

Edwin F. Holmes
London, July 1982

Acknowledgements

I owe much to the kindness of the curators and staffs of those collections of needlework tools in museums on both sides of the Atlantic. They were patient and helpful in discussing their collections, allowing the use of their specialized libraries and in furnishing photocopies of articles and pictures otherwise inaccessible. Particular thanks go to Susan Swan, Curator of Textiles, Winterthur Museum, Delaware; Linda Baumgarten, Curator of Textiles, and Margaret Gill, Registrar, The Colonial Williamsburg Foundation, Virginia; Lina Steele, Index of American Design, National Gallery of Art, Washington, D.C.; Doris Bowman, Curator of Textiles, and Valentine Chilk, docent, Museum of American History, Washington, D.C. They spent much time taking me through the nooks, crannies and seemingly endless drawers holding the impressive collection of needlework tools of the Smithsonian Institution.

Although I never had the opportunity to meet the late Edward Pinto, I relied heavily on his research on wood needlework tools. I profited much from studying his great collection of 'wooden bygones' now in the Birmingham City Museum and Art Gallery. I also gained needed advice in identifying the odd tool without any markings from the helpful curatorial staff of the Victoria and Albert Museum.

The splendid collection of workboxes formed by Queen Mary, in the Bethnal Green Annex of the Victoria and Albert Museum, amply repaid repeated study as did the assorted needlework tools and accessories in the Costume Museum in Bath. The staffs at the London Museum and the Guildford Museum were very helpful in discussing their diverse collections of needlework tools. The curator of the Tunbridge Wells Museum explained precisely the process by which those distinctive wood needlework tools were manufactured.

Almost every person interested in needlework tools knows at least one dealer who has made a special contribution to his or her knowledge of the subject. I have been particularly fortunate in knowing my good friend, Sylvia Scott. She sold to me my first needlework box, invited me to accompany her on antique-hunting expeditions, taught me from her great knowledge of antiques, and most important, gave me an insight into English life, past and present, which I could never have gained on my own. Because I could not have acquired much of my knowledge about needlework tools without her help over the past decade, this book is dedicated to her.

I am also in debt to those friends, who allowed me to photograph their needlework tools for use in this book. In particular, I want to thank Estelle Horowitz, Kathleen Sweeney, Grace Blackburn and Patricia Caras for their co-operation and valued information which they freely shared with me.

Edwin F. Holmes, whose superb book on thimbles is known to every serious collector, did me a great service by writing the preface to this book for which I am most grateful. It was also important to me that he read the manuscript. I would never have had the courage to publish the chapter on thimbles if it had not undergone his careful scrutiny and profited by his specific criticisms and suggestions.

Sheila Smith, that excellent source for needlework tools in Bath, also kindly consented to read the entire manuscript and sent me detailed criticism and suggestions for which I am very grateful. Her knowledge not only of the tools but also of the social history of which they are a part is extensive, and the book gained much from her careful reading.

The photographs, with the exception of those by Kathleen Sweeney, are my own. I am indebted to Jerry Breault for his valuable suggestions regarding many of the photographs.

Finally, I want to express my debt for advice, criticism, and above all, patience, to my husband. His research for his own work on social and technological change in the nineteenth century led me to see the history of needlework tools in a perspective I would otherwise have lacked. Any errors of fact or interpretation which remain are mine alone, and I would welcome their correction.

Introduction

Previous writing on old needlework tools has focused primarily on the higher quality tools produced from the late seventeenth to the early nineteenth century. These were the needlework tools most valued and collected in the past. The great majority of women, however, had no access to these expensive tools. The more utilitarian needlework tools from that early period have usually survived only by accident as they were more often worn to breaking point, and discarded when beyond repair. When we study the larger number of needlework tools available from the nineteenth and early twentieth century, we acquire a more complex view of domestic life than is possible by analysing the smaller number of earlier tools.

There is a myth that European needlework tools before the middle of the nineteenth century were made largely by hand processes by individual craftsmen and were superior in quality to those tools made by machine later in the century. This is misleading as it misconstrues the concept of craftsmanship. David Pye has defined craftsmanship as 'workmanship using any kind of technique or apparatus, in which the quality of the result is not predetermined, but depends on the judgment, dexterity and care which the maker exercises as he works'.[1]

Pye's distinction is between workmanship of risk (craftsmanship) and workmanship of certainty (automation) rather than between manual and machine labour. Many production processes involved both types of workmanship. When John Lofting patented his 'engine or instrument for making thimbles for men, women and children' in England in 1693, he set up a process of production whereby he could turn out two million thimbles a year. The quality of the thimbles was largely predetermined by his 'engine or instrument' so that this was mostly a workmanship of certainty although the necessity to use some skills introduced a degree of the workmanship of risk.

By contrast, when the artisans of the Palais Royal area of Paris were making mother-of-pearl thimbles and other needlework tools more than a century later, they relied more on their skills in using tools and machines to control the quality of their fragile needlework implements. They practiced a workmanship of risk rather than of certainty although both elements were present.

There is no doubt that some needlework tools of the eighteenth century were unique in design and execution and were at the same high level of craftsmanship as other objects of vertu made of precious metals and stones. The vast majority of needlework tools from the late eighteenth century, and especially from the nineteenth century, even at the higher levels of quality, were not the product of individual craftsmanship but of manufacturing processes where the quality was often largely predetermined.

The use of machinery, standardization of parts and various techniques later associated with mass production made possible the manufacture of articles for both the luxury trade and wider markets at increasingly lower prices.[2] So well accepted were some of these attractive, machine-made products at all levels of society, that Matthew Boulton of Birmingham, for example, was able to insist that the aristocracy pay for crest-design dies if it wanted crests stamped on individually ordered items.[3]

To enlarge their sales, the Birmingham manufacturers began to issue pattern books in the 1760s which were the precursors of modern trade catalogues. The first pattern books containing needlework tools appeared towards the end of the eighteenth century. The widespread distribution of English pattern books in the United States suggests that many Americans continued to furnish their houses with English needlework tools and accessories well into the nineteenth century. When manufacturers in the United States began to make needlework tools in significant quantities after the 1830s, they often followed the designs of the English pattern books to which Americans had become accustomed.[4]

By the middle of the nineteenth century, the pattern books of the Birmingham manufacturers and others illustrate clearly how they were able to supply various needlework tools, assembled from several standardized parts, to different economic levels of society. For example, in one pattern book of the 1840s, the plainest netting vice sold for fourteen shillings a dozen wholesale; the fanciest, with ornamented surface and the addition of a pincushion, for fifty-four shillings a dozen. With the exception of these minor quantitative changes, the two clamps were identical in quality.[5]

The ability to make needlework tools more elaborate and much more expensive simply by adding standardized parts and ornamentation marked the triumph of the workmanship of certainty over that of risk, and the disappearance to a large degree of craftsmanship from the manufacture of needlework tools. The major exceptions (aside from those tools imported from the Far East and India) were those particular needlework tools which by their inherent properties or their specialized function were not easily amenable to automated production at that time. A good example are high quality scissors of the small, delicate embroidery type.

It was not machine production itself, however, which sometimes lowered the quality of needlework tools in the latter half of the nineteenth century. It was instead the temptation to undercut the competition by using the machines to produce inferior and cheaper standardized and interchangeable parts often in imitation of more expensive materials. These parts were then likely to be put together by simplified and cheaper methods. An example is the bent metal tabs used to assemble some brass needlecases in the 1870s which eliminated the expense of soldering the parts together and of hiding the soldering marks.

While there is a general decline in the quality of the highest level of needlework tools in the nineteenth century compared to their eighteenth-century counterparts, the quality of the middle level of needlework tools remained amazingly sound. Moreover, the quality and diversity of factory-produced needlework tools available to the majority of women in the nineteenth century were far better than the utilitarian tools available to the masses in the eighteenth century and earlier. Craftsmanship may have disappeared from the manufacture of most needlework tools during the nineteenth century, but that loss must be balanced against the gain to most women in the new accessibility of more diverse, cheaper and, sometimes, even better needlework tools.

At the beginning of the nineteenth century, the ability to sew and to dc needlework remained a central part of the training of almost every young girl regardless of her circumstances. By the beginning of the twentieth century, that intensive training continued in some Western societies, but in many, it was beginning to be the exception rather than the rule. The reasons usually given for this change of interest are the availability of cheap and well-made fabrics; the introduction and widespread distribution of sewing machines; the advent of cheap, ready-made household furnishings and clothing; and the increasing participation of women in work or careers made possible by the modernization of Western society.

Although modernization and the industrial revolution may explain why needlework was no longer at the centre of most women's lives in the twentieth century, it does not explain why needlework continues to be enormously popular to the present time. Susan Swan, in her book on American women and their needlework in the eighteenth and early nineteenth century, suggests that needlework was a relief from the tedium or pressures of household activities for nearly all women of that period. Moreover, for many it was also their most important contribution to the decorative arts, the most acceptable outlet for creative expression, and often the only concrete evidence of their craftsmanship.[6]

By the twentieth century, needlework was no longer either the only important nor the only acceptable outlet for creative expression for most women. Nonetheless, it was still for many women a welcome respite from their work, whatever that might be, as well as a contribution to their own domestic decorative arts. It was also for some an important means of communicating and sharing with other women an enjoyable experience.

Finally, needlework remained for many women concrete evidence of their craftsmanship just as it had in earlier centuries. When various kinds of needlework by hand were rendered commercially obsolete by automated versions, as happened to netting in the 1840s, some women still continued to do them. The workmanship of certainty provided by automation did not satisfy their need to do creative work where the quality is not predetermined but instead depends on their skills. It is this basic and creative need for craftsmanship that continues to interest women in needlework, and consequently, in needlework tools of the past and present.

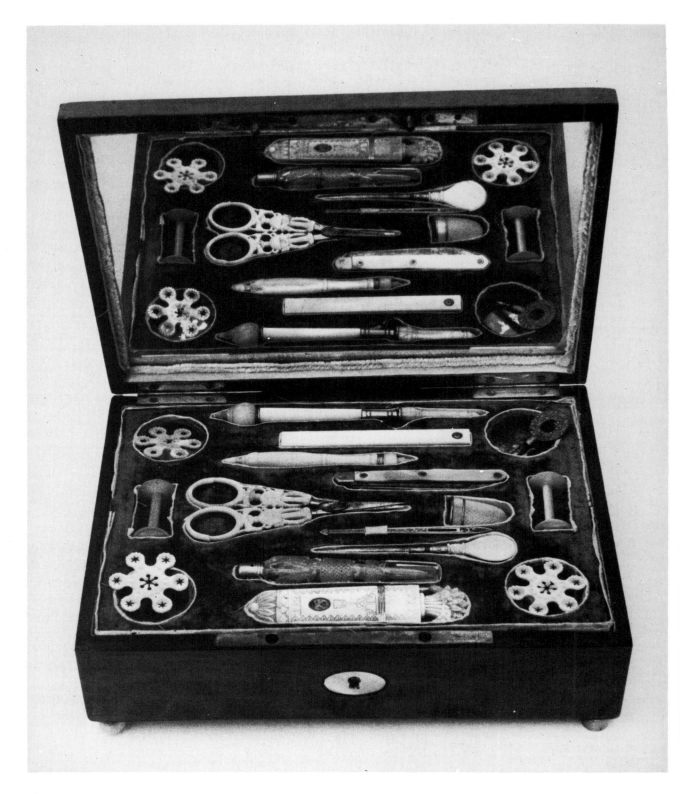

18

1 Fitted Needlework Boxes

In the history of needlework tools, the fitted needlework box occupies a special place. Unlike other needlework tool containers, such as the *étui* and *chatelaine*, which have been in use for several centuries, the fitted needlework box came into favour towards the end of the eighteenth century and disappeared from general use about a century later.

The fitted needlework box, although referred to as a workbox, is, in fact, a specialized version of the general workbox. Numerous museums on both sides of the Atlantic have examples of caskets and workboxes used for sewing and needlework in the seventeenth and eighteenth centuries. Some of these early workboxes had interior compartments for individual tools and pincushions. But none had, until the late eighteenth century, the detailed and fitted interiors designed expressly for a variety of needlework tools and supplies.

The fitted needlework box became more than a mere container for needlework implements. Under the influence of French and English furniture styles of the late eighteenth and early nineteenth centuries, this box became a fine piece of small furniture to which the most able cabinetmakers in Europe and Asia did not hesitate to apply their skills. Artisans working in precious metals, as well as ivory, bone, mother-of-pearl, tortoise shell and other exotic materials, fashioned matching sets of needlework tools for these valuable miniature chests. The workboxes illustrated on the following pages suggest the care with which these unusual containers were made.

The fitted needlework box was not a gift to be given or accepted lightly. Jane Austen in *Mansfield Park* describes Fanny surveying the presents she has received from her cousins: 'The table between the windows was covered with work-boxes and netting-boxes which had been given her at different times, principally by Tom; and she grew bewildered as to the amount of the debt which all these kind remembrances produced.'

The fitted needlework box was carefully made and exquisitely decorated because it was an integral part of the social life of privileged women in the North Atlantic countries during the first half of the nineteenth century. By the latter part of the century, less elaborate workboxes were accessible to most women. By the beginning of the twentieth century, giant American stores like Montgomery Ward and Co. sold mass-produced and fitted needlework boxes of celluloid for fifty cents to three dollars.

In the first half of the nineteenth century, women often carried their elegantly fitted needlework boxes on visits to one another. The boxes furnished an endless source of conversation and amusement for those in need of something delightful to occupy their time. Implements would be admired as needlework and conversation went on together.

Plate 1: *Palais Royal satinwood workbox, tray lined with purple velvet holding mother-of-pearl needlework tools. Beneath tray is music box. French, c. 1800–1825. 21.5 cm. wide.*

For longer trips by coach or ship, there were special needlework boxes covered with leather. Large brass feet kept such boxes well removed from any soiled surface while large brass handles made the box easy to carry. At home, many women had, in addition to work tables, larger and more elaborate multi-purpose boxes which might include, in addition to a fitted needlework tray in the top, a jewellery drawer and a lap writing desk.

Such compendiums were not uncommon. The accomplished woman of the time was expected to be as proficient in calligraphy as in needlework, and the implements she used for both reflected, as did her jewellery, her station in life. It was not unusual to find in a fancy workbox, writing utensils and needlework tools of precious metals, appropriate for those evenings when women occupied themselves at social gatherings with needlework.

To understand the extraordinary popularity of needlework and of the fitted needlework box, it is necessary to understand the profound transformation of European life which took place at the end of the eighteenth and the beginning of the nineteenth century. Rapid political, industrial and social change brought to the forefront a new and affluent middle class eager to use its wealth to imitate the way of life of the older patrician and gentry families.

Servants were relatively cheap and even a moderate income allowed for several. This furnished abundant time for the women of the house to study genteel pursuits such as music, drawing and needlework. Governesses educated young girls at home and taught them the same polite accomplishments that their mothers had learned. When these girls married, they could decorate their clothes and houses with needlework, and thus pass their time in an acceptable manner.

More mundane tasks such as mending were often left to servants as was some of the plain sewing. All essential household sewing, including the making of underclothes, bedclothes, towels, linens and the like, was considered plain sewing. The women of the house might do plain sewing before receiving visitors during the day. Fancy sewing or needlework, which was decorative work, was often done while receiving or paying calls. It had become an accepted practice for women to take their fancy needlework into their own drawing rooms when entertaining guests as well as to private and public social gatherings.[1]

The amount of fancy needlework done in the nineteenth century was incredible. By the second half of the century, the Victorian manuals of embroidery were offering ingenious advice on how to decorate with needlework almost any domestic item of household or personal use. When their own households were satiated with fancy needlework, women could always do fancy work for the charity bazaars which were so popular in the nineteenth century.[2]

All this needlework pursued so avidly by the new middle-class women seeking to fill idle hours at home in some respectable activity sometimes resulted in a monomaniacal cult of the needle. It drove some husbands to seek refuge elsewhere, which *Punch* satirized in 'The Law of Crochet' (1852):

'Parliament has at length been compelled to give its over-tardy attention to the question deeply affecting the domestic happiness of her majesty's subjects. We allude to the Crochet question. The miseries arising from the unsettled state of the law upon this subject have resulted in an agitation which has made itself constitutionally heard. Meetings have been held in all the smoking clubs . . . and in the various places of refuge to which sufferers have been driven by Crochet persecution . . .'[3]

To carry the needlework tools and supplies from room to room, to the garden, to visit friends, and to attend public assemblies, an elegant and practical container was needed. Some women used small pouches or bags, others used an étui or small sewing case. But the most admired and convenient container was the fitted needlework box.

Because these boxes were highly valued by their owners, and because the needlework tools, with the exception of court presentation or jewelled pieces, were also objects of everyday utility, the tools usually broke or were lost before the box itself disappeared. The boxes were rarely refitted with a matching set of new needlework tools. The refitting was done, as would be natural, piece by piece as each implement was lost or broken beyond repair.

This meant that the owner in 1880 of a box originally made in 1830 might find, if she studied the contents very carefully, that many of the implements did not match the style of the box or each other. Since such an owner might have watched her mother, and possibly her grandmother, working out of the same fitted and partially refitted workboxes, she would probably not have been aware of the gradual change in implements. The visitor to the Costume Museum at Bath, or to the collection of workboxes formed by Queen Mary at the Bethnal Green Annex of the Victoria and Albert Museum, will notice that the boxes exhibiting signs of wear have only a few matching tools.

The collector of fitted needlework boxes will find that the majority of surviving boxes have no helpful markings, and neither do most of their implements. To a large extent, the collector must rely on a comparative analysis of style to establish approximate dates of manufacture.

Occasionally a box may have a recorded date of design or purchase mentioned in other documents if it comes from an historically prominent family, and this helps date similar boxes. Other boxes may carry the mark of the reigning monarch on the lever lockplate. The English patent for the lever lock was issued in 1784 before the fitted needlework box became common. Since nearly all fitted needlework boxes have the lever lock, the lock itself is of little help in dating a box if it is not engraved with a date or mark.[4]

Sometimes the letter of presentation is preserved in the storage envelope so often found under the lid of a box. It is necessary, however, to be careful about presentation dates. These boxes were considered suitable gifts to celebrate the engagement of a young woman, or some important event in her life. The purpose of the gift was to help her prepare her trousseau and household furnishings. How close the date of presentation was to the date of manufacture is sometimes a matter of conjecture. The engraving of the nameplate on the top of the box normally took place, if at all, upon the first presentation. It is not unknown, however, for boxes to be engraved with a date marking the passage of a mother's box to her daughter or even to her grandaughter. That is why some dates of presentation seem to be much later than the date of manufacture.

Boxes of similar style which have hallmarked implements, such as silver tea containers in tea caddies or silver cosmetic aids in cosmetic cases, can be identified by their hallmarks as to the year and place where the silver was assayed. Both tea caddies and cosmetic cases are often similar in exterior appearance to fitted needlework boxes and are an excellent guide to the establishment of a comparative chronology of style.

A careful examination of the workbox also offers a guide to its period of manufacture. The quality and type of wood or other material used, the pattern of inlay work, the shape of handles and feet, or their absence, all offer clues as to the origin of a given box. In addition, the arrangement of the interior compartments of a box, the types of built-in needlework tools, the absence or presence of paper or cloth to cover the tray are all indications of its age and country of manufacture.

Most fitted needlework boxes available to the collector today are one of three basic types: French, Far Eastern and Indian, or English. Workboxes for sewing and needlework were obviously made in many other parts of the world, but few of them were fitted needlework boxes of the type discussed here. Moreover, the large number of surviving English and French boxes, as well as Far Eastern boxes fitted for the European trade, suggest that northwest Europe was the chief user and often exporter of the fitted needlework box to the rest of the world.

The Japanese, for example, had an indigenous sewing box in the nineteenth century which was similar in size and shape to their writing, counting and vanity boxes. They were often made of mulberry wood with a delicate bamboo design on the wood, and with elegant metal handles or pulls for the three to five drawers which made up these boxes.

The Japanese called this sewing box, *haribako*, literally needlebox. The drawers held various sewing implements and supplies, and sometimes they also held secret savings which came to be known as haribako gin or sewing box gold. Sometimes these boxes had a *kukedai* or workholder mounted on one side of the box which held one or more drawers, and a pincushion to which the needlework could be attached to hold it tight while working on it from the other end. It was not, however, this indigenous type of sewing box which was exported to Europe, but the traditional Japanese lacquer ware box fitted with a European style interior tray and matching needlework implements.

There were, of course, other types of sewing and needlework tool containers which developed in various parts of the world including Europe. Pedlar's dolls, for example, were another form of work table companion and stood about eight inches tall. They were mounted on a stand and their costume was designed to hold sewing and needlework tools, pins, needles and threads. Various home-made folding fabric as well as wood containers were made everywhere, and were particularly popular in North America. There, most of the fancy fitted needlework boxes were imported and expensive, and as a result, were largely owned by the privileged. The many Victorian embroidery manuals were very ingenious on the making of sewing containers in various shapes and sizes out of scraps of old cloth and other cheaply available material.[5]

The design of the nineteenth-century fully fitted needlework box had several sources. English wood caskets, similar to the compendium (plate 11), from the seventeenth and eighteenth centuries were fitted with general compartments for needlework and writing implements and for jewellery. Large French workboxes, some made of ivory at Dieppe, were in use at the French court in the eighteenth century. These usually had open compartments for needlework tools and other implements.

What was novel about the nineteenth-century fitted needlework box was that it was designed specifically for needlework implements, and many of its compartments or recessed openings held only certain types of tools. This specialization may also have owed something to the design of the étui and *nécessaire* which were fashionable in the eighteenth century as very small fitted containers for needlework tools and other implements.

The new type of French fully fitted needlework box appeared about 1790. It was larger than the étui but smaller than the earlier workboxes. Like the étui, but unlike the workbox, it had no all-purpose compartments in the tray. Instead, every tool was displayed in a recessed opening in the velvet tray. This made it nearly impossible to replace the tools unless they were made to order. That approach to the crafting of needlework tools was expensive, and it is not surprising that French boxes of this period usually had tools of gold, silver or mother-of-pearl banded in gold or gilt metal.

The most recognizable of these early French boxes are the so-called Palais Royal sets. The name may have come from the shops clustered around the Palais Royal in Paris where these fitted boxes were supposedly made or sold. In these sets, the scissors, thimble or needlecase may be marked with an enamelled pansy, or with a silver or copper diamond or shield design. Surviving sets of these tools, if carved from mother-of-pearl, are relatively rare because of their fragility.

A typical Palais Royal box (plate 1) is about twenty-one and a half centimetres wide, fifteen centimetres deep and eight centimetres high. The box is of veneered satinwood inlaid with mother-of-pearl set in ebony stringers with an abstract floral design at each corner of the top. The escutcheon and small bun feet are also of mother-of-pearl. All fifteen tools are fitted into lined compartments of the purple velvet tray which is reflected in the Venetian mirror of the lid. The elaborately carved scissors and needlecase reflect the preoccupation of Directoire and Empire craftsmen with variations on classical motifs. Beneath the tray is a music box which plays two tunes. The handle of the key which winds the music box is in the shape of the laurel wreath of

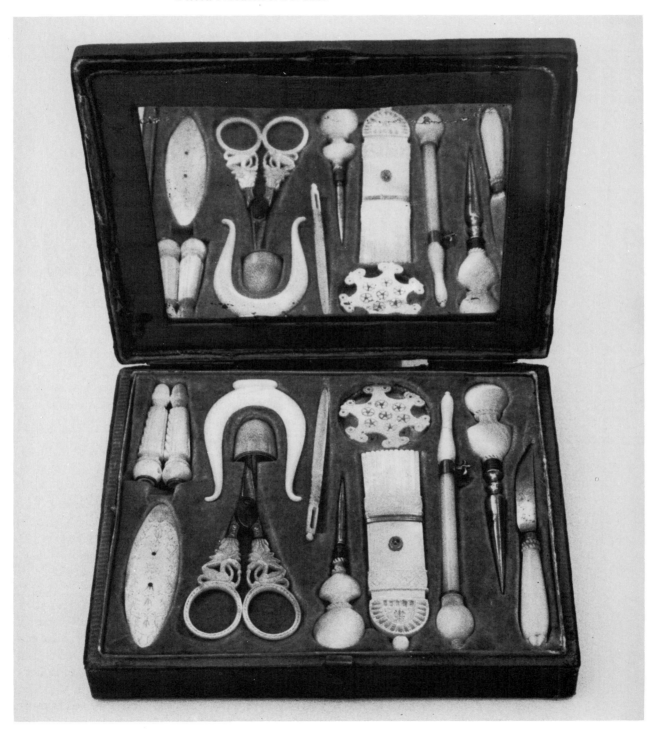

Plate 2: *Red morocco leather sewing box, lined with grey velvet, holds mother-of-pearl needlework tools. French. Tools, c. 1800–1825. Box, c. 1850. 16 cm. wide.*

victory with which Napoleon surrounded his monogram.

Not all tools of this period necessarily came in similar boxes. Plate 2 shows a box made about the middle of the nineteenth century to accommodate an owner's varied collection of tools from the early nineteenth century. The red morocco leather box with its fitted gray velvet tray makes a very smart, flat and practical travelling needlework box to protect one owner's valued collection of mother-of-pearl implements.

The other type of French fitted needlework box of this early period is more rare, and is sometimes in the shape of a spinet (plate 3). This spinet is of faded mahogany inlaid with satinwood stringers and edging. It stands on five turned ebony legs. The keyboard section is of inlaid strips of white and stained ivory. In some examples, the keyboard is inside the spinet rather than outside as here. The top of the spinet opens to reveal a tray of purple velvet with two built-in cushions embroidered with silver spangles. Four of the needlework implements are of French silver, elaborately embossed in the fashion of the time. Beneath the tray is a music box which plays two tunes.

These spinets can also be found with gold or mother-of-pearl tools. The cases are usually of wood although a few are covered entirely with mother-of-pearl. Some are decorated with ormolu fittings. Whatever the type, the spinet is attractive to collectors and commands a correspondingly high price.

These early French boxes have a number of characteristic details in common. The trays are covered with velvet and the colour of the velvet is picked up in the chenille which outlines the mirror on the lid and the flat silk pad placed between the top of the tray and the mirror. The recessed openings for the tools are lined with paper. Where they hold round silkwinders, the bottom of the recessed opening is lined with a mirror. The tools fit so snugly into these lined compartments that they usually appear too large rather than too small for the openings.

It is no problem to recognize these distinctive and elegant French boxes. The problem is usually missing or mismatched tools, missing silk pads, and replaced chenille around the mirror. The most serious of these is the mismatching of tools. Matching tools will have similar motifs on the body of the tool as well as on any banding used where parts join. The tools will be of the same material with the exception that the silkwinders and reels are often of mother-of-pearl. If the storage area was meant to have a music box, there will be telltale holes drilled through the bottom by which the music box was attached. The music box of this period had a revolving cylinder, on which spikes struck the teeth of a comb to produce one or more tunes.

Although the fitted needlework box is a European invention, Far Eastern craftsmen had long exported to Europe fine boxes of superb workmanship and exquisite design. It was natural for Europeans to turn to these Far Eastern craftsmen with patterns for the interior fittings of the workbox. Not only were the fitted boxes well made in the Orient, but the materials used were often exotic, such as lacquerware, sandalwood, ivory, horn, ebony and others.

Fitted needlework boxes of lacquerware were among those most in demand in Europe in the late eighteenth and nineteenth centuries. Lacquerware had been known in Europe at least since the seventeenth century, and had been much prized because of its lightness, delicate design and durability. It resisted heat, water and alcohol equally successfully. The durable properties of lacquer derived from its base of urushi acid found in the sap of the sumac tree (*Rhus vernicifera*) indigenous to the Orient.

The interior of the fitted needlework lacquer box, whether it dated from 1790 or 1850, was very similar. The interior tray was usually, but not always, of lacquerware, sometimes trimmed with ivory or bone. Although Far Eastern craftsmen made precisely engineered boxes, they did not necessarily

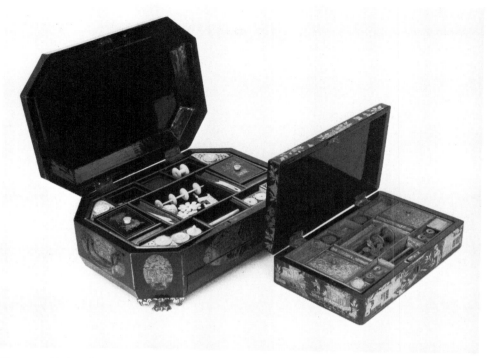

Plate 4: *Left: Octagonal black lacquer workbox, lacquer tray holding carved bone needlework tools, c. 1840. 33 cm. wide. Right: Rectangular black lacquer workbox, sandalwood tray holding carved sandalwood needlework tools, c. 1800–1820. Both Chinese exportware.*

understand the function of the European fitted tray and matching needlework tools they were asked to copy. As a result, the tools are sometimes not functional.

The small Georgian-style lacquer box on the right of plate 4 with its characteristic proportions dates from about the end of the eighteenth century and reflects the careful work that distinguished the early lacquerware. The box is lightweight, finely proportioned, and the heavy painting covers all surfaces as was customary with the finer boxes.

The interior tray appears to have been added to the box after it was constructed as it is made entirely of sandalwood with no relation to the exterior at all except for some matching carved motifs. This was not uncommon in the early Asian fitted needlework boxes. Europeans would order a copy of a particular interior tray and matching implements that would fit into an Asian box they already owned or intended to buy.

The larger lacquer box in the same plate on the left with its shaped top, carved and gold-leafed feet, and its elegant handles and octagonal form, reflects the whimsy of the late Regency period. This style was manufactured readymade for the European market with interior compartments of lacquer and matching implements of carved ivory or bone. Many of these boxes had,

Plate 5: *Horn workbox, sandalwood and horn tray holding horn needlework tools. Indian, c. 1830. 37 cm. wide.*

as does this example, a drawer at the bottom with a folding writing desk.

The green horn box in plate 5 can possibly be dated about 1830 because a similar box, made in ivory, has been documented as of Indian origin about the same time.[6] The reason that the dating is only tentative is that craftsmen in the East tended to repeat the same box design decade after decade. The horn box is unusual because of its large size (thirty-seven centimetres wide) and because of its construction. Each side of the box is covered with carefully matched pieces of tusk laid vertically on the wood carcass. The pagoda-style lid is constructed of matching individual tusks tapering to a central finial.

The interior reveals a sandalwood tray trimmed with matching horn. The underside of the lid opens to a small space for patterns and letters. The compartment lids are made of carved horn in the design of the exterior pagoda-style top. Two red velvet pincushions and a set of matching horn tools complete this unusual box.

The large Indian box of carved wood with the two-tiered pagoda-style top in plate 6 appears to be about the same age as the horn box from the arrangement of the interior tray. The wood carving is in a traditional animal and floral pattern found in many Indian pattern books. The sides and top of the box are outlined in marquetry set in narrow ivory stringers. The marquetry is applied in small rectangular sections to the box to form a continuous band. These sections were cut in thin slices from the end of a rectangular rod made of long thin strips of ivory, ebony and silver glued together to form a geometric pattern. This technique of 'prefabricated mosaic' predates the very similar 'end-grain mosaic' used later to decorate Tunbridgeware in England.[7]

The interior tray has six compartments with lids of carved wood, each outlined in the same marquetry and set in ivory stringers. It also has four fitted cotton barrels of ivory, also with inlaid marquetry tops, and a tape-measure fitted and inlaid the same way. What is fascinating and significant is that not one of the highly decorated needlework implements in this box is functional as each lacks the necessary hole or slot to allow the thread or tape to emerge.

Many Asian boxes had built-in cotton barrels and multiple winders used to

Plate 6: *Carved wood and mosaic marquetry workbox, carved tray holding mosaic marquetry and ivory needlework tools. Indian, c. 1830. 32.5 cm. wide.*

wind thread. This might suggest that these boxes date well before the middle of the nineteenth century. The cotton spool had been commercially manufactured by the second quarter of the nineteenth century and it made these barrels and winders seemingly obsolete. They continued, however, to appear in many needlework boxes long after the introduction of the modern cotton spool.[8]

The early nineteenth-century English workboxes reflected some aspects of the late Georgian and Regency style of furniture. Regency boxes often had modified pagoda-style tops and shaped boxes with elaborate handles and feet. The Regency style reflected a mixture of tradition and innovation. It carried on the tradition of well proportioned work of the Georgians but it carried much further the Georgian vogue for chinoiserie. Indeed, the latter became a passion of the Regency period and has left its monument in the Indian-Chinese architecture and furnishings of the Royal Pavilion at Brighton. The Regency style also reflected the influence of the French Empire style.

A discussion of Regency style is vital to an understanding of the enduring design of the English fitted needlework box. These boxes had to remain portable and practical regardless of their exquisite workmanship. This functional aspect meant that their basic architectural design largely escaped the Victorian obsession with reproducing past historical styles. By comparison with the design of larger pieces of Victorian furniture, which changed drastically over the course of the nineteenth century, the basic design of the English fitted needlework box remained amazingly stable, having only one major change about mid-century.

Two boxes, one from the Regency period, the other from the very end of the Victorian in plate 7 illustrate this continuity and change in design. Both are veneered in rosewood and are approximately the same size. Both have mahogany trays with carefully mitred compartments for diverse needlework tools and supplies. Beneath each tray is a storage space for sewing and needlework.

The major change in form becomes more apparent if the lids of the two boxes are closed. The Regency box has a modified pagoda-shaped top and the sides of the box have a slope to them. With its handles and feet, it resembles the closed late Regency box in plate 9. The late Victorian box, by contrast, has a flat top, the sides of the box are straight, and it has neither handles nor feet. This change from the shaped body of the Regency-style workbox to the straight-sided Victorian box took place in the 1840s. There are few exceptions to this change except for boxes not of wood which lent themselves to moulding.

Two early English needlework boxes in plate 8 show the influence of late eighteenth-century design. The black leather box on the left has a modified pagoda top. It may also have been used as a travelling case because of its oversize brass handles and feet. The abundant chased brass work is unusually handsome in detail on the escutcheon, the medallion on top, and the brass fittings at each corner.

Plate 7: *Left: Rosewood workbox with ebony and brass trim, mahogany tray with red morocco leather compartments. Leather storage envelope inside lid. English, c. 1800. 27 cm. wide. Right: Rosewood workbox trimmed with ebonized wood, silver and abalone shell, mahogany tray and interior pink silk lid to hold implements. English, 1891.*

Plate 8: *Left: Black leather workbox with brass trim, tray lined with yellow paper and silk. English, c. 1800. 20 cm. wide. Right: Gold-tooled red leather workbox with brass trim, tray lined with aquamarine paper and gold-tooled green leather. English, c. 1810.*

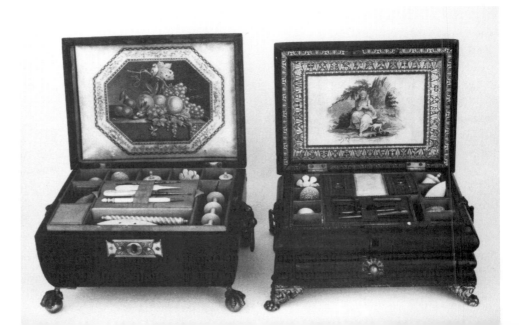

The interior has a wood tray covered in plain yellow paper matched by a small built-in yellow silk pincushion and a compartment with a silk lid on top of which rest scissors and other tools. There is also a built-in multiple thread winder of ivory. In this period the tray and the implements may not always have been designed together. Beneath the tray is a storage space and above it on the interior of the lid is an engraved still life printed on silk.

On the right, the red box repeats in gold-tooled morocco leather the elaborate shape of the pagoda top of the Indian horn box. Beneath the key hole is a brass knob for a lower drawer lined with acquamarine paper. The interior tray, covered with the same paper, has three leather lids over compartments. A matching gold-tooled green leather frame surrounds a silk transfer painting of a pastoral scene in the interior of the lid. What is new in this tray is a compartment fitted with a recessed holder for a thimble to lie on its side. This was the practice in French boxes around 1820 but it is less common in the English box of this period.

This style of red morocco leather workbox appears to have been fashionable. There is a nearly identical one which belonged to Lady Blessington (1789–1849). She became the hostess of Gore House where she entertained such notables as Bulwer Lytton, Disraeli, Thackeray, Dickens and the Duke of Wellington.[9]

The 1830s and 1840s saw the development of the English fitted needlework box into its most luxurious form with elaborately carved and matching needlework tools. While retaining the careful craftsmanship of the earlier period, the makers of these boxes experimented with exotic materials and luxurious interiors which, with a few exceptions, are not to be found in the generally smaller boxes of the second half of the nineteenth century.

A good example of the boxes of this period is the large tortoise-shell box trimmed with ivory in plate 9. Unlike the tortoise shell worked in Asia where it was often carved, engraved or incised in some manner, here the light and unadorned tortoise shell has been applied to each side in two matching sheets and to the top in six matching and curved sheets. The bracket feet, reminiscent of Regency furniture feet, are also covered in tortoise shell and trimmed with ivory. European craftsmen had long before learned how to soften tortoise shell by moisture and heat and to mould it under pressure into the desired shape and pattern.

The interior tray is covered with light blue paper with matching silk on five of the compartments, the two pincushions, two needlebooks and the interior of the lid. Seven open compartments hold matching carved mother-of-pearl reels. Each has a separable top and bottom to fit over the commercially-produced spool of thread. These reels now begin to displace the built-in multiple thread winder and cotton barrel as a means of storing thread in workboxes. Behind the reel compartments are three holes for tape-measure, emery and waxer.

In the 1840s, the lavish interiors characteristic of the earlier Regency period continue to brighten the interior of the workboxes, but the boxes

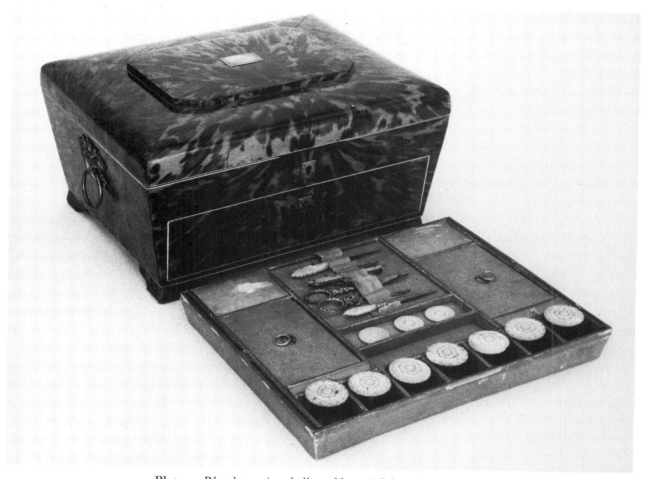

Plate 9: *Blond tortoise-shell workbox with brass handles, tray lined with blue paper and moiré silk holding mother-of-pearl and silver needlework tools. English, c. 1840. 30 cm. wide.*

themselves now begin to be flat-topped and straight-sided. Sometimes they are of exotic woods, but the detailing is sparse and the boxes rarely have feet or handles.

Another luxuriously-fitted rosewood box of the 1840s is on the left in plate 10. The exterior has two simple rectangular inlays of mother-of-pearl for the escutcheon and the medallion on top as well as mother-of-pearl for the stringers. The interior tray is covered with silver paper as is the storage area below. All the compartment lids as well as the recessed holders for thimble and fingerguard, again in the French style on their sides, are covered with green silk which matches the puckered silk in the interior of the lid framed in green gold-tooled leather.

This box has two unusual features. The six carved mother-of-pearl reels are stored in a single compartment on the upper right rather than in the usual

Plate 10: *Left: Rosewood workbox with mother-of-pearl trim, tray lined with silver paper and gold-tooled green leather holding mother-of-pearl needlework tools. English, c. 1840. 34.5 cm. wide. Right: Coromandel workbox with mother-of-pearl trim, tray lined with rose silk and velvet holding mother-of-pearl needlework tools. English, c. 1850.*

manner. Behind the usual storage envelope in the lid is a mirror framed in gold-tooled leather with compartments of silver paper on each side to hold various stationery and sewing supplies.

An example of restrained sumptuousness of about 1850 is the coromandel box on the right in plate 10. Aside from an inlay of mother-of-pearl for the medallion, escutcheon and stringers, the pattern of the coromandel wood is its major decoration. The entire inside of the box is lined with rose silk. None of the mother-of-pearl tools has incised carving. Near the front of the box are two recessed openings to display thimble and fingerguard on their sides. The London dealer, W. Leuchars, 38 Piccadilly, signed his name to this box.

It is rare to find an English needlework box that is signed because such boxes were the result of several craftsmen: cabinetmaker, upholsterer, cutler, carver, locksmith, inlayer and others. It was usually the London retailer, selling the more intricate workboxes, who signed his name to the box.

A different type of box from this period is the rosewood compendium which is an abridged or miniature bureau of drawers (plate 11). With the two doors of the compendium open, three drawers with mother-of-pearl inlay and handles are visible. The first drawer with matching paper is for needlework. The second has two tiers of compartments to hold jewellery. The third has a small writing desk with compartments for pens, knives, an ink well and sand container. This compendium is large and heavy, and while it is in a technical sense portable, it is not a convenient travelling companion.

Plate 11: Rosewood compendium inlaid with mother-of-pearl, tray and three drawers lined with paper and rose silk for holding mother-of-pearl needlework tools, needlework, jewellery and writing materials. English, c. 1840. 31 cm. wide.

On the top and front of the compendium are abstract floral patterns inlaid in mother-of-pearl. Because of its size, the compendium has both handles and bun feet, but they are of rosewood rather than of brass which was so characteristic of the earlier Regency period. Flowered paper covers the interior tray and all the compartments. Rose silk covers the built-in pincushions, needlebooks and all compartment lids. The interior of the lid has a mirror framed in

Plate 12: *Rosewood and satinwood marquetry workbox, tray lined with rose paper and silk holding mother-of-pearl needlework tools. English, c. 1850. 30 cm. wide.*

polychrome gold-tooled leather, and behind it, a storage space for patterns and letters covered in flowered paper to match the tray.

In shape, this compendium is similar to the large English caskets of the seventeenth century. The Irwin Untermyer Collection had a seventeenth-century walnut cabinet in beadwork with four drawers which, with the exception of the lack of an interior tray, is similar in size and shape.[10]

The Victorian workbox at mid-century was generally less ornate on the interior and more decorative on the exterior than its predecessors. The interior arrangement of the tray was now standardized with matching reels clustered three or four on each side or all in a row in the back of the tray. The built-in cotton barrels and multiple winders have largely disappeared although narrow slots to store thread winders remain in some boxes.

The workbox in plate 12 is a good example of the fitted Victorian needlework box at mid-century. The rosewood veneer has an elaborate border of light wood marquetry on the top and front of the box as well as around the escutcheon and the centre medallion on top. The interior is lined with a deep rose paper and matching silk for compartment lids and recessed openings. Eight matching and elaborately carved mother-of-pearl reels suggest the Victorian sensibility which now becomes predominant in the surface decoration of both the needlework boxes and their implements.

Looking at the elaborate marquetry on this workbox, it would be tempting to ascribe its relatively cheap price at mid-century to the introduction of the power-driven jig or scroll saw. It is generally assumed that the excessive ornamentation of the Victorian period would have been impossible without the introduction of power-driven machinery which made mass production possible. In fact, the economic reality was more complex. Some companies were able to afford power-driven machinery even by the end of the eighteenth century, but they were in a very small minority, and this change had little, if any, effect on the design of their manufactured goods. For most cabinetmakers working alone or with a few employees, the high cost of power machinery prevented them from utilizing it for most of the nineteenth century.[11]

The first major break with the dominance of the wood carcass workbox, which had been the most fashionable material for workboxes since the Regency, came near the middle of the nineteenth century with the renewed popularity of papier-mâché. The Victorians constantly searched for new and more efficient ways to use materials and styles of the past. Papier-mâché was previously known in England as japanware because it was an attempt to imitate Japanese lacquerware which was considered superior to all other Asian lacquerware. The English 'japan' was a varnish made in a variety of ways and coloured black. It dried to a hard and brittle surface, and could be used for wood-graining and ebonizing other woods as well as for coating papier-mâché.[12]

Although papier-mâché was an Asian invention, it lent itself to large-scale production through two major English improvements. The first was by Henry Clay of Birmingham, who in 1772 took out a patent for his papier-mâché panels which were suitable for japanning and could be treated like wood without danger of warping. Clay's invention was to paste together a number of sheets, each covered on both sides with paste, soak them in linseed oil to make them waterproof, and then to dry them at a temperature of 100 degrees Fahrenheit. The second improvement was by the firm of Aaron Jennens and John Bettridge (the ultimate successors to Clay's firm) which took out a patent in 1825 to ornament papier-mâché with pearl shell, and another in 1847 to apply steam to soften papier-mâché so that it could be pressed or moulded by machines into any form desired.[13]

The firm of Jennens & Bettridge (1816–64), which had become Japanners in Ordinary to George IV, was the best known of the Birmingham japanneries because of the high quality of its products. The company exported its wares to North America and even had its own showroom on Pearl Street in New York City. Jennens & Bettridge trained its artists professionally to paint the thousands of patterns at its disposal on the various items of furniture, trays, boxes, screens, and other domestic articles which it manufactured. Although the artists did not sign their paintings, Jennens & Bettridge usually signed the firm name to its products.

Jennens & Bettridge fitted workboxes came fully equipped with needlework implements in ivory or mother-of-pearl set in velvet linings and patterned papers. Often the small silver locks were stamped with the royal patent, a crown and the initials V.R. as in the workbox in plate 13. That box is in design similar to an earlier Hepplewhite tea caddy although treated with flamboyance in its Victorian curves. The entire papier-mâché surface is covered with floral motifs of inlaid and tinted mother-of-pearl combined with gilt and other painting. Painters did not hesitate to tint the shells with translucent paints, or even to cover them with opaque colours to achieve their overall design.

Mother-of-pearl was not only popular as an inlay for the exterior of workboxes of other materials. Many boxes were entirely covered with it. The popularity of mother-of-pearl reached its peak in the middle of the nineteenth

Plate 13: *Papier-mâché workbox, tray lined with gold-patterned paper and purple velvet holding mother-of-pearl and silver needlework tools. English, c. 1850. 29 cm. wide.*

Plate 14: *Left: Mother-of-pearl workbox with abalone decoration, tray lined with silver paper and blue silk holding mother-of-pearl needlework tools. English, c. 1860. 25 cm. wide. Right: Mother-of-pearl workbox, tray lined with green silk and velvet holding wood, steel and mother-of-pearl tools. English, 1854.*

century although needlework tools were carved of it well into the twentieth century.

The thin veneer of nacre cut from the pearl oyster and abalone also made a shimmering cover for the workboxes in plate 14. The larger workbox is covered with diamond-shaped pieces of mother-of-pearl contrasted with abalone shell at the escutcheon, medallion and each corner. The Victorians repaired several pieces with glass covered with iridescent fish scales.

The smaller workbox is made up of larger, square pieces of mother-of-pearl. The medallion on top is engraved 1854 which is probably close to the date of manufacture for both boxes. The interior lid of this small box contains netting needles but its other implements suggest that it was probably a general workbox. In the very centre of the green velvet tray is a small, faceted steel corkscrew with buttonhook which may have come from R. Timmins & Sons, steel toymakers of Birmingham. The company's trade catalogue published in the 1840s has an identical corkscrew and hook. It could also have come from another company as it was common practice to produce identical products and even to use the same pictures from the trade catalogues in the days before designs were registered.[14]

The two boxes in plate 15 illustrate the decorative changes in the English workbox by the last quarter of the nineteenth century. The box on the left is elaborately decorated in a manner that has come to be synonymous with Victorian. The front and top have a highly figured walnut burr veneer. Every edge of the box has ebonized wood trim. Two wide strips of ebonized wood set within narrow, crossgrain stringers also extend from the top of the box to the front. Eight-pointed abstract flowers of ivory attach to the ebonized wood by brass studs placed between the points of the flowers. Double strips of ivory, attached by brass studs, separate one flower from another.

The top medallion is an abstract twelve-pointed flower of tapered ivory petals meeting together at a centre circle of ivory surrounded by large brass studs. Each petal of ivory, inlaid with abalone shell, has engraving to create a separate flower within the petal. This forms a wreath of flowers as does the eight-petal circle of ivory surrounding the escutcheon. The effect is one of unmitigated excess although not without some interest simply for the technical virtuosity displayed. The interior of this box is, by comparison, quite simple. Silver paper lines the tray and storage area below while blue silk covers all the compartments, holders and storage envelope.[15]

The workbox on the right shows the further development of the Victorian workbox in its general decline. Walnut burr veneer covers the entire box. The top has a diagonal design with inlaid bone, abalone shell, ebonized wood, and

Plate 15: *Left: Decorated walnut burr workbox, tray lined with silver paper and blue silk holding mother-of-pearl needlework tools. English, c. 1870. 27 cm. wide. Right: Inlaid walnut burr workbox, tray lined with silver paper and rose silk. English, c. 1890.*

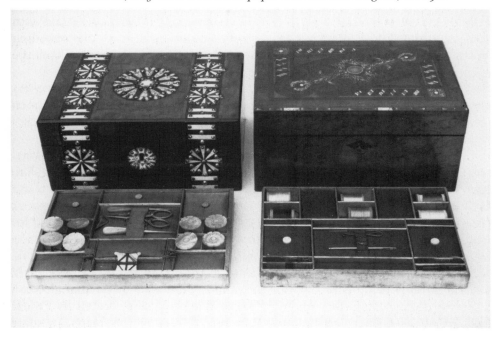

Plate 16: *Maple Shaker workbox lined with pink silk holds needlebook, emery and pincushion. American, c. 1900–1920. 26.5 cm. wide.*

various incised and painted veneers. The edging is ebonized wood inlaid with abalone shell alternating with a white painted design. Unlike all the preceding boxes, the front of the box does not repeat the design or any part of it from the top.

The interior tray and storage area have silver paper lining. Rose silk covers the rest of the interior but there is no storage envelope in the lid. The six open compartments hold commercially-produced spools of thread. The four narrow compartments are for thread winders in the front of the tray.

By the end of the nineteenth century, the workbox still had a functional purpose but it was more utilitarian than decorative, and of less interest to those still doing fancy sewing and needlework. They now turned to the revived fashion of chatelaines or other sewing cases if they carried needlework with them at all. As the Victorian era came to a close, opportunities opened for women outside the home, and proficiency with the needle was no longer the necessary and admired accomplishment it once had been.

The sewing machine had done away with much of the drudgery of plain sewing. The growing emancipation of women meant for many emancipation from needlework, whether plain or fancy. Workboxes continued to appear well into the twentieth century but they took less elaborate forms. In some cases they were charming playthings with no practical use for those who could afford to have their needlework done by someone else. Or they were simple oval American-style boxes as in plate 16, often called Shaker boxes. Americans had used similar boxes from the eighteenth century, and many continued to use them well into the twentieth century.[16]

After the First World War, the workbox often gave way in a more egalitarian age to the simple wicker workbasket imported from China and sold for a trifling sum. Decorated with Peking glass rings, tassles and pierced Chinese coins on the top (plate 17), it provided ample and lightweight storage space for the utilitarian scissors, thread, thimble, darner and bits of cloth needed for occasional mending, plain sewing, or more rarely, fancy work. The majority of women, even of the middle classes, were voluntarily or involuntarily losing the genteel status, servants and enforced leisure which had divided women in the nineteenth century. Nearly all women now began to look for every possible labour-saving device and to make use, when they could afford them, of readymade clothing and household furnishings.

The collector of the fitted needlework box will find that it is rapidly disappearing from the market and that its price is rising accordingly. Even empty boxes, and some were originally sold in that form, command a premium price today. If an English workbox is completely fitted with matching tools,

Plate 17: Chinese wicker workbasket decorated with coins, tassles and Peking glass beads and ring. 29 cm. diameter. c. 1900–1930.

whether or not they are original to the box, it commands a better price. If the tools are appropriate to the age of the box, it is more expensive still.

The Palais Royal and Asian boxes can sometimes be found with their original tools since these were built into the box or into special compartments and are almost impossible to duplicate. This is not to say, however, that the attempt is not made. Any Palais Royal or Asian box should be examined very carefully to make certain that the tools do in fact match each other and fit snugly into the recessed compartments. Asian boxes, unlike French and English workboxes, rarely, if ever, have paper or silk lining.

The collector should also check the veneer, marquetry, edging, and the escutcheon and medallion plates on the boxes, looking for missing or chipped pieces or for hidden repairs made with wax. The fabric is sometimes replaced on the inside, usually on the interior of the lid where the built-in storage envelope often suffered heavy wear. Replaced silk is rarely of as fine quality as the original and is usually obvious by its heavy and dull look as well as by the lack of skill in applying it.

Both handles and feet are often replaced, but this is fairly easy to judge. To replace the handles, it is necessary to tear off the inside paper covering the hole where the handle was joined to the storage section of the box. There is no other reason for the paper being torn at that point. Replaced feet are nearly as obvious: there are telltale holes left by the screws which held the original feet.

The most difficult problem in vetting these nineteenth-century workboxes is how to judge major repairs done by the Victorians themselves. These later repairs often resulted in the boxes being stripped for other uses, or being so badly recovered that they inspire no interest. The Victorians were the last to have cheap, skilled labour for inexpensive repairs on expensive objects.

For example, I have a fitted Regency workbox covered with tin painted to look like green marble. The box and its tools hold together as a single entity with two exceptions: the raised top of the box is covered with Victorian green velvet held in place by edging of stamped-out gilt metal, and the interior storage envelope has white puckered silk instead of the fine green silk used everywhere else in the box.

On careful examination, it is apparent that this Regency box of the 1830s suffered some damage which made a hole in the top of the box, the interior of the lid and the storage envelope. The green velvet, gilt edging and white silk were an attempt in Victorian times to salvage what must have been a prized possession. This box may now be a testimonial to the curious Victorian taste in repairs, but it also suggests the Victorian appreciation of a basically sound and well designed workbox. What the box loses in authenticity, it gains as evidence of how these workboxes were prized and repaired in their own time.

2 Sewing Cases and Chatelaines

Although the fitted needlework box was unusually popular in the nineteenth century, there were occasions when a smaller sewing case was more convenient and appropriate. It could be tucked in one's bag or carried inconspicuously in one's hand. The concept of a small sewing case goes back at least to the eighteenth century in the form of the étui such as the silver-mounted shagreen étui (plate 18). An étui was an all-purpose small case convenient for carrying sewing implements, writing tools, medicinal necessities and other personal items.[1]

The étui continued to be popular into the first quarter of the nineteenth century, but was soon superseded by the small flat sewing case often of French manufacture. The flat sewing case, in various forms, has always been well received since then and fills the need for a small container carrying the basic needlework tools: scissors, thimble, bodkin and needlecase. Flat sewing cases differ from fitted needlework boxes not only by their smaller size. They are, with some exceptions, finished with the same outer covering on all sides, including the bottom, so that there is no apparent 'bottom' side when they are carried in the hand.

In the twentieth century the small flat sewing case has often been of leather with silver tools. These cases are sometimes of precious metals in the eclectic styles of the nineteenth century as well as in later motifs from the Art Nouveau and Art Deco periods. Needleworkers have always prized these small cases not only for their convenient portability but also for their attractive designs. The better cases often serve now, as in the past, as functional pieces of jewellery. In this limited sense, these cases are a direct link to the eighteenth-century objects of vertu which included exquisitely decorated boxes and containers for sewing and writing tools, snuff, powder, scent, patches and other personal conveniences intended not merely to be utilitarian, but to enhance the appearance of the bearer.

As elegant and well made as nineteenth-century sewing cases may appear to the modern eye, they are not the result of the same standards as were applied to the one-of-a-kind object of vertu made in the eighteenth century for the privileged of the Ancien Régime. The specialized guilds with their standards, rules and individual training for the luxury trades were, however, rapidly disappearing by the end of the eighteenth century.

The transition between the eighteenth-century object of vertu for sewing tools and the nineteenth-century flat sewing case can be seen in the satinwood case in plate 19. This type of French flat sewing case was, in some ways, a miniaturized version of the contemporary Palais Royal fitted needlework box. All tools fitted into recessed openings, there was often a mirror in the interior

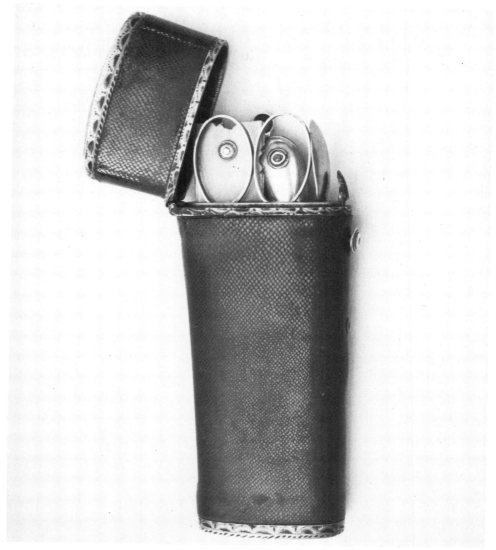

Plate 18: *Silver-mounted shagreen étui with silver tools. English, c. 1800. 9 cm. long.*

of the lid, and between that mirror and the tools was a flat silk pad to protect both when the case was closed.

Some flat sewing cases, such as the one illustrated here, are of unusually high quality. The inside of the box has a white velvet-covered tray in which are inset scissors, bodkin, needlecase and thimble, all of two-colour gold. The design on the needlecase and the shanks of the scissors incorporates Egyptian and classical motifs and is similar to designs commemorating Napoleon's Egyptian campaign which can be seen in Malmaison today. The gold work is finely and delicately done as is the cut glass of the small perfume bottle and the snowflake-shaped mother-of-pearl thread winder.

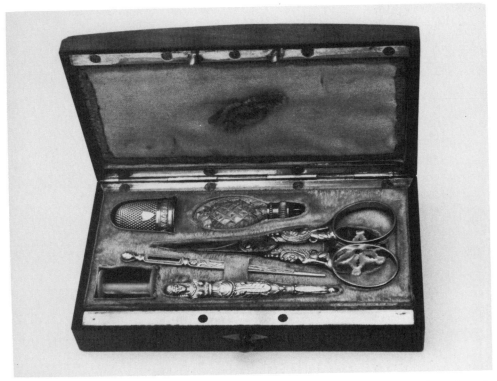

Plate 19: *Satinwood sewing case lined with white velvet holds gold needlework tools marked for Paris, 1809–1819. 11 cm. wide.*

Multi-coloured gold which is often found in French sewing tools of this period, had become fashionable in Paris in the middle of the eighteenth century. The French goldsmiths had discovered how to make gold in four basic colours: white, red, green and blue. White gold was more silver than gold; red gold was one part copper to three parts of 24 carat gold; green gold came in three distinct shades of green and was an alloy of gold and silver whose proportions determined the exact shade of green; blue gold was achieved by adding either arsenic or steel-filings to gold.[2]

The three flat sewing cases in plate 20 are another variation in that they open from the end rather than from the side. Although they differ widely in the date of their manufacture, the arrangement of the interior fittings is similar: scissors and thimble in the centre, needlecase or pencil on the left, bodkin and either a stiletto or needlecase on the right. This type of case, opening from the end, does not as a rule, have a mirror in the interior of the lid; instead it is lined with silk.

The sewing case on the left is of faded mahogany with stringers of satinwood. The small mother-of-pearl medallion is engraved: 'S.K. 1784'. The date is repeated on the silver bodkin inside the case. The date is too early for the case and may refer to the owner's birth-date. The silver tools are of a typical French design, and indeed, appear in a later version in the green, gold-tooled leather case on the right which dates from about the 1840s.

The black lacquer case in the centre of the illustration has implements of gold, with thimble and pencil of two-colour gold. It is the scissors, however, which are of special interest. Delicately modelled in steel, they are decorated on the top of the handles, the shanks and the bottom of the blades with miniature sunbursts of gold. They are reminiscent of scissors designed by Nicolas Pelletier of Poinson-les-Nogent in the nineteenth century.[3]

French flat sewing cases also came in ivory. The top and bottom sections of the case were designed in such a manner that each tool fitted into a recessed opening carved directly from the solid ivory. Considering the fragility of

Plate 20: *Left: Mahogany case lined with rose silk and velvet holds silver needlework tools. French, c. 1800–1830. 12.5 cm. long. Centre: Black lacquer case lined with black silk faille and velvet holds gold and steel needlework tools. French, c. 1860–1880. Right: Gold-tooled green leather case lined with green silk and velvet holds silver-gilt needlework tools marked for Paris after 1838.*

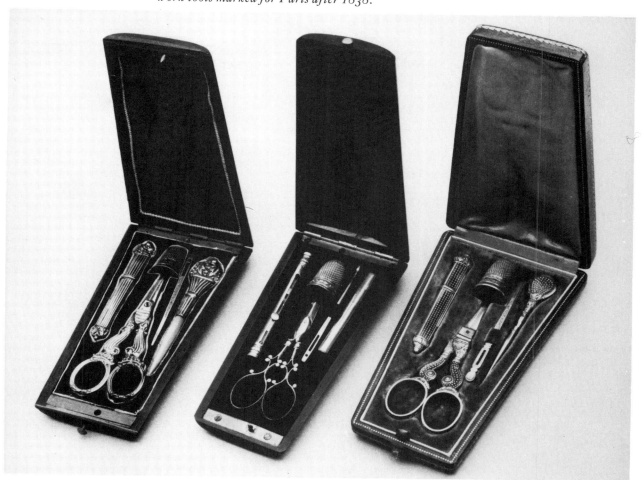

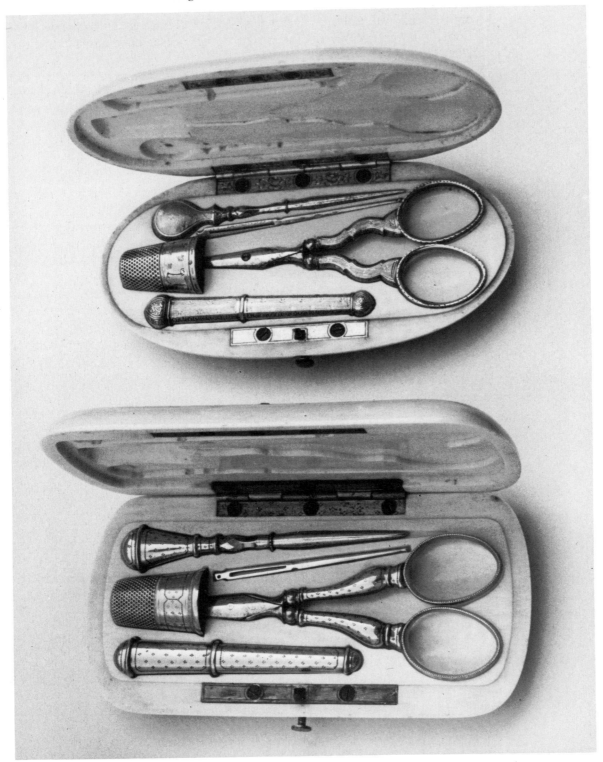

ivory and its vulnerability to cracking under changing atmospheric conditions, it is remarkable that so many of these cases have survived to the present time.

Two examples of these ivory cases are in plate 21. The case on the top has five tools of silver gilt: scissors, thimble, bodkin, stiletto and needlecase. The engraved design on the tools, hinges and upper lockplate is somewhat arabesque in form. The case on the bottom also has five implements, but they are of rose-coloured gold decorated with a chaste engraved design. The same motif is repeated on the hinges and upper lockplate as well as on the opener. The top of the ivory case has an inlaid coronet with the initials 'E E' worked in matching gold. Both of these cases date from the 1840s although the style of such ivory cases changed little throughout the nineteenth century.

Another popular small sewing case by the middle of the nineteenth century was the 'lady's companion'. This was the successor to the French and English nécessaire of the late eighteenth and early nineteenth century which had been an all-purpose container holding sewing and other tools. Like the nécessaire, the lady's companion opens from the top to reveal a number of tools each fitted into its own slot. Unlike the nécessaire, however, the lady's companion holds only sewing and writing implements.[4]

The lady's companion in plate 22 includes scissors, thimble, needlebook, stiletto, scent bottle, pencil and penknife. In addition, the tiny post which furnishes the support for the thimble, forms the top of a container which opens to reveal a small pin box. The implements are silver with typical Victorian floral decoration, and are fitted into a blue silk-lined box. The exterior is veneered in tortoise shell while the top and the front have inlay of mother-of-pearl. The exotic materials used on the surface of the box make it closer in appearance to the earlier nécessaire than the lady's companion in plate 23. The latter is of gold-tooled leather, a more common material for these containers. Its more straightforward and plain design is also more typical of the lady's companion.

There are many other small sewing cases besides the flat case and the lady's companion. Some are in fanciful shapes and not very portable despite their small size, such as the opaline egg container on the left in plate 24. The opaline egg, edged in gilt brass, contains miniature tools: scissors, thimble, bodkin, stiletto and needlecase on a white velvet tray. The egg itself rests on a fanciful bird's nest of gilt brass curled spring wires. The nest sits between two poles crossed at the top by ropes realistically modelled in gilt brass with brass leaves and vines covering the poles.

The lack of portability was no problem for this sewing case as the tools were too small to be usable. Such cases may have been gifts to young girls to celebrate the attainment of a certain standard of proficiency in needlework. Others may have been primarily for display in a Victorian parlour. The same is true of the mother-of-pearl egg on the right in plate 24. Pressing down the scrolled top opens one or both sides of the egg edged in gilt brass. Inside, on a blue velvet stand, are five miniature gilt brass tools: scissors, bodkin, thimble,

Plate 21: *Top: Ivory case with silver-gilt needlework tools marked for Paris after 1838. 11 cm. wide. Bottom: Ivory case with inlaid gold coronet and initials 'E E' on top hold rose-coloured gold needlework tools marked for Paris, 1838–1847.*

Plate 22: *Tortoise-shell and mother-of-pearl lady's companion lined with blue patterned paper and silk holds silver needlework tools. English, c. 1850. 10 cm. wide.*

Plate 23: *Polychrome-tooled black leather lady's companion lined with maroon leather holds silver needlework tools. English, c. 1850.*

stiletto and needlecase. The egg rests on four grape leaf vines which in turn lie on a round white marble stand.

These small sewing cases reflect one result of the decline of sewing and needlework, plain and fancy, in the last years of the nineteenth century. The sewing machine, readymade clothing and household furnishings, and new careers for many women outside the house, lessened the earlier emphasis on proficient needlework. For many women, the sewing case was only symbolic of an earlier function and now was for display alone.

Not all small sewing cases, however, came to this. Some took on the actual appearance of portability. The blue velvet purse and the purple velvet trunk in plate 25 are literally portable sewing cases with functional sewing tools. The taste for representational novelty displayed in these two sewing cases can be seen in many sewing tools in the last third of the nineteenth century as manufacturers satisfied, on a mass production basis, the public taste for the novel and whimsical in pseudo-realistic and miniature form.

Just as there was a revival of eighteenth-century furniture styles and the

Plate 24: *Left: Pink opaline egg resting on gilt brass nest holds miniature gilt brass needlework tools. 21 cm. high. Right: Mother-of-pearl egg supported by gilt brass leaves on marble base holds miniature gilt brass needlework tools. Both French, c. 1880.*

Plate 25: *Left: Blue velvet purse with ivory strips holds gilt metal needlework tools and pincushion. 14 cm. wide. Right: Purple velvet trunk with gilt brass mounts and bun feet holds gilt metal needlework tools. Both French, c. 1880.*

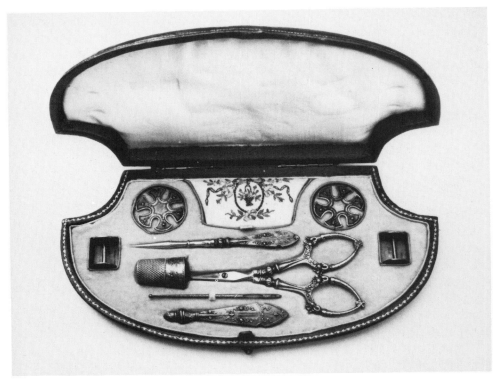

Plate 26: *Brown leather sewing case lined with white silk and velvet holds silver-gilt needlework tools marked 'Sterling, France' (for export). c. 1900. 19.5 cm. wide.*

establishment of the 'Queen Anne' style in architecture during this time, there was also a revival of the interior style of French Palais Royal boxes. This style now appeared, however, in a flat sewing case (plate 26). Both the brown leather case and the silver-gilt tools are more flamboyant in design than the early nineteenth-century Palais Royal boxes. The attempt to recapture the feeling of the style is, nonetheless, quite obvious and extends even to such minor details as the same placement of the reels, silkwinders and the small, built-in, embroidered pincushion. In this later version, however, the pincushion also functions as a small lid to a compartment holding needles and pins.

Finally, there are the home-made small sewing cases which defy description in their infinite variety. Directions for their manufacture filled the pages of women's magazines in the nineteenth century. These cases are often available on the market, but are difficult to vet because of the inconsistency so often found in the style and fabric of the case which is usually compounded by the mismatched implements inside.

It is not difficult, by contrast, to vet the small flat sewing cases nor the miniature and novelty sewing cases. Nearly all of them have recessed openings or distinct places for the sewing implements so that it is fairly obvious whether the tools belong and match one another in design. The major problem with these small sewing cases is not so much mismatched tools as missing tools which are nearly impossible to replace. They also require careful examination of the exterior veneer or fabric for any hidden repairs, chips, tears or other damage. The fabric and paper used on the interiors should match one another. Finally, attention should be paid to the latching mechanism to make certain that the case will close firmly and stay closed. One of the reasons for missing tools is unrepaired faulty latching mechanisms.

The collector will find that these small sewing cases, if in good condition with a complete set of tools, are becoming scarce on the market. Many women collect them for their own use, and as a result the price seems to rise each year.

Another form of the sewing case was the chatelaine, worn suspended from the waist, and known from the middle ages. It derives its name from the French for the mistress of a castle or château. It is an ornamental plaque, attached to the waist by a clasp, from which hang several chains holding keys, scissors, penknife, thimble case, and the like.

The chatelaine was popular throughout the eighteenth century with both sexes as an all-purpose hanger or as a specialized holder for watches, seals and expensive trifles. In the late nineteenth and early twentieth century, it again became for women a specialized ornamental hanger for purses, watches and other items of display.

Our concern here is only with the specialized sewing chatelaine which is primarily a Victorian creation. Chatelaines had gone out of favour during the first part of the nineteenth century. Regency dress with its high-waisted, slim and diaphanous appearance did not lend itself to such encumbrance but with the arrival of the full-skirted Victorian costume, the chatelaine once again became an object of utility and decoration.

It was never meant to replace the workbox or the workbag but it was an alternative to the small sewing case, being the most portable of all needlework containers. The chatelaine furnished in an ornamental manner the necessary sewing tools for unexpected repairs or for working on a piece of needlework wherever one might be.

The Victorian chatelaine consisted of a head with a clasp behind to attach to the waistband. It usually had three or more linked chains from which hung sewing tools and related objects such as disc pincushions, sheathed scissors, thimble buckets, needlecases, pencils, ivory aide-mémoires, small scent bottles and the like.

The chatelaine head alone sometimes appears in nineteenth-century advertisements under the term chatelaine, while the implements may be called chatelets. This is really rather misleading as the entire ornamental hanger with its chains and sewing items is the chatelaine.

There is a fairly clear distinction between early and late chatelaines in the Victorian period. The early ones were usually of steel (often faceted and of a bluish hue), utilitarian, sturdy, and fairly simple in design although not without elegance. They often combined needlework tools with writing tools and others.

The simple steel chatelaine in plate 27 with its clasp (visible behind the head) was probably manufactured by the steel toymakers of Birmingham. Machines for rolling, stamping and piercing steel made the manufacture of such items relatively cheap. At the same time, the process retained the sturdy and simple qualities characteristic of these early sewing chatelaines. The implements of the illustrated chatelaine are all in steel: disc pincushion, button-hook and corkscrew opener, mesh purse, acorn-shaped tablet, and tape-measure.

The term, toymaker, can be confusing when referring to artisans in the nineteenth century unless it is used in a context which makes the specialized function of the toymaker obvious. Toymaker usually meant the producer of a large range of domestic items of polished iron or steel.[5]

Plate 27: *Faceted steel chatelaine with four charms and five household accessories. English, c. 1850. 25 cm. long.*

Plate 28: *Steel chatelaine in imitation niello work with penknife, scissors, disc pincushion, tape-measure and thimble bucket. English, c. 1860. 38 cm. long.*

The wholesale trade catalogues of these toymakers can sometimes give us information about steel sewing tools. For example, the chatelaine from plate 27 probably dates from the second quarter of the nineteenth century. The button-hook/perfume opener is identical to one in the 1840s trade catalogue of Richard Timmins and Sons, steel toymakers of Birmingham.[6] The tape-measure has a silk tape with stencilled calibration marks and other decoration, a feature rarely found on tapes after the third quarter of the nineteenth century.

The chatelaine in plate 28 is an example of the transition between the two types of Victorian chatelaines. The stamped and embossed head and linked chains have been treated so that the design stands out brightly against a dark background giving the impression of niello work in silver although this chatelaine is of steel. The original five tools of steel are only for needlework.

Chatelaines from the last quarter of the nineteenth century became increasingly decorative and specialized as their utilitarian function waned. Princess Alexandra, wife of the Prince of Wales (the future Edward VII) also made the wearing of chatelaines fashionable just at the time they were needed less. This paralleled the change in other needlework tools brought about by the widespread use of the sewing machine and the beginning of women's emancipation from careers centred on domestic duties alone.

The chatelaine of gilded base metal in plate 29 is an example of the mass-produced chatelaine accessible in price and attractive in design to those of more modest incomes towards the end of the nineteenth century. The elaborately embossed head has at its centre a round medallion depicting, amid much foliage, a cherub astride a bird, perhaps an inspiration from the contemporary sewing clamps which presented three-dimensional models of such scenes. The same medallion, without the elaborate surround, also forms a subsidiary head to tie together three of the linked chains. These chains are only an embossed imitation of filigree work as can be seen on the reverse side of two of the upper links of the first chain on the left. The five implements are of a matching design.

This type of elaborate and mass-produced sewing chatelaine of base metal was popular and cheap in England and North America from the 1880s. Many of these chatelaines have a certain charm in their ingenious combination of design and function. Others are tawdry exercises in ornamentation for its own sake and reflect the eclecticism which often dominated traditional styles in the waning years of the nineteenth century.

By the 1880s chatelaine heads were worn not only with a clasp at the waist but also as a brooch to be pinned elsewhere. Sometimes they were replaced by a bow from whose ribbons the needlework implements could hang. As a result, chatelaine heads and the needlework implements to go with them were often sold separately so that it was possible to design one's own chatelaine.[7]

Whether a self-designed chatelaine had a silver or a ribbon head, the outfitting of the basic needlework implements in silver of sheathed scissors, thimble case, needlecase, disc pincushion and tape-measure cost a consi-

derable sum at the end of the nineteenth century and may explain why base metal chatelaines readymade with matching implements dominated the popular market.[8]

The collector, who is unaware of the historical evolution of the chatelaine in the nineteenth century, may be under the impression that the only authentic chatelaine is one with matching needlework implements, chain and head. This is probably true for the early Victorian sewing chatelaines and for the late base metal imitation of the expensive, precious metal chatelaine, all of which were designed as a single unity. Separate chatelaine implements often could, however, be purchased for these matching sets.

The self-designed chatelaine, whether the head was of silver or of ribbon, had no necessary single motif or design. The lack of those ribbon heads today (very few have survived) and the many chatelaine implements originally manufactured as separate tools, may explain why many separate chatelaine needlework implements are available on the market.

The collector of chatelaines can expect to pay a higher price for matching chatelaines, even if of base metal, than for those which appear to be in some way mismatched. Today, many stitchers design their own chatelaines, as was done at the end of the nineteenth century, but they do it for a different reason. They want to use their own implements so that they will have a functional chatelaine where the thimble fits and the scissors are sturdy and sharp.

If the stitcher does not want to use a ribbon as a chatelaine head and chain, then she must search for a metal chatelaine head. A helpful clue to determine whether a chatelaine head and chains are original to one another is to examine carefully the links by which the chains are attached to each other. They should match in design and in size and they should have for connections to the implements all links of one kind whether they be all swivel links or all clasp links or whatever.

Chatelaines are often like the fitted needlework box in that normal usage resulted in the breakage or loss of some tools over time, which were then replaced to avoid discarding the entire chatelaine.

Plate 29: *Gilded base metal chatelaine with decorated heads and square tape-measure, needlecase, scissors sheath, thimble bucket and book-pincushion. English, c. 1880. 31 cm. long.*

3 Needles and Needlecases

Looking at the variety of cheap and well-made needles available today, it is easy to forget what a costly and rare item a needle was only a few centuries ago when John Taylor wrote his ode to the needle in *The Needles Excellency*:

> Flowers, plants and fishes, beasts, birds, flies and bees,
> Hills, dales, plains, pastures, skies, seas, rivers, trees,
> There's nothing near at hand or farthest sought
> But with the needle may be shaped and wrought.

No one knows the origin of the steel needle. The Islamic invasions along the Mediterranean in medieval times brought the steel needle, as part of the advanced Islamic steel technology, to Spain. From there it passed slowly to the rest of Europe. Nuremburg produced steel needles by 1370 and England by 1650.

Redditch in Worcestershire was only one of several towns engaged in needle making. Its location was critical however, in disseminating knowledge of needle making to the surrounding region. As this became a major cottage industry, Redditch and nearby towns became the centre of that industry in England, and later, of Europe.

The hand fabrication of needles was slow and tedious as was the conversion of iron into steel by the heating of iron bars packed in charcoal. It was only the invention of crucible steel in the eighteenth century, and needle-making machines in the second quarter of the nineteenth century, that made possible the high quality, smooth and strong needle that we take so much for granted today.

Although the introduction of machinery lightened the burden of human labour in producing needles, it by no means dispensed with it even toward the end of the nineteenth century. Workers cut Sheffield steel wire into lengths sufficient to make two needles. Then they straightened bundles of these cut wires and placed them in pointing machines which pointed each end of the wire. The stamping machines then flattened the centre of the wire. Breaking the wire in two pieces at this place produced two crudely formed needles. Filing the heads and burnishing the eyes so that they would not cut the thread completed the shaping of the needle. Then the needles were hardened and tempered for strength and flexibility, scoured, polished and packed into papers, 'envelopes' (wrappers or packets), and boxes for shipment.[1]

The pointing, grinding, stamping and press machines had, nonetheless, sufficiently reduced the need for hand labour by the end of the century that steel needles sold wholesale for one to five shillings per thousand.[2] This was a dramatic decrease in price from that of the hand-forged needle a century earlier. For the better type of mass-produced needle, it was also an equally dramatic improvement in quality. Advances in steel technology, the careful attention paid to the burnishing of the eye of the needle, to the hardening and tempering of the shank, and to the grinding of the point produced a superior steel needle. Comparing the machine-made needle with the more crudely hand-made needle of earlier times can only lead to more respect for the work of early needlewomen.

Redditch factories turned out millions of needles a day for many different types of needlework: 'Long-eyed Sharps' or the variation known as 'White-chapel' in numbers one to ten were preferred for embroidery in silk or wool. 'Sharps' were the common sewing needles, usually with round eyes, and came in a variety of sizes. Some had gold burnished on the eye, as well as grooves on each side of the eye, to ease the passage of the thread. Tapestry needles with a long and oval eye were blunt at the point and came in sizes from fourteen to twenty-five for common use. Because steel was so subject to rust, these needles were often made of gold or silver for wet and tropical climates.

So popular were English steel needles that Redditch became the major centre of the needle industry for the Western world. Even the United States had not developed to any significant degree a needle industry by the First World War, but continued to import its needles largely from Redditch, with a much smaller number coming from Aix-la-Chapelle in France, as well as from Germany and Japan.

American distributors usually sold Redditch needles in their original wrappers because of the prestige carried by English needles. By contrast, English firms, such as drapers, pasted their own name and address over one side of the needle wrapper. The leading needle manufacturers of Redditch had regular American distributors in the nineteenth and early twentieth centuries. Crescent needles, for example, were distributed only by Canfield Rubber Company of New York. That was an exception, however, as most English needle manufacturers had more than one major American distributor.

T. Harper needles of Redditch were distributed by Brainerd & Armstrong of Connecticut and by Montgomery Ward and Company of Illinois; T. Hessin and Company needles by S. S. Kresge Company of Michigan; H. Milward & Sons needles by Clark's Thread Company of New Jersey, and by Sears, Roebuck & Company of Illinois. Other major Redditch needle manufacturers included: W. Avery & Sons; A. Shrimpton & Sons; Leaf, Sons & Company; J. Thomas & Sons; Kirby, Beard and Company; Abel Morrall; Wells and Company; J. Burston, and Franklin. Some examples appear in plate 30.

The English needle manufacturers were careful to secure United States patents for their needles and wrappers exported to the United States as well as for any innovations tried on the United States market such as 'calyx-eyed' needles. These were oval-eyed needles with a very narrow open slit from the top of the needle down into the eye. 'This needle was made to meet a long felt want,' explained the Clark Thread Company catalogue of 1916, 'that of a needle which could be threaded without any strain on the eyes. To thread the Calyx-Eyed Needle, the cotton is looped over the head of the needle and drawn downward. . . .'[3]

Other English innovations included the 'Scientific Needle' by Kirby, Beard and Company in plate 30, second from upper right. The needle is so formed, the company explained, 'that the eye when threaded only equals the size of the body of the needle and works in consequence most easily and rapidly'. With such unstartling innovations, the competitive needle manufacturers tried to distinguish their mass-produced, high quality, very similar needles one from the other.

Not only did the needle manufacturers advertise on their wrappers or on their folding cards of needles, but so did trains, the Chicago World's Fair, a Southern California grocery chain, dirigibles, silk shops, sewing machine companies, political candidates, and dairies among many others (plate 31). By the beginning of the twentieth century, needle packets were sometimes so cheap that the advertisers distributed them without cost, just as American restaurants and hotels today give free book matches.

American insurance companies preferred the cheapest needles for advertising purposes, and turned more to Japanese, and after the First World War, to Czechoslovakian needles than to English ones. During the First World War, Japan and others supplied the United States with the popular Army and Navy needle packets.

The bodkin dates from the earliest times and is often associated with the needle which it probably preceded. By the eighteenth century, if not earlier, bodkin also came to mean a needle-like instrument. The bodkin can be made of almost any hard material and usually has a flattened knob at one end. That end may contain an earspoon as do the two early nineteenth-century examples on the left in plate 32. The next seven bodkins, more typical of later nineteenth-century bodkins, are essentially large and thick needles with a slit in the larger end of the needle. The slit held the cord, tape or ribbon while the sharper end of the bodkin entered the fabric which was to be laced. Some bodkins, such as the sixth from the left in plate 32, had slits at both ends so that either end could be used to enter the fabric.

The competition among bodkin manufacturers was as fierce as among needle manufacturers. The R. J. Roberts Co., whose bodkin wrapper is seventh from the right in plate 32, complained of the competition in rather strong, if Victorian, language: 'Numerous dishonest manufacturers have closely copied our labels. They put up in purple envelopes like ours, similarly arranged, worthless, rotten, brass-headed needles, and many deceived customers buying the ineffable trash, have supposed they had "Parabola". Thus the high repute of the "Parabola" Needles has oft-times suffered. See that the label reads: R. J. Roberts' Patent "Parabola". You will thus save yourselves from imposition.'[4]

Plate 30: *English and German packets of needles and pins, c. 1875–1900. Upper left packet 4 cm. wide.*

Plate 31: *American needlepackets, c. 1900–1940. Upper left packet 18 cm. wide.*

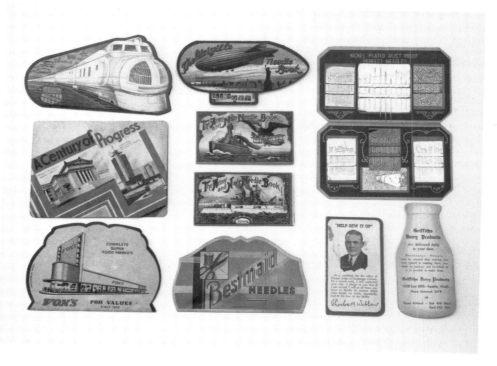

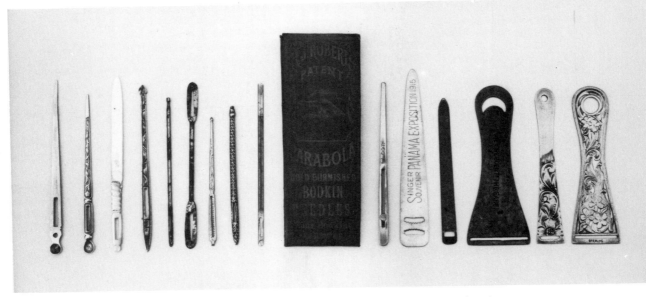

Plate 32: *Bodkins. From left: 1–9: Typical bodkins of silver, gold, mother-of-pearl and steel from English and French workboxes, c. 1800–1870. 10: Paper packet of bodkins. 11–16: Ribbon threaders of base metal, brass and silver, English and American, c. 1880–1915. Left bodkin 7.5 cm. long.*

The other common shape of the bodkin was less like a needle. Six examples are on the right of plate 32. These bodkins have a slit or eye through which ribbon, tape or cord passes for threading the holes punched in a hem or in a fabric for lacing. Bodkins are sometimes called ribbon threaders. Before the nineteenth century, men as well as women used bodkins since both had clothing fasteners which needed lacing.

These bodkins came as single implements or as matched sets of three or more, with variations in the size of the eyes and slits to accommodate a wide range of sizes in the ribbons, cords and tapes used. The makers of gold or silver bodkin sets usually decorated the bodkins, signed them, and sold the sets in presentation cases (plate 33). Cheaper sets of brass or steel bodkins were often for commemorative or souvenir ware. Others of base metal were sometimes distributed freely for advertising-related products such as sewing machines.

While bodkins are collectable, and in matching sets of gold or silver command a good price, the ordinary bodkin is still an inexpensive needlework tool and requires no caution other than the ordinary careful examination given to any needlework implement before purchasing it.

In the late eighteenth and early nineteenth centuries, bodkins were often carried in bodkin cases or in all-purpose cylindrical cases. These had two parts which closed by threading together or by inserting one in the other for a tight friction fit. While the all-purpose cases remained large, the later bodkin cases were smaller in size than those used in the eighteenth century. The earlier cases were often, within their spatial limits, a substitute for the étui or for the nécessaire, and held an equally varied collection of implements.

Bodkin cases came in every decorative material and were popular as souvenirs and gifts. Four examples are shown in plate 34. The English bodkin case in tortoise shell on the left has a classical swag and urn design, a typical Regency motif. The piqué work is piqué posé, inlay work formed with very thin strips of gold or silver. The strips of metal are cut to the desired shape, embossed and pressed into the heated shell. As the shell contracts, it holds the metal firmly in place. Burnishing both the metal and shell brings them to a high gloss. Piqué work made use of a number of other methods as well. The German porcelain case with painted roses and gilt metal bands at the juncture

Plate 33: *Silver ribbon threader set in green and white silk case. American, marked: 'Sterling', c. 1900. 9 cm. long.*

Plate 34: *Bodkin cases from left: Tortoise-shell and silver piqué case. English, c. 1815. 9 cm. long. Painted porcelain case. German, c. 1815. Two wood cases, French, c. 1800.*

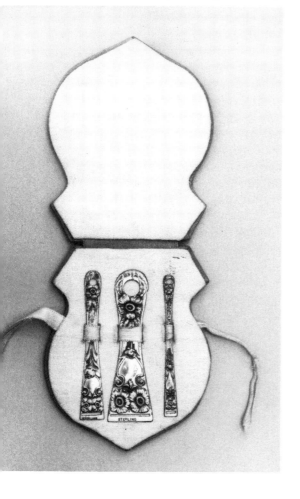

is also early nineteenth century and is typical of German bodkin cases of the period. The third bodkin case from the left is French and dates from about 1800. It has gold mounts, a painting on ivory of a cherub set behind bevelled crystal, and the inscription, 'donné par l'amitié', also set behind another crystal. The last bodkin case on the extreme right of plate 34 is unusual because it is a Palais Royal case of wood rather than of mother-of-pearl, ivory or precious metals. It has the Palais Royal blue and gold pansy inlaid in the centre of the case and surrounded by faceted steel studs which also ornament other parts of the case. Like other Palais Royal tools it dates from the early part of the nineteenth century.

Needlecases, by contrast with bodkin cases, were generally smaller in size although the two could overlap. The French needlecase in plate 35 is similar in shape to a bodkin case but smaller in size. The needlecase is of white enamel on gold decorated with birds, flowers and turquoise and set with gold mounts. It closes with a friction fit. When needles were hand-made and relatively expensive, it was important that they be kept in tight fitting cases to prevent rusting.

The design of nineteenth-century needlecases reflected fashion, the search for novelty and sometimes the nature of the materials, such as mother-of-pearl, of which the needlecase was made. Artisans generally used mother-of-pearl in one of two ways. Either they cut marquetry pieces of mother-of-pearl for application over wood or they carved or hollowed out a thick piece of mother-of-pearl to form a needlework implement. Not only did the thickness of the mother-of-pearl dictate the thickness of the implement, but the relative lack of patterned lustre on each cut side forced the artisan to display the patterned lustrous parts to their maximum. This is why mother-of-pearl needlework implements like needlecases tend to be somewhat flat in shape. The major exceptions are the thimble and the bottom of the tambour handle where the small size, polish and design tend to obscure the lack of patterned lustre.

Mother-of-pearl needlecases, either plain or elaborately incised and carved (plate 36), usually came from France or Italy. Those needlecases with the small oval enamel pansy, second and fourth from the left, probably came from the Palais Royal area in Paris. Other so-called Palais Royal needlecases may have copper, steel, or silver diamond- or shield-shaped inlays in place of the enamel pansy. Some are without any of these inlays.

All mother-of-pearl needlecases should be carefully examined by the collector for cracks, chips, and repairs, especially on the inside area of the friction fit which is hidden when the case is closed. Most have gilt metal or gold bands at the juncture of the friction fit, and these bands should adhere firmly to the body of the case. Above all, the two sections of the needlecase should not wobble when closed. That is a sign of a defective friction fit which is difficult, if not impossible, to repair.

Needlecases of silver or gold have always been in demand because of their inherent value. Silver and gold are chemically similar and are often found

Plate 35: *Decorated white enamel needlecase with its own red leather case. French, c. 1820. 7 cm. long.*

Plate 36: *Mother-of-pearl needlecases from Palais Royal workboxes. French, c. 1800–1825. Left case 7 cm. long.*

together in ores. Before the late nineteenth century, nearly all commercial silver contained some trace elements of gold which could not be removed by the means then available. Testing for the presence of gold is thus an accurate method for exposing restorations and forgeries of pre-twentieth century silver.[5]

To make the three French needlecases on the left in plate 37, a sheet of thin silver was embossed to raise in relief the ornamentation desired. The ornamentation not only decorated the needlecase but also helped to obscure the seams where the two embossed sheets of silver were soldered together to form the needlecase. The three Georgian silver needlecases on the right in plate 37 form a striking contrast to the French ones. They reflect the skill of the silversmith in hiding the soldering marks without resorting to relief work, and in adding decoration by chasing the silver.

Two of the three silver figures in plate 38 on the right appear to be nineteenth-century replicas in silver of the popular folk figures, especially

Plate 37: *Needlecases from left: 1–2: French silver marked for Paris, 1819–1838. 3: French silver, c. 1880. 4–5: English silver made by Samuel Pemberton, c. 1800. 6: English silver made by Cocks and Bettridge, c. 1800. Left case 9 cm. long.*

Plate 38: *Silver figural needlecases. European, c. 1820–1860. Left case 7 cm. high.*

Plate 39: *Needlecases from left: 1–4: Beadwork on bone, and straw. English, c. 1840–1850. Left case 9 cm. long. 5: Pink and green opaque glass. English, c. 1850. 6–7: Wire and silver. French, c. 1840–1870. 8–9: Silver case and mitrailleuse from chatelaines. American, c. 1890. 10–11: Silver filigree needle and bodkin cases. English, c. 1830.*

fisherfolk, worked in ivory in such port cities as Dieppe from the seventeenth century.

The increased use of silver in the nineteenth century was made possible by the great silver discoveries in the Western part of the United States. These were rapidly exploited in the last third of the nineteenth century and brought about a continuous decrease in the price of silver. This made silver relatively cheap, particularly after the American Panic of 1893. In the Sears, Roebuck Company catalogue, for example, the price of sterling silver embroidery scissors went down from one dollar and seventy-five cents in 1897 to seventy-five cents in 1908.

Silver was only one of many materials used to make needlecases. The three needlecases on the left in plate 39 are covered with beaded work. Beaded needlecases were popular from the late eighteenth century well into the Victorian era. The better beads usually came from France and Italy. The underlying cases were often of bone or ivory or sometimes of wood. The three needlecases illustrated give only a slight idea of the extraordinary variety of designs available in beaded needlecases. Although these designs are contemporary with Berlin work, they are more restrained than the designs copied from Berlin work patterns.[6]

The mosaic-pattern straw needlecase, fourth from the left in plate 39, is a good example of nineteenth-century straw work. This type of straw work was known in both England and on the Continent at least from the eighteenth century. The manufacture of straw articles received a great impetus from the work of the many foreign prisoners of war held in England from about 1750 to 1815. These were mostly of French origin but included Dutch, American and other nationals.

Because every prison had within its gates a market where local people sold food and articles to those prisoners who could afford them, the poorer prisoners began to make such articles as straw work and bone carvings to barter or sell. French prisoners were good at both skills which were traditional artisan work in France.

Today this straw work is usually called Napoleonic-prisoner-of-war work, but this may be misleading as much of it was done before and after the Napoleonic wars, and by other than French nationals. Moreover, artisans living near the prisons quickly added the foreign techniques to their own skills. In any event, most of the prison work was of fairly high quality and much of it was not cheap, even in its own time. This is remarkable considering the circumstances under which the prisoners were forced to sell their wares.

The prisoners prepared the straw by running it through a straw splitter which cut a single piece of straw into several strands. These strands were then applied to the surface to be decorated using several different techniques. One of the most common methods was marquetry where the straw in flattened strands of various shades of colours was used like wood veneer to make marquetry patterns. Another technique was mosaic where very small pieces of straw of different colours were fitted in precise designs. A third technique was embossing where strips of straw were applied one on the other in various depths to build up a surface texture of bas-relief.[7]

More rare than the straw needlecase is the English pink and green opaque glass needlecase fifth from the left in plate 39. It dates from the middle of the nineteenth century. Because glass needlecases are at risk for chipping and breaking, particularly at the juncture where the two threaded sections meet, relatively few glass needlecases have survived.

The needlecase to the right of the glass one is a rather odd French case from the last half of the nineteenth century. At first glance it appears to be covered with filigree work but closer examination reveals a cover of coiled wire interwoven with blue yarn over a metal base. More common are the next two silver needlecases, late French and American cases, the latter from a chatelaine.

The American silver needlecase, third from the right in the same plate, illustrates an inventive adaptation from the implements of war. In 1868 the French introduced into their armaments a breech-loading machine gun with a number of barrels fitted together so that it could discharge its bullets simultaneously or singly in rapid succession. This machine gun became known as the mitrailleuse, a name which was subsequently adopted for needlecases working on somewhat analogous principles.

In the 1880s, the Crescent Manufacturing Co. advertised the mitrailleuse needlecase consisting of a cylindrical needlecase divided into five compartments, each of which contained twenty needles of one size. By turning the revolving cap of the needlecase with its indicator pointed to the size of the needle required, and tilting the needlecase downward, a needle of the desired size would fall out. Such needlecases became very popular and were made in various materials besides silver. By the end of the century, Sears, Roebuck and Co. as well as Henry Dobb sold them cheaply as did Crescent Co. which advertised its mitrailleuse needlecase with one hundred needles for only twenty-five cents. The Sears and the H. Dobb mitrailleuse cases appear in plate 40, second from the left and from the right.

Silver filigree work, which has an ancient history, also appears on silver needlecases. The needlecase and the larger bodkin case on the extreme right in plate 39 are good examples of this art where ornamental work of fine silver wire is applied over solid silver. The artisan, who made the filigree needle-

Plate 40: *From left: 1 and 6: Metal needle threaders. American, c. 1900–1930. 7 cm. long. 2–5: Mitrailleuse, brass needlecase, brass nanny's brooch with goldstone, and mitrailleuse for export to Sears, Roebuck Co. All English, c. 1880–1910.*

case, second from the right, used the filigree wire as the outline for delicate flower patterns which appear in several places on the needlecase. By filling the space between the wires with enamel, which was then fired, a needlecase was produced combining cloisonné and filigree.

In the nineteenth century, many needlecases were also made of brass as in plate 40, third from the left. Stamping machines and dies usually provided the decoration found on brass needlecases. To the right is a nanny's brooch, a rather interesting Victorian needlecase supposedly worn by nannies, which conveniently held needles and thread needed for unexpected repairs. On the extreme left and right in this plate are the cheap needle threaders invented in the United States and often given away as advertisements by insurance and other companies. The other side of the needle threader, as shown on the extreme right, explains precisely how this implement works.

The most popular material for the making of needlecases in the nineteenth century may well have been bone, and to a lesser degree, ivory. The difference between bone and ivory is not always evident. They are chemically similar and have tubular cells running lengthwise. Both yellow with age, grow brittle and are subject to warping. The difference appears when they are cut open.

Bone contains small channels which once carried blood. When bone is cut across the end, these small channels appear as very small dark holes. When cut lengthwise, the channels are exposed as long dark lines. When turned on a lathe, the small channels are penetrated and exposed as pitted areas. Looking at bone through a magnifying glass will reveal a pitted surface that is less shiny and more opaque than ivory. Elaborate carving makes visual identification more difficult as it tends to conceal those surface characteristics which differentiate bone from ivory. The collector will find that more needlework implements have been made of bone than of ivory as bone is more plentiful and cheap. The shin bones of horses, cattle and sheep have been widely used because of their large size and minimum cost.

Ivory from the tusks of elephants is more dense than bone and is made of the same hard material, dentine, as is the human tooth. When ivory is cut in a cross section, the characteristic arc lines, made up of the cut ends of very minute tubes radiating out from the centre are clearly visible. This profusion of overlapping circles has been called the 'engine-turned' effect. When cut lengthwise, ivory reveals long, parallel lines alternating between a lighter and darker effect. Some of these lines are straight while others are wavy.

Ivory takes a better shine than bone because the tubular structure of the ivory, when alive, was filled with an oil-like substance. This also explains why old pieces of dessicated ivory often take on a new life when polished with oil. Ivory is also porous and takes stain very well whether intended or not. It also bleaches strongly when exposed to sunlight.[8]

There are imitations of ivory such as ivorene made of ivory dust, glue and other ingredients. Ivorene lacks the characteristic striations and lustre of ivory. More common is the plastic, celluloid, invented by an Englishman, Alexander Parkes in 1862. This first artificial polymer was made of xylonite cellulose nitrate stabilized with camphor, and was often referred to as xylonite. An improved form of celluloid by the American, John Hyatt, in the 1870s, made the product commercially feasible.[9]

Celluloid may appear to have a grain like ivory and bone. This grain is achieved by casting celluloid in thin layers of alternating shades of an ivory colour. It is not like the grain of any natural substance. The grain effect appears the same however celluloid is cut because it has neither a natural cross section or length. Moreover, celluloid as a thermoplastic material is subject to melting when touched by fire which does not effect ivory or bone in that way.

Whether of ivory, bone, wood or similar material, needlecases were often turned on a lathe to give them shape and decoration. The lathe also made threaded cylindrical parts so that the needlecase in two parts could be closed by rotating the top and making the needlecase air-tight.

The invention of the ornamental turning lathe at the end of the seventeenth century, and its improvement later, made possible more precise ornamentation. The basic difference between plain and ornamental turning on a lathe is that in plain turning, the object revolves horizontally while the cutting tools and their angles are varied to achieve the desired result. In ornamental turning, it is the tool rather than the object, which revolves, cutting a surface pattern on the object.[10]

While ornamental turning changes the surface texture, plain turning, which is done first, produces the basic needlecase profile and can add some

Plate 41: *Ivory and bone needlecases from left: 1–2: Italian, c. 1800. Left case 10 cm. long. 3: French, c. 1830. 4–7: Possibly English, 19th century. 8–10: Chinese, c. 1840–1880.*

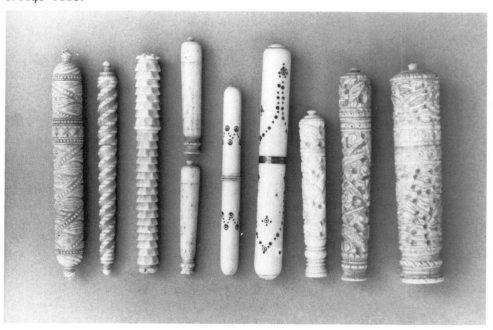

ornamentation. The first two bone needlecases on the left in plate 41 are good examples of ornamental turning with their flowing lines of incision. They are probably Italian, late eighteenth and early nineteenth century. The careful workmanship suggests the experienced and precise control exercised over the ornamental tool cutter by the worker.

The third needlecase from the left is turned in a pattern popular for tape-measure cases and other needlework implements made in France before the middle of the nineteenth century. The two plain needlecases to its right are typical utilitarian English needlecases of the early nineteenth century. The sixth and seventh needlecases from the left are interesting because similar markings appear on English clamps, pincushion bases and other implements. The dots and circles are made by pressing and smoothing hot coloured wax into holes pierced in the needlecases by hot needles.

The dots with the circles around them appear to repeat the same markings found in the pierced holes and bas-relief bands on the three Chinese needle-cases on the extreme right of plate 41. The middle needlecase of the three appears to be the oldest, probably early nineteenth century. The other two needlecases have less fine carving and may reflect the decadence which had overtaken craftsmanship in China during the very late Ch'ing dynasty. At the juncture of the parts of the two needlecases on the right are the ubiquitous dots and circles pierced and carved into the needlecases.

The dot and circle decoration appears to be universal and its origin is unknown. It is often found incised on ivory objects from Roman times, and it also appears in medieval bone and ivory objects and in Scandinavian ones as well. In any event, whatever its origin, it had become a commonplace motif in painted, inlaid, pierced and carved needlework implements by the nineteenth century whether made in Asia or Europe.

Still other examples of bone and ivory needlecases, as in plate 42, suggest the wide range of designs and shapes popular in the nineteenth century. The two dark cases (fourth from the left and third from the right) in the form of a fish and umbrella, are stained red. Occasionally, the collector will find an ivory or bone implement stained green although the colour is more rare than red. The folk-figure of the woman with an apron (sixth from the right) is probably eighteenth-century although such figures were carved in Dieppe from the seventeenth century. Umbrella and bean or pea pod needlecases (the four cases to the right of the ivory woman case) were perennially popular shapes for needlecases in the nineteenth century.

The first implement on the left in plate 42 is not a needlecase but a needle gauge made by Rodgers & Sons. It has a hole at the top for needles, sizes nine to twelve, and one at the bottom for sizes four to eight. The third needlecase from the left with gilt ends is also English and from the first half of the nineteenth century. The last needlecase on the extreme right is a late nineteenth-century German quiver-shaped case with a carved stag and deer.

The needlecases in plate 42 with small holes near the top (from the left: numbers 2, 4, 5, 7, 8 and 9) contain viewers known as Stanhopes. When held

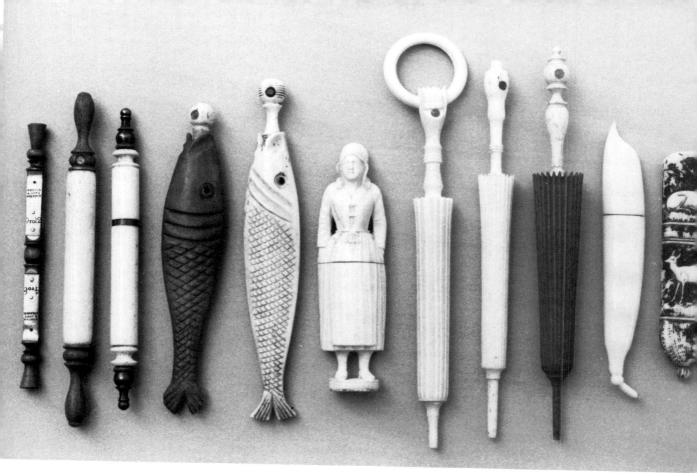

Plate 42: *Ivory and bone needlecases from left: 1: Needle gauge. English, c. 1870. 8.5 cm. long. 2, 4, 5, 7–9: Needlecases with Stanhope viewers. European, after 1860. 3: Ivory. English, c. 1840. 6: Ivory woman with seal base. French, c. 1790. 10: Ivory bean or pea pod. English, c. 1820. 11: Quiver case. Bavarian, c. 1870.*

close to the eye, the Stanhopes reveal scenes of famous resorts, cities and other tourist attractions. The viewers are called Stanhopes after the inventor of the lens, Charles Stanhope, 3rd Earl of Stanhope (1753–1816), a prolific inventor.

The Stanhope lens was a tiny glass rod approximately one-fourth of an inch long and one-tenth of an inch in diameter. The end through which one looked was convex in shape to produce high magnification for the very short focal length. The other end had an extraordinarily small black and white transparent image in the centre of the rod measuring not more than one-thirtieth of an inch in diameter.

Although Stanhope's lens made possible the later invention of micro-photos, that did not occur until 1860 when the French chemist, René Dagron, used Frederick Archer's collodian or wet-plate process to make transparent microphotos on the flat end of the Stanhope viewer. Needlework implements with Stanhope viewers include not only needlecases but tape-measure cases and various multi-purpose needlework tools. They were made from the 1860s until the First World War.[11]

Plate 43: *Needlecases from left: Wood umbrella. English, c. 1870. 9 cm. long. Three wood cases. Tyrolean, c. 1880. Indian sandalwood case, c. 1800. Two carved coquilla nut cases. English, c. 1850.*

That the ornamental lathe could construct ornament as easily as it had ornamented construction is shown by the needlecases in plate 43. The five wood ones on the left may include hand carving as well. The two needlecases on the right are made of the shell of the coquilla nut. They each have two parts with lathe-turned cylindrical threads for making an air-tight fit. The somewhat medieval-looking heads are traditional in coquilla carving as late as the first half of the nineteenth century. Later in the century, there was a tendency to use bands composed of dots with circles in bas-relief as a way of concealing the line where the two parts of the needlecase threaded together. (For a discussion of the coquilla nut and the difference between it and vegetable ivory, see pp. 127–129.)

It is not difficult to vet these cylindrical needlecases whether made of silver and gold, straw work, bone and ivory, celluloid or other plastic, beaded work or wood. The major problem is to know whether they are needlecases since other small cases or containers are sometimes confused with needlecases.

Other problems in vetting needlecases include the authenticity of the material, knowledge of the manufacturing technique used, and how both of these relate to the age of the object. Silver and gold needlecases usually have marks to identify them but this is not always true. Straw work, aside from the condition, is not a problem unless one is asked to pay a premium price for Napoleonic prisoner-of-war work for which a specialist opinion may be needed.

Bone and ivory needlecases should be carefully checked for chips and cracks which are not uncommon, and for functioning threaded or friction fit closings. The vast majority of needlecases are of bone, and this assumption should be kept in mind unless powerful evidence to the contrary is presented. Celluloid is used only from the 1870s and is easily detected by a magnifying glass. Any needlecase with a Stanhope viewer must date from after 1860 and will usually command a premium in price. But the viewer must be in working condition with the lens and microphoto intact; it is not uncommon for them to slip or fall out. Beaded and wood needlecases are judged by their design and condition and command corresponding prices. Needlecases are among those needlework tools unlikely to be reproduced.

Needlecases were not the only receptacle for needles in the nineteenth century. Needlebooks were equally popular, and like needlecases, go back several centuries. In the nineteenth century, they were made of every conceivable decorative material as shown in plate 44. When open, the needlebooks are about eight by ten centimetres or slightly larger and reveal pages of flannel into which needles are stuck. Most workboxes have one or two small needlebooks finished in fabric to match the interior of the box.

From England came carved and pierced needlebooks of ivory, bone and mother-of-pearl as well as of sandalwood. The fretted cover placed over silk may be a typical example of prisoner-of-war bone carving as in the needle-

Plate 44: *Needlebooks from top left: 1–6: English, c. 1840–1880. Left book 5 cm. high. From bottom left: 7–9, 11–12: English, 19th century. 10: American, c. 1900.*

book at the top left of plate 44. The remaining needlebooks on the top row are all of English manufacture and represent a painted scene on bone, carved ivory, shell work on cardboard, straw work and pierced mother-of-pearl lined with silk, all dating from the second half of the nineteenth century.

The needlebook on the left of the bottom row of plate 44 is a Bristol board lined with silk. Bristol board was a fine pasteboard of a smooth but unglazed surface. Worked in needlepoint as though it were canvas, Bristol board produced an unusual effect. The fine leather needlebook with silver mounts as well as the silver filigree book are both English. The silver Art Nouveau book, third from the right, is of American manufacture about 1900. The last two books on the right are nineteenth-century Tunbridgeware in the familiar mosaic and cube patterns.

Not all needle containers were made for individual needles as were the cylindrical needlecases and most needlebooks. Some needle containers were designed to accommodate the needle packets in which mass-produced needles of the nineteenth century were wrapped. These packets not only made the needles easy to transport and display but, equally important, they identified the size and type of the needle as well as the name of the manufacturer.

Artisans soon made small containers with partitioned steps that would

Plate 45: *Gold-tooled red leather needleboxes in shape of books, knifebox and workbox. English, c. 1840–1860. Left box 5 cm. high.*

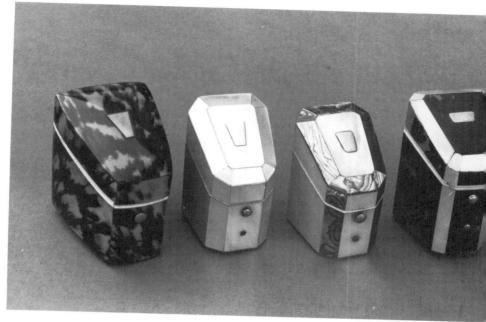

Plate 46: *Ivory needlebox with thimble post. English, c. 1860. 4 cm. wide.*

Plate 47: *Needleboxes holding needle packets. 2nd from left marked: 'Middleton's. 7 King William Str. CITY'. 3rd marked: 'Lund'. English, c. 1860. Left box 5 cm. high.*

make each needle packet visible. Sometimes these containers looked like miniature leather books or caskets (plate 45). More elaborate containers looked like miniature Georgian knife boxes and were of ivory, mother-of-pearl, abalone shell, or tortoise shell or a mixture of these (plates 46, 47). These containers rarely date from after the 1860s.

The high quality of the mass-produced steel needle led the manufacturers to compete by calling attention to the unusual containers in which they carried their packets of needles. The most successful manufacturer of unusual needle containers was probably William Avery and Son of Redditch, who produced a series of brass and bronze needle containers in the last half of the nineteenth century which have become very collectable. They are easily recognizable, and are usually stamped with the name, W. Avery & Son, Redditch, and with the British Registry mark which gives the precise date of registration of the design. Properly marked, they present no difficulty for vetting and dating.

Avery brasses, as collectors have since called them, are often ingenious devices for holding and retrieving needles. The brass needlecases in plate 48, for example, each hold four packets of needles in sizes six through nine. The easel at the left in plate 49 also holds four needlepackets while the top of the Temple Bar to its right lifts to reveal a storage compartment for needles. The bronze elephant with the brass howdah also stores needles in the top of the

Plate 48: *Avery brass needlecases. Left marked: 'Alexandra'. Right marked: 'The Quadruple Golden Casket'. English, c. 1870.*

Plate 49: *Avery brass needlecases clockwise from left: Easel on stand, 11.4 cm. high. Temple Bar; bronze elephant with brass howdah; windmill; footstool; and hat box. English, c. 1870.*

howdah. Turn the arms of the windmill and the top opens to raise and lower compartments holding needlepackets. At the bottom are a hat box and a footstool which both store needles.

Although the Avery brasses were cheaply produced and cheaply put together, in some cases with bent metal tabs, they often produced a distinctive

Plate 50: *Avery brass needlecases clockwise from left: Rose on shield, 9 cm. high; crab on plate, butterfly and scallop shell. English, 1870s–1880s.*

bas–relief or texture, of better quality than one might expect in such cheaply made, promotional containers. In plate 50, for example, the modelling of the rose on the shield case, the texture of the bronze crab, the clearly ridged scallop shell and the butterfly wing markings are surprisingly well done.

There is no reason, of course, why stamped brass decoration should be vasty inferior to hand-worked brass. There was no more likelihood of defective work when stamping a large number of brass objects than when the same number were made by hand as long as the dies were originally well made and were discarded when worn. The stamping of brass, and metal in general, has acquired a bad name because it made the design subservient to the capabilities of the machine, curtailed the creative artistry of the workers, made superfluous decoration economically possible and made slipshod work the norm only when the worker used inferior dies or inadequate techniques.

Avery brasses were, with some unfortunate exceptions, well stamped by comparison with much of the stamped metal of the Victorian era. The collector will sometimes find stamped brass needle containers similar or identical to Avery brasses but with the names of other companies stamped on them. It is possible that they were produced by the same company, probably in Birmingham, that may have made Avery brasses. It seems rather unlikely that Avery and Son would manufacture its own brass containers for the competition. Avery and Son did, however, sometimes stamp its brass needle containers with the names of its leading retailers or its licensees.

4 Thimbles and Thimble Cases

Of all needlework tools collected, the thimble has inspired the most literature, the most enthusiasm and the largest number of collectors. Its history is ancient and its distribution universal. As a result, there is no end to the variety of thimbles encountered. Made of bronze, leather, bone, ivory, brass, porcelain, gold, silver, various base metals, mother-of-pearl, aluminium, plastic, and other materials, thimbles have assumed nearly every decorative finish imaginable.

Thimbles have also appeared in wood, stone, glass, tortoise shell, horn and other such materials which are usually too soft or too brittle for the basic function of the thimble: to prevent the blunt end of the steel needle from penetrating the middle finger as it forces the needle through the fabric.

Thimbles in the past were not only a functional needlework tool. They were sometimes a piece of jewellery, a token of love or esteem, or an expression of social status. By the seventeenth century, silver thimbles were common in society, and gold thimbles not at all rare. The collector of thimbles will find that most thimbles available in the market today date from the nineteenth century or from the early twentieth century. Some of the available thimbles from this period will be discussed here.[1]

The thimble usually has four basic parts: the top of the thimble, often called the dome or top; the indentations on the side of the thimble called the knurling; the band beneath the knurling which usually carries whatever decoration may exist; and the rim at the bottom of the thimble, although not all thimbles have rims.

Before the nineteenth century, artisans often built metal thimbles in two pieces, the top being attached to the seamed cylinder below. They made the indentation or knurling by hand or by knurling wheels making one or more rows of indentation at a time. Decoration was usually done by hand or by rollers imprinting a design on the band.

By the beginning of the nineteenth century, some thimble manufacturers made metal thimbles in northwest Europe and in the United States out of a sheet of metal pressed or stamped into a thimble shape and then worked, if necessary, on a lathe for decoration.[2] The non-metal thimbles were usually carved or fabricated by hand, and consequently produced in fewer numbers.

Gold thimbles became very fashionable in France in the eighteenth and early nineteenth centuries. They usually were of two or more colours of gold, one colour of gold for the thimble, the other colours for the design around the band which was often a classical motif of swags and garlands. See example in plate 51.

French gold and silver marks can be extraordinarily difficult to read

Plate 51: *Rose gold thimble with green gold swags. French, c. 1800–1825. 2.5 cm. high.*

Plate 52: *Thimbles from top left: 1: Mother-of-pearl, 2.25 cm. high. 2–3: Palais Royal mother-of-pearl. French, c. 1800–1825. 4: Ivory. English, c. 1820. From bottom left: 5–6: Chinese bone and Indian ivory, after 1830. 7: Vegetable ivory, c. 1860–1880. 8: Ivory. English, c. 1880–1900.*

because of their small size, and equally difficult to decipher because of the many changes made in the type of mark used from the eighteenth well into the present century. To discover if a mark is a French hallmark, it is necessary to look at its reverse side. From 1818, the French struck their hallmarks against specially designed anvils known as *bigornes* which left a bigorne mark on the reverse.

The collector of needlework tools should note that the French usually hallmarked such tools with a special category called restricted warranty or *petite garantie*. This signified items which were approximately of the legal standard but which had not been tested by a complete assay but only by touchstone. For these petite garantie items, the French hallmarks are the following, with numerous exceptions. Before 1838, the cock is often the mark for both gold and silver although the rabbit's head marks Paris petite garantie silver from 1819–38. After 1838, petite garantie gold from Paris is marked by the eagle's head, and from the provinces by a horse's head until 1919 when it is also changed to an eagle's head. Petite garantie silver from Paris is marked by a boar's head and from the provinces by a crab.[3]

The early nineteenth-century thimbles, such as the one in plate 51, are usually taller, thinner and with finer rims than those made late in the century.

This may be the result of the introduction of new manufacturing techniques in the late eighteenth century. In the case of gold thimbles, it may also be the result of a conscious sense of design and an attempt to minimize the amount of gold used in a given thimble.

Often as costly as gold thimbles were mother-of-pearl thimbles banded in gold or gilt metal (top left of plate 52). Mother-of-pearl had been used to make thimbles at least from the middle ages in the West and had long been known as a carving material in the East.

The two taller mother-of-pearl thimbles to the right are in the so-called Palais Royal style. The middle mother-of-pearl thimble has the blue and gold pansy which so often identifies these unusual and fragile thimbles. Both mother-of-pearl thimbles on the right also have rows of gilded metal outlining the band, a characteristic of Palais Royal thimbles.

The shorter mother-of-pearl thimble to the left could also be a Palais Royal thimble, but it lacks the proportions and gilt band associated with that type. It seems possible that it may be a Chinese export thimble intended for the European market. In 1884, the author of an article in *Dorcas Magazine* on the origin of thimbles commented: 'I saw some very beautiful ones in China that were exquisitely carved, of pearl, and bound with gold.... These pearl thimbles are quite as costly and far prettier than those made entirely of gold.'[4]

The ivory thimble, to the right in the same row as the mother-of-pearl thimbles, is carved from one piece of ivory and decorated with the ubiquitous dot and circle design which became so widespread in the nineteenth century. What is unusual about this thimble is the knurling which is of concentric circles of ivory rather than the usual indentations. This may be intended to make the thimble smoother for working with lace and embroidery work. Such smooth ivory thimbles were popular in the late eighteenth and early nineteenth centuries. This thimble probably dates from the early nineteenth century. It is similar in its unusual knurling to a Tunbridge wood thimble made about 1800.[5]

On the bottom row, on the left, the squat bone thimble is from a Chinese lacquer box and is very typical of its kind. This type, widely exported from the second quarter of the nineteenth century to Western Europe, is carved in two pieces, the top being fitted to the stubby cylinder. The bone thimble to the right, without knurling on the sides or top, is also from an Asian export workbox and again may reflect the Western desire for smoother thimbles to use with fine needlework. It is carved from a single piece of bone.

The thimble on the bottom row, second from the right, is of vegetable ivory. For a discussion of vegetable ivory, see pp. 127–129. Carved in one piece, it has a matching vegetable ivory acorn thimble case. Although vegetable ivory is considered by some to be inferior to ivory as a substance, in fact, thimbles made from it are comparatively rare. This is a paradox since ivory thimbles are rarely made in the twentieth century while vegetable ivory thimbles continue to be a staple of the souvenir trade in South America.

The thimble on the far right, bottom row, is difficult to identify. It is carved of one piece of ivory and is probably late nineteenth century. It does not have the strong convex top of the earlier thimbles. The crosses on the band may reflect the Gothic Revival or the Arts and Crafts movement of the last half of the nineteenth century in England.

The thimbles in plate 53 are all typical English thimbles of the nineteenth and early twentieth centuries. At the upper left is a 14 carat two-colour gold thimble with a fleur-de-lis design on the band and rim. It came in a tortoise shell thimble case from the Isle of Man. The next three-colour gold thimble is also 14 carat with a garland design. The middle thimble of the upper row is 15 carat gold which places it somewhere between 1854 and 1932, probably closer to the former. In 1854, 15, 12 and 9 carat gold became legally recognized gold standards. In 1932, 14 carat gold replaced the 12 and 15 carat gold standards.[6]

The silver thimble, second from the right on the upper row, is typical of a whole genre of English engraved thimbles. Elegant and slim, these thimbles were common during the Victorian period and did much to enhance the

Plate 53: *English thimbles from top left: 1–2: Two and three colour gold, c. 1860 and 1900. Left thimble 2.25 cm. high. 3: Gold marked '15 ct'. c. 1880. 4: Silver, c. 1850. 5: Silver, marked 'friendship'. c. 1850. From bottom left: 6: Silver filigree, c. 1800–1830. 7: Silver with purple agate stone top, c. 1850. 8–9 coronation souvenirs, 1902 and 1911. 10: Silver, hallmarked Chester, 1903.*

reputation of English silversmiths for careful work and fine design.

There were several ways to make silver thimbles during the nineteenth century from a single sheet of silver. If dies were used, this might also produce some pattern or design on the thimble itself. The thimble then received its indentations from knurling wheels while cutting tools trimmed the edges and cut the basic design.

The decorative pattern could be done in several ways. The engraving for a thimble such as the one illustrated above could be done manually or by machine. To give it extra brightness, the artisan cut additional details with beveled tools by hand. Steel rolling wheels could also emboss patterns on the band as in the silver thimble on the far right of the upper row where the word, 'friend', is in bas-relief. It was also possible in the forging process itself to emboss or stamp the pattern on the thimble blank.[7]

The decorative pattern was sometimes a part of the thimble structure itself as in the silver filigree thimble shown on the far left of the bottom row. Filigree thimbles date approximately from the last third of the eighteenth century to the first third of the nineteenth century. They often had an oval or shield plate for the owner's initials. Georgian filigree thimbles sometimes formed the top for a scent bottle or pincushion beneath which was a letter seal. These late Georgian combination filigree thimbles are somewhat scarce today and command a corresponding price.

The second silver thimble from the left on the bottom row is interesting because of the purple agate stone on its top. Stone tops with their indentations were supplied to the thimblemaker readymade, and in England, were associated with the thimblemakers of Birmingham. They fixed the stone in place by a rim around the edge of the top of the thimble so that the stone appeared translucent when held to the light. This was in contrast to the practice in Germany where the stone rested on a silver or metal plate.[8]

The two coronation thimbles in the bottom row celebrating the coronations of Edward VII (1902) and George V (1911) are part of a genre of royal commemorative thimbles which began to gain widespread popularity with the coronation of Queen Victoria in 1837. The relatively cheap cost of Victorian mass-produced thimbles, and the prosperity of the time, made it possible to distribute these thimbles to an increasingly large audience interested in celebrating births, weddings, coronations and other significant events in the family of the reigning sovereign.

Toward the end of the nineteenth century, English silver thimbles became somewhat shorter and heavier. Some sacrificed an elegant appearance for practicality as in the hallmarked Chester thimble at the far right of the bottom row. Substantial and heavy, this thimble has no decoration other than the knurling itself. It was assayed and hallmarked at Chester in 1903.

Hallmarks are an excellent guide to dating English thimbles after 1890. Before that time, thimbles and all other articles weighing less than ten pennyweight (later reduced to five pennyweight – a pennyweight being one-twentieth of an ounce) were exempted by statute since the eighteenth century from the requirement of hallmarking. The most common hallmarks found on thimbles (following the Lion Passant which is the mark for sterling) are those for Birmingham, Chester, or London. The other mark often found on English thimbles after about 1880 is a size number. Before this time, English thimbles came in only three sizes: for girls, young women, and women.

The only way to date non-hallmarked English silver thimbles with any accuracy before 1890 is by their style, chiefly the type of decoration and proportions, and in some cases, by the technique of manufacture. Early Victorian thimbles tend to be tall, narrow and light, like their Regency predecessors. One of the major differences between eighteenth- and nineteenth-century thimbles is that most eighteenth-century thimbles did not have rims. The later Victorian thimble, with notable exceptions, had a heavier and more ornate design and usually a large bevelled or rolled rim. Toward the end of the nineteenth century, English silver thimbles tended to be shorter and heavier than those at mid-century.

English sterling thimbles are ninety-two and a half per cent pure silver alloyed with seven and a half per cent of another metal such as copper. This makes a relatively strong thimble, but it is nonetheless vulnerable to punctures from the needle and to general wear. To strengthen the silver thimble, some thimble manufacturers in the eighteenth and nineteenth centuries added steel tops to their silver thimbles as in plate 54. The first four rimless thimbles are early nineteenth century while the fifth thimble with its heavier rim dates from the last half of the nineteenth century.

An improvement on the steel top thimble received a patent on 14 June 1884 when Charles Horner of Halifax produced his Dorcas steel core thimble. The core had an inner lining and outer decorated casing, both of silver.[9] Horner later improved his steel core thimble for which he received a new patent. The core of hardened steel now underwent heavy plating with silver rather than

Plate 54: *English silver thimbles with steel tops. 1–4: c. 1800–1830. 5: 1850–1875. Left thimble 2.75 cm. high.*

being sandwiched between lining and casing. These Dorcas thimbles usually carried the name Dorcas, the thimble size number and Horner's initials, C.H. Examples of these improved Dorcas thimbles are in plate 55. Two of Horner's solid silver thimbles, which unlike the Dorcas thimbles, could be hallmarked as sterling appear in plate 55 on the extreme right of the bottom row.

On the back of the box in which Horner sold his improved Dorcas thimble, he gave the following guarantee: 'Exchanged free if rendered useless from any cause whatsoever. Made of Sterling silver with inner lining of hardened steel. None genuine without the name "Dorcas". C.H. British Made.' The Dorcas was not a cheap thimble and sold for two shillings and six pence in the late 1880s or not quite twice the price of a cheap silver thimble. In the United States at the same time, the cheapest silver thimble sold for about twenty-five cents which was roughly the equivalent of one shilling.[10]

Horner's idea of a steel core sandwiched between silver layers had its predecessors. Several years before Horner's original patent of 1884, the French made gold thimbles with a steel core in a single piece. They first made a steel thimble, complete with indentations and any decoration, and then plated it with gold. The gold was not expected to last a lifetime, but rather the

Plate 55: *English thimbles made by Charles Horner from top left: 1–2: Plain Dorcas thimble and its box. 2 cm. high. 3–5: Dorcas floral (1893), star (1889) and square (1887) patterns. 5–6: Silver, square pattern hallmarked Chester, 1897, and star pattern hallmarked Chester, 1902.*

Plate 56: *English thimbles made by Henry Griffith and Sons from left: 1–2: Dreema thimble and its box. 2.25 cm. high. 3: Marked: 'HG&S, Dreema, Made in England'. 4: Silver Spa thimble hallmarked Birmingham, 1927.*

user was to replate the steel thimble when the gold wore away.[11]

Charles Horner's steel core thimbles met competition from the Dreema thimbles manufactured by Henry Griffith and Sons, Ltd. Griffith was the major manufacturer of thimbles in England from 1856. When the market for thimbles began to collapse in the second quarter of the twentieth century, Griffith concentrated on the production of a souvenir type of thimble called the Spa. This could not, however, keep up the former sales in the face of the decline in both fancy and plain sewing. In 1956 Griffith ceased the production of thimbles altogether.

Examples of Griffith's Dreema thimbles, original box and one of the Spa thimbles are in plate 56. On the bottom of the Dreema box was not a guarantee like the one offered by Dorcas, but only the following statement: 'This thimble has a steel lining between two layers of solid sterling silver. The beauty of silver with strength of steel.' It would appear that fewer Dreema thimbles were either made, or fewer have survived than the number of existing Dorcas thimbles. As a result, the Dreema thimble commands a slightly higher price in the market today. Other silver thimbles with an inner core of steel were also marketed under such names as Dura (by Walker and Hall of Sheffield) or Doris, but fewer still of these seem to have survived.

Innovation in thimble making, as shown by British and American patents, was prolific toward the end of the nineteenth century. An interesting example is the pair of thimbles in plate 57, which are in the shape of a fingernail. The one on the left is of cupro-nickel and on the right of silver, hallmarked London, 1901. For some reason, these thimbles were considered sanitary or hygienic. The idea was not new at the end of the nineteenth century but it seemed to acquire popularity at that time as these thimbles also appeared in brass and celluloid. Patents for variations on the hygienic fingernail thimble were taken out in the United States as late as 1952.

The two silver finger guards or shields in plate 58 are typical of mid-nineteenth century Victorian finger protectors worn on the first finger of the left hand on which fabric was laid and held by the thumb. The point of the needle would hit the wide covered part of the finger guard rather than the uncovered section. Moreover, the guard had indented lines or a smooth surface rather than knurling so that the point of the needle would easily slide off the finger guard. Finger guards date from the late eighteenth century and are usually of silver although there are examples in gold, ivory, bone and later of celluloid. In general, finger guards are rather plain by comparison with thimbles although later finger guards are more ornate than earlier ones.

American thimbles of the nineteenth and early twentieth centuries were the result of the same mass production methods used in England. But there was a difference in design which paralleled the general difference between English and American decorative arts. American thimbles with some excep-

Plate 57: *English finger nail thimbles. Left: Cupro-nickel. 2.5 cm. high. Right: Silver, hallmarked London, 1901. Pat. no. 19157.*

Plate 58: *English silver finger guards, c. 1850. Left guard 2.5 cm. high.*

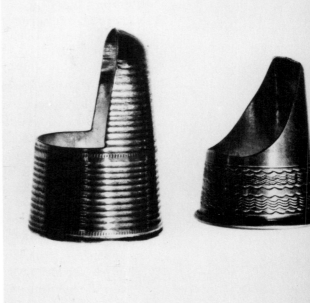

tions were more simple in design. However, gold thimbles studded with diamonds, as well as other fancy thimbles, were available from American manufacturers.

American thimble manufacturing goes back at least to the eighteenth century, and a few brass and silver thimbles may have been made in the American colony as early as the late seventeenth century.[12] Until the nineteenth century, however, the Americans relied heavily on European thimbles, a reliance resented by the fledgling American thimble manufacturers. Benjamin Halsted, silversmith, in an advertisement of 1794 informed the public that 'he has brought the manufactory of Gold, Silver and Pinchbeck Thimbles with steel top to great perfection and thinks he could make a sufficient quantity to supply the United States. Citizens, consider your interest, and encourage American Manufactures.'[13]

Before the 1840s, there were no silver factories as such in the United States. Silver and gold thimbles were ordered directly from the silversmith. What encouraged the growth of factories manufacturing silver was the passage of a protective tariff in August of 1842 which levied a duty of thirty per cent on all imported gold and silverware. The new manufacturers of silver came from several origins: some companies which had manufactured metal goods now moved into silver, such as Reed & Barton; former silversmiths sometimes banded together as in the case of The International Silver Company; or jewellers founded companies such as Unger Brothers, or Tiffany Company, or the Gorham Company, and others.

Because the United States has no hallmark or official dating system for silver, one of the guides to the identification of thimbles is the mark of the silversmith or the trademark of the silver manufacturer, if it exists, under the top or on the band of the thimble. The American system is complicated by the marks often added to silver and other metals by the wholesaler and retailer in place of the trademark of the manufacturer.

Another guide to American thimbles is the patent date which sometimes appears. This differs from England where it is the patent number rather than the date that is stamped on the thimble. American thimbles received patents both for innovations and for designs while English thimbles were patented only for innovations. English thimble designs, however, were registered from 1884, and the registration number was usually stamped on the registered item.

If United States thimbles lacked official hallmarks, they did have size numbers on the side of the thimble which before the 1880s distinguished them from European thimbles. After that time, many English thimble manufacturers also added size numbers, but other European thimble makers did not necessarily follow suit.

American silver, like that of England, is ninety-two and a half per cent pure silver in its sterling form. Only Baltimore silver was marked sterling in the period from 1814. For the country as a whole, the sterling mark came into general use only after 1857. Some silver thimbles may be marked 'coin' which indicates that the silver is ninety per cent pure. Silversmiths sometimes used silver coins for making small silver articles.[14]

Simons Bros. Co. of Philadelphia is the only American manufacturer of silver and gold thimbles still in existence in the fourth quarter of the twentieth century. Founded in 1839 by George W. Simons, the company at first specialized in the manufacture of such articles as gold and silver thimbles and mechanical pencils. Simons Bros. thimbles have a few basic shapes, and it is more in the design than in the shape that variety must be sought.

The attitude of American manufacturers toward the comparative importance of shape and design reflects the impact of early industrialization on the manufacture of American thimbles. A number of patents issued in the nineteenth century to American inventors were for the manufacture of thimbles, including rims and stamped designs in a single mechanical operation. Unlike Europe, where thimble manufacturers tried to increase the variety of shapes and designs, most American manufacturers tried to limit that variety, and to introduce repeat patterns which could be easily altered for machine application.

Some examples of Simons Bros. thimbles in gold and silver are in plate 59.

Plate 59: *American thimbles made by Simons Bros. From top left: 1: Gold inscribed '1887'. 2 cm. high. 2: Gold with Greek key band marked '14 kt'. 3: Gold with panel band marked '14 kt'. 4: Silver 'Cupid' thimble marked 'Patent, November 21, 1906'. From bottom left: 5: Silver with enamel band. 6: Silver, originally a Waite Thresher design. 7: Silver 'Priscella' thimble marked 'Patent, May 31, 1898'. 8: Silver. All silver thimbles marked 'Sterling'.*

Plate 60: *American thimbles made by Waite Thresher from top left: 1–2: Gold. 2 cm. high. 3: Gold with panel band marked '14 kt'. 4–5: Silver with gold bands. 6, 9–10: Silver. 7: Silver with Dogwood band. 8: Silver with harbour scene. All silver thimbles marked 'Sterling'.*

They did not, with some exceptions, usually give names to their designs but instead assigned them numbers accompanied by descriptions such as 'Fluted Octagon'. The names have usually come from collectors and have not always been accurate. For example, the 'Cupid' thimble, which is in one list as Simons Bros. no. 146 for sterling silver, has been called by some the 'Cherub' thimble. In any event, Simons Bros. sterling silver and gold thimbles were trademarked with the Old English letter S set in a shield. Their thimbles of nickel silver (so-called German silver made of an alloy of copper, nickel and zinc) and of oroide (an alloy of copper and zinc or of copper and tin the colour of gold) carried the trademark of S.B.C. set within an outline of a thimble.

Simons Bros. bought out in 1927 the thimble part of Waite Thresher Company of Providence, Rhode Island. That company's thimble trademark was a plain star or a star with a thimble inside.[15] Examples of Waite Thresher thimbles are in plate 60.

The only equal to Simons Bros., and the leading thimble manufacturer in

New York was Ketcham & McDougall, a company which had ties to the earlier thimble company, Roshore and Prime, established in 1832. Edward Ketcham, who became a partner of Roshore, was first his apprentice, while Hugh McDougall acquired silversmith training in the Prime company. The retail shop of Ketcham & McDougall became known as 'The Thimble House'. Their factory in three large six-storey buildings in Brooklyn turned out gold and silver thimbles like the ones in plate 61.

In September of 1881, Hugh McDougall received a patent for a new and cheaper method of manufacturing thimbles. In his patent application, McDougall explained that 'the invention consists in a novel method of making a thimble – namely, in so rolling a [thimble] blank as to form a thick portion for the rim, and if desired, also an embossed ornamentation, in cutting or trimming the blank to the desired form, in bending the blank and soldering its ends together, and in closing the end thereof. . . . By my invention I simplify the manufacture of thimbles, and I enable thimbles having embossed ornamentation to be produced without materially increasing the cost of manufacture.'[16]

Some of the best Ketcham & McDougall thimbles were made by this new

Plate 61: *American thimbles made by Ketcham & McDougall from top left: 1: Gold marked '14 kt'. 2 cm. high. 2: Silver with gold band. 3–4: Silver with Wild Rose band, and with fluted band. From bottom left: 5: Silver marked 'Souvenir of St. Augustine, Florida'. 6–8: Silver. All silver thimbles except no. 6 marked 'Sterling'.*

Plate 62: *American thimbles made by Stern Bros. and by Goldsmith, Stern & Co. from top left: 1: Silver with gold band marked 'gold, sterling'. 2 cm. high. 2: Silver with band of four-leaf clover and horseshoes. 3: Silver with band of two cherubs and banner. 4: Silver with Greek key band. 5: Silver with band of grapes and leaves. From bottom left: 6: Gold. 7: Gold-filled. 8–9: Silver with panel bands. 10: Silver. All silver thimbles marked 'Sterling'.*

process, such as the Florida souvenir thimble in plate 61, far left, bottom row. McDougall continued to improve his new process of manufacture and to lower the cost of producing thimbles. The company trademark for thimbles after August of 1892 was a K placed between M and D with a c on the upper part of the straight line of the K and a & below the lower diagonal line of the K. Some of the earlier thimbles made between September of 1881 and August of 1892 are marked: Pat. Sep. 20, '81. Although the company of Ketcham & McDougall is still in operation, it ceased to make thimbles in 1932, a century after the founding of its parent company.

Another important manufacturer of thimbles was Stern Brothers and Company of New York City which later became Goldsmith, Stern and Co. of New York. The trademark for Stern Bros. was the letter B over C set within a large square S. Next to this was an anchor or sometimes the anchor was the only mark. Goldsmith, Stern and Co. changed the top letter from B to G but left the C below set within a square S, according to *Trade Marks of the Jewelry and Kindred Trades* (p. 66). Examples of these companies' thimbles are in plate 62. Other thimbles of these companies show variations from the trade marks described above.[17]

A prolific breeding ground for silver factories, some of which made thimbles, was North Attleboro, Massachusetts. One of the best known of the

North Attleboro silver factories was the Webster Company, which made among other things, needlework tools and thimbles. It was preceded by the company of G. K. Webster, who began manufacturing silver novelties and thimbles in 1879. The Webster Co. trademark was a W superimposed on a C bisected by an arrow pointing to the right. The Webster Co. became a subsidiary of Reed & Barton of Taunton, Massachusetts in 1950, but went out of business in 1971.[18] Four of its thimbles are in plate 63.

What is interesting about American thimble manufacturers is how similar the thimbles of one company are to the others in shape, design and decorative techniques. There is a concentration on reducing production costs by the standardization of shapes, by an avoidance of any unnecessary hand work, and by using simple repeat patterns mechanically impressed on the thimble blank or the thimble itself.

Not all thimbles distributed by American companies under their trademark were American made. For example, Gabler Brothers of Germany produced some silver thimbles with ninety-two and a half per cent silver content which some American companies ordered for their own use to be stamped with the name of their company followed by the designation, 'Sterling'. Not all Gabler thimbles, however, were sterling. Some were only eighty per cent silver and were marked 800 while the sterling ones were marked 925. A collection of both types of Gabler Bros. silver thimbles is in plate 64.

The Gabler Bros. thimbles illustrated here are of silver and enamel although they made thimbles of many other materials as well. The Gabler Bros., and Germany in general, had acquired by the nineteenth century an installed capacity to produce an enormous quantity of export thimbles. The founder of Gabler Bros. was Johann Ferdinand Gabler, a silversmith of the late eighteenth and early nineteenth centuries, who invented a thimble-making machine. His sons continued his work, and founded in Schorndorf the firm of Gebrüder Gabler. This company became one of the world's leading exporters of thimbles by the end of the nineteenth century. It survived well into the twentieth century, ceasing production of thimbles only in the 1960s. The Gabler Bros. trademark was an abstract eight-pointed daisy moulded on top of the thimble rather than under the top as in American thimbles.

Not all thimbles are trademarked. Perhaps the majority carry no identifying marks. In these cases, the collector is dependent on a study of comparative style and method of manufacture. Also helpful are inscriptions on the thimble. It is curious how many gold and silver thimbles were apparently gifts and were engraved with the date of presentation. Some examples of these thimbles are in plate 65.

Brass thimbles are in a category all their own. One of the earliest thimbles known to have been made in the American colony in the late seventeenth century appears to have been brass. The first major thimble manufacturer in England to use machinery to make thimbles was John Lofting. After emigrating from Holland, the centre of a thriving thimble industry, he took out a

Plate 63: *American thimbles made by Webster Co. from left: 1: Silver. 2 cm. high. 2: Silver with small band of acorns. 3: Silver with fluted band. 4: Silver with Greek key band. All thimbles marked 'Sterling'.*

Plate 64: *German thimbles made by Gabler Bros. from left: 1, 3–5: Silver with enamel marked '800'. Left thimble 2.25 cm. high. 2 and 6: Silver with enamel marked '925'. All 20th century.*

patent in 1693 for a machine to make brass thimbles. Although silver thimbles became common among the middle-class by the seventeenth century, brass thimbles remained the most widely used for plain sewing because of their cheap cost and durability.

Brass thimbles played an unusual role in the United States where they were traded for fur and other items with American Indians, who wanted them for jewellery and to decorate the fringes of their clothing. The Indians strung brass thimbles together to make decorative necklaces, and attached thimbles to their clothes with beads inside the thimbles to make a tinkling noise as they moved about.

Plate 65: *Thimbles from left: 1: Gold inscribed 'Mathilda Casey, May 11th, 1816'.
2.5 cm. high. 2: Gold with city scene inscribed 'Jennie, Dec. 25th 1871'. American. 3:
Silver with city scene inscribed 'September 20, 1881'. American. Silver gilt with enamel
band marked '925'. Norwegian. 5: Silver, Indian, c. 1875–1890. 6: Gold marked '585'.
c. 1930.*

Plate 66: *Brass thimbles from top left: 1: Greek key band. 2 cm. high. 2–4: Floral,
'friendship' and palmate designs. 5: Child's plain thimble. From bottom left: 6: Gilt
brass with carnelian top. 7: Base metal with brass lining. 8–10: Gilt brass from French
sewing cases. All c. 1880–1930.*

Brass thimbles were usually not marked by the manufacturer. The decorative designs on them often appear less clear than those on gold and silver thimbles. This may, in some cases, be the result of cheap production, such as the use of worn dies, but it may also be the result of use. Since brass thimbles were the housewife's constant companion, they wore out more quickly than thimbles made of precious metals. This wear is seen in several of the brass thimbles in plate 66.

The more elaborate thimbles of gold and silver, or of fragile substances like ivory, often came in thimble boxes designed to guard or protect the individual thimble. The use of special thimble cases goes back several centuries, but the collectable thimble cases available today date primarily from the nineteenth century. Some of these boxes were constructed with the same care as the fitted needlework box, and indeed, appear as miniature versions of such boxes. The five boxes in plate 67 have veneers of leather, tortoise shell, ivory, mother-of-pearl and abalone shell. The interiors are lined with velvet and ivory edging and have posts or recessed compartments to hold thimbles.

Other popular thimble containers were made of Scottish transferware (plate 68). The older ones had transfer prints of well-known scenic attractions

Plate 67: *Thimble cases clockwise from back left: 1 and 3: hold thimbles horizontally. 2, 4–5: have thimble posts to hold thimbles vertically. English, c. 1860. Left case 3.5 cm. wide.*

Plate 68: *Scottish transferware thimble cases. Left: Pasted oval print of Brig o'Balgownie, Aberdeen, c. 1900–1920. 3.25 cm. wide. Right: Oval transfer print of Old Church Clevedon, c. 1875–1900.*

Plate 69: *Vegetable ivory acorn thimble case and original thimble with matching leaf motif on band. English, c. 1850–1890. 5 cm. long.*

on the top of the box while those from the early twentieth century often had a photo pasted on the case. Equally popular was the carved vegetable ivory acorn where the top unscrewed to reveal a matching carved thimble of the same material (plate 69).

Still other thimble cases reflected the tendency to treat needlework tools as novelties, toys or miniatures. The eggcup thimble holder at the top of plate 70 is a good example of this tendency. On either side of it are miniature cases lined with velvet to hold thimbles which, when closed, look like jewellery cases. In the centre of plate 70 is the popular acorn-shape thimble case made here out of Tunbridgeware in the stickware pattern. To its right is a beaded, all-purpose case which was often used as a thimble case; in shape it was nearly as popular as the acorn case. A more whimsical thimble case is the blue slipper at the bottom of the plate with its feather stitching, beaded flowers and pre-1840 coil-head pins.

Thimble cases also commemorated public events, such as Queen Victoria's Diamond Jubilee in 1897, as on the right in plate 71. Other thimble cases of the same yellow sheet metal were often stamped with floral designs as in the other example on the left.

Silver thimble containers of various types meant to hang from chatelaines became fashionable once again in the last third of the nineteenth century.

Several examples are in plate 72: the first on the left has a thimble post; the next is in an acorn shape; the third is a thimble bucket while the last is in silver plate lined with rose silk. These hanging silver thimble holders are very collectable today as they are still sometimes used, hung from a ribbon, by those who do fancy sewing or needlework.

A thimble serving as the threaded cap of a silver sewing case was another way to help prevent a thimble from being lost and to hold together the contents of a small, portable sewing kit known as a hussif. The word is derived from housewife and describes various types of sewing containers. Hussifs were made in Germany, primarily in Augsburg, from the late seventeenth century. Many hussifs had a foot adapted to serve also as a letter seal. An example from the eighteenth century appears on the left in plate 73. An

Plate 70: *English thimble cases made of silk, leather, wood and vegetable ivory, velvet and brass, beadwork on bone, and Tunbridge stickware. Light blue slipper holder 7 cm. long.*

Plate 71: *English thimble cases of yellow sheet metal. Left: Egg shape lined with white plush velvet. c. 1890. 4.5 cm. wide. Right: Queen Victoria's Diamond Jubilee souvenir lined with rose plush velvet, 1897.*

Plate 73 (opposite): *Left: Silver hussif with thimble, small thread reel and needlecase. German, 18th century. 7.5 cm. high. Right: Silver sewing kit with thimble, needlecase and multiple reel made by Waite Thresher, c. 1900.*

Plate 72: *Four silver and silver plate thimble cases from chatelaines. American and English, c. 1890. Left case 3 cm. high.*

American adaptation of the hussif dating from about 1900 appears on the right.

In the twentieth century, a cheaper form of the hussif appeared in other countries as well for use by both men and women (plate 74). Some carried advertising such as the second and third from the far right. Others reflected styles such as Art Nouveau seen on the extreme left with its inner container to its right. Many modern hussifs were amusing novelties, and most were of cheap materials such as brass (third from left) or of celluloid (extreme right).

The end of the nineteenth century and the beginning of the twentieth saw a plethora of inventions having to do with sewing and particularly with the thimble. When one considers that this was precisely the time when plain and fancy sewing and needlework were losing their central importance for many

Plate 74: *Sewing kits from left: 1, 3 and 5: Brass. 2: Needlecase and two thread reels from inside no. 1. 4: Metal kit with needlecase, four spools and thimble advertising Lydia E. Pinkham's Vegetable Compound. American, c. 1900–1920. 6: Celluloid kit with needlecase and three spools. All except no. 4 are German, c. 1900–1930. Left case 5.5 cm. high.*

women, it seems surprising that so much attention was paid to 'improving' the ancient form and function of the thimble.

Patents issued for innovative thimbles in Great Britain and the United States during this period cover everything from magnetic devices (for picking up steel pins and needles), needle pulling devices, needle threaders, and thread cutters to ventilated thimbles and stretchable thimbles so that the manufacturer would not have to make so many different sizes.

One of the most amusing innovations is the thimble invented by Alfred Constantine of Birmingham, England for which he received an English patent in 1909 (No. 6253) and an American patent in 1911. Mr. Constantine's thimble was to have a curative effect on ailments such as rheumatism. It reflected the medical folklore of its time as well as the public interest in technology. The thimble had an outer casing of silver with an inner lining of magnetic metal. The top of the magnetic lining had a saw cut on it which formed a horse-shoe magnet. Inside the bottom of the magnetic lining was placed another lining of zinc with holes in it. Directly behind the zinc lining was a smaller one of copper with studs which protruded through the zinc lining holes and made contact with the magnetic lining. When the thimble finger became moist, its contact with the three linings set up a galvanic action which supposedly cured rheumatism. Mr. Constantine in his patent application did not specify the size of the area that was cured.[19]

Vetting thimbles for authenticity presents a number of problems. Dating the thimble can be difficult when there are no hallmarks, trademarks, or inscriptions. Style and method of manufacture may be a guide in some cases, but a knowledge of both can only come from the experience of looking at many thimbles and comparing them with known examples. Each type of thimble presents its own problems of authentication.

Enamel thimbles, if expensive when in mint condition, are unfortunately worth the expense of careful restoration by the unscrupulous seller. A good magnifying glass may show the break lines in repaired enamel or it may reveal that a supposedly enamel thimble is in fact a silver thimble gratuitously enamelled to increase the price.

Gold-plated silver thimbles passing as gold thimbles should be guarded against. It is not unknown for someone to imply that the size number of the thimble may be the carat number for a gold-plated thimble. It is also not uncommon to find silver and gold thimbles newly embellished with stones such as turquoise which are attached by glue or fitted into drilled holes.[20]

One of the most difficult problems in vetting thimbles is presented by reproductions of nineteenth-century ones passing as originals. The great interest in thimbles, the growing number of collectors, and the rising prices in the thimble market sometimes bring thimbles, originally made and sold as honest reproductions (often from original dies and moulds), or as tourist souvenirs, back into the market as 'antique' thimbles after their surface has been sufficiently aged by appropriate treatment.

The best defence against fraud in thimble collecting is knowledge of the subject gained through reading, experience in the marketplace, study of thimble collections, and above all, making an effort to know and to deal only with reputable dealers. There are many such, who can be extraordinarily helpful in broadening one's knowledge.

Because thimbles are the most widely collected of all needlework tools, they are also the subject of the largest amount of literature about needlework tools. In addition, the thimble is the single needlework tool for which there exists a scholarly monograph: *Thimbles* by Edwin F. Holmes, 1976.

The minor problem when vetting a thimble case is simply to make certain that it is not damaged on the surface, that its hinges and closing device function and that it has its original interior intact. The major problem is to distinguish thimble cases from cases similar in size and shape which may have been used as thimble cases but are either all-purpose cases or cases which originally had another specific function. The true thimble case has usually, but not always, some special feature to facilitate the carrying of the thimble. This may be a thimble post, an approximate thimble shape on the outside or a thimble-shaped recessed compartment on the inside. In addition, for carved thimbles there may be matching motifs on the thimble and its case.

5 Scissors

'We are but the two halves of a pair of scissors, when apart,' Charles Dickens wrote in *Martin Chuzzlewit*, 'but together we are something.' This metaphorical view of scissors as two individuals necessarily connected for their happiness and utility sometimes appeared as part of their decoration. When scissors were rare and expensive in the eighteenth century, they were often carried in small steel cases with surfaces finely worked with pictures of cupids, hearts and flowers. Surrounding inscriptions played on the metaphorical theme of each blade needing the other to survive: 'l'amour pour l'amour'; 'l'amour nous unis'; and 'inséparable nous sommes'.

Neither the necessity of scissors to human civilization nor their antiquity is in doubt. Modern cross-bladed scissors secured by a centre pivot go back at least to Roman times while the double-bladed, spring-back shears date back some two thousand years before the Romans. About the seventeenth century, cross-bladed scissors began to replace shears for cutting fabric.

Early scissors varied widely in design, but all had the familiar handles (bows), shanks and blades. Steel scissors introduced in the eighteenth century were superior to iron in terms of strength. The cutlery of Sheffield, England, including its scissors, acquired its early fame because of the high quality of its steel and workmanship. Improvements on eighteenth-century Sheffield crucible steel set the standard for a homogeneous, slag-free, high-carbon steel not only for Sheffield cutlery but for other countries which soon imported Sheffield steel for their cutlery industries.

Before the 1830s, all scissors were made by hand, and the finest scissors often continued to be hand-made well into the twentieth century. Sheffield scissors makers secured an enviable reputation for their scissors which went through nine major steps: forging, boring, hardening, shaping, grinding, filing shanks and handles, assembling with rivet or screw, polishing and burnishing. To hand-forge steel scissors, the Sheffield scissors maker took two lengths of steel rod and hammered out blades at one end. The two pieces of steel were from the same crucible so that the carbon content would be identical. The hammering out of the blades to get the right variation of thickness from the back of the blade to the cutting edge was a severe test both for the plasticity of the steel and for the skill of the scissors maker.

At the other end of the steel rods, if the scissors were to be all-steel, the scissors maker forged the handles by punching a hole through each flattened rod which was then enlarged. Next, the filer bored the hole for the screw to join the blades. This hole was graduated in size so that each blade would be held firmly by the screw and yet have sufficient play to work evenly.

The next step in fabricating scissors was the grinding of the cutting edge of the blades. The revolving grinding stones were driven by the water power of streams along which many of the early cutlery factories were built, or by human power. After grinding, blades were hardened and tempered. Highly skilled artisans, working with engraving tools, chisels, drills and scissors files, then decorated the shanks and handles. They worked out those elaborate and sometimes whimsical designs of flowers, animals or abstract subjects which make these hand-forged scissors so attractive. Finally, the scissors were polished, assembled and finished.[1]

The variety of scissors in plate 82 (with the exception of the third pair from the left) is a good introduction to the various scissors parts and their names from the hand-forged period. Some of this terminology continued to be used through the die-stamped period although the drastic curtailment in the variety of designs made much of it obsolete. Today, because of advancing technology, even the fancy die-stamped scissors are becoming more scarce.

Scissors blades were one of three types: rapier, bodkin or flat. Handles also had various names such as wire, flat, fluted and bevel. The shanks had an even larger variety of names, which used in combination, made a seemingly infinite list: square swamp or square curl; square sarum or square reverse; reverse glass or reverse glass fiddle joint or winged reverse square neb swamp joint, and so on.[2]

All-steel scissors were the strongest but until the last half of the nineteenth century, they remained relatively expensive and limited in production. Small scissors, like embroidery scissors, might be made entirely of steel but larger scissors and shears were still often made of iron.

The theoretical distinction between scissors and shears is somewhat arbitrary. Embroidery scissors usually range in size from six and a half to nine centimetres, sewing scissors from ten to fifteen centimetres. According to some cutlery standards, scissors must have identical blades and handles. This is not necessarily found in some of the smallest scissors, and as a result, the common distinction between scissors and shears is size. Shears and trimmers tend to be larger than fifteen centimetres while scissors are usually smaller, although the rule is not without exception.[3]

One of the oldest producers of needlework scissors has been France. The centre of scissors production was in Thiers, but Paris, Nogent, Langres and Chatellerault were also important nineteenth-century producers of quality scissors. French scissors had variety, excellent design and individuality and a lack of uniformity in the industrial techniques employed. Before 1830 all scissors of French origin were hand-forged. By that time, some 12,000 people were employed in the cutlery industry in Thiers.[4]

A good example of French scissors are in plate 75. These scissors with hand-forged blades of crucible steel and intricately carved mother-of-pearl handles were designed for fitted needlework sets. Made largely during the Empire period, these scissors with their carved swans, urns, dolphins and foliage reflect the motifs popularized by Napoleon and his entourage to associate his regime with his military triumphs and the empires of antiquity.

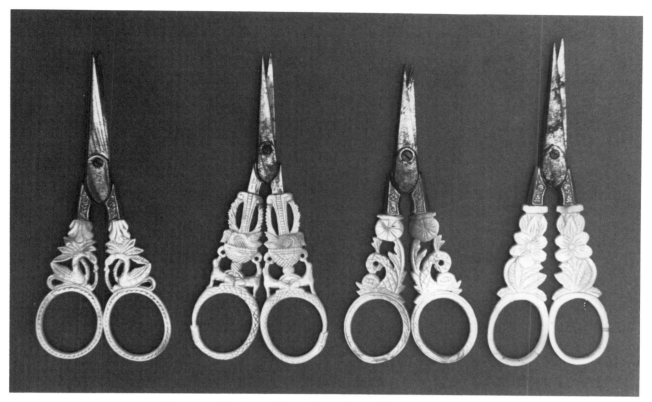

Plate 75: *Scissors with mother-of-pearl handles and gilt bands with swan, urn, dolphin and floral motifs. From French workboxes, c. 1800–1825. Left pair 9.5 cm. long.*

French silver scissors with steel blades were equally decorative as in plate 76. The first two pairs on the left contain on the shanks a typical French scroll motif of the early nineteenth century. While these scissors were still hand-forged, the pair on the extreme right which date from the second half of the nineteenth century, were probably forged mechanically by a steam- or water-driven hammer. Thiers was on the fast-flowing river Durolle, which furnished power for most of the mechanical processes employed in the French cutlery industry. From the 1830s until the 1880s, French cutlery factories introduced mechanization of production wherever possible. In Thiers the process of mechanical modernization was largely complete by 1862. Scissors makers used machinery to forge the blades, grind them, stamp out the shanks and decorations, pierce the handles and polish the parts.[5]

Unlike France, England did not begin to machine-forge scissors until the 1880s, long after France, Germany and the United States had mechanized their cutlery industries. Sheffield, nonetheless, retained its pre-eminence as the maker of high quality cutlery. So highly regarded was Sheffield cutlery, that some foreign exporters trans-shipped their cutlery through England to acquire the coveted mark: 'Made in England'. Others simply usurped the name of Sheffield for their products. To protect the reputation of their wares,

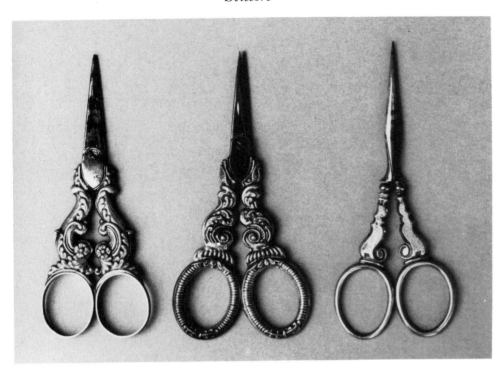

Plate 76: *Scissors from French workboxes. Left and centre: With silver handles, c. 1820. Left pair 9.5 cm. long. Right: With silver-gilt handles marked for Paris after 1838.*

Plate 77: *Scissors with silver handles and silver sheaths from English workboxes from left: 1: Imitation filigree. 11 cm. long. 2–4: Floral and scallop designs, c. 1830–1860.*

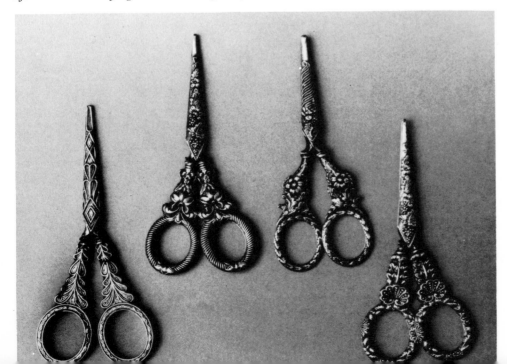

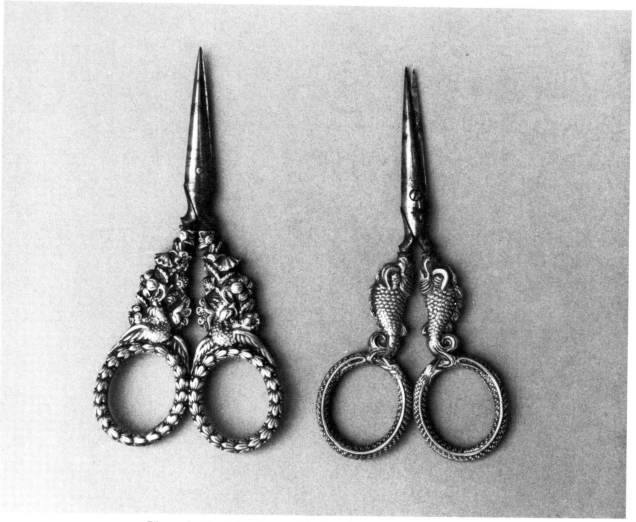

Plate 78: *English scissors with silver handles, c. 1830–1860. Left pair 9.5 cm. long.*

the Sheffield cutlers' companies were instrumental in bringing about the passage of the Trade Mark Act of 1862. The word, Sheffield, was registered as a community trademark for metal goods made only in Sheffield, England. By this time, the best known of the Sheffield cutlers' companies was Joseph Rodgers & Sons, Ltd, which had been founded in the seventeenth century. In the 1860s, this company produced each week some 7,200 pairs of scissors in addition to large quantities of other cutlery.[6]

In plates 77, 78 are some good examples of mid-nineteenth century English scissors in typical Victorian designs. The hand-forged crucible steel blades are attached to shanks ornately chased in silver. The scissors in plate 77 have sheaths to protect the points, a not uncommon practice at the time. Relatively few of the fragile sheaths have survived as a common mishap at the time was to open the scissors still in their sheaths, irrevocably ruining the latter. The designs on the sheaths usually matched the design or motif on the shanks of the scissors and made it difficult to find a matching replacement.

American scissors makers took their lead from English manufacturers, and primarily from those in Sheffield. The first large Sheffield fortunes came from the American trade. The American cutlery industry did not come into existence until the 1830s, and even then it was heavily influenced by Sheffield styles. The earliest cutlery companies were located in Connecticut, Massachusetts and New York. These companies imported much of their raw material and many of their craftsmen from Sheffield, but their method of production reflected the high price and scarcity of labour in the United States. Almost from the beginning, American cutlery companies introduced power-driven machines to forge scissors and other cutlery mechanically.[7]

Where the machine could not be adjusted to the cutlery product, the Americans tried to adjust the product to fit the machine. The result was cutlery of a more simple design, and with fewer variations in patterns from which to choose. By contrast, English cutlery companies often had pattern books with several thousand designs for scissors. Where cutlery could not be cheaply adapted to American machine production, it was sometimes imported from Europe despite the fifty per cent import duty. The penknife or small pocketknife, often found in fitted needlework boxes, is a good example of imported cutlery where American manufacturers found it difficult to compete with the European product because of the extensive hand labour necessary for its manufacture.[8]

The manufacture of scissors presented another challenge to American mechanical ingenuity. Although American cutlery companies drop-forged the scissors blades and stamped out some all-steel scissors and did the first grinding mechanically, they soon discovered that there were limits to the mechanization of scissors manufacturing. As late as 1927, an article in *Scientific American* claimed that despite all attempts at mechanization, ninety per cent of the manufacturing costs of scissors came from the cost of skilled labour just as it had nearly a century before when Americans began to manufacture scissors. This was the result of the necessary hand grinding, polishing and adjusting of one scissors blade to another. Machines for these tasks took so much hand adjustment that they resulted in no saving of labour costs.[9]

The difficulties encountered in manufacturing scissors mechanically led to a specialization in labour not only in the cutlery factory but also between countries. The scissors in plate 79 show this specialization, and date from the late nineteenth and early twentieth centuries. By this time, German scissors blades had become competitive with English steel blades in cost for common scissors.

Germany was soon exporting either the finished blades or scissors blanks to the United States, France and even to England. The first and fifth pairs of scissors from the left were made in the United States but with imported German blades. The French and the English, particularly in their finer

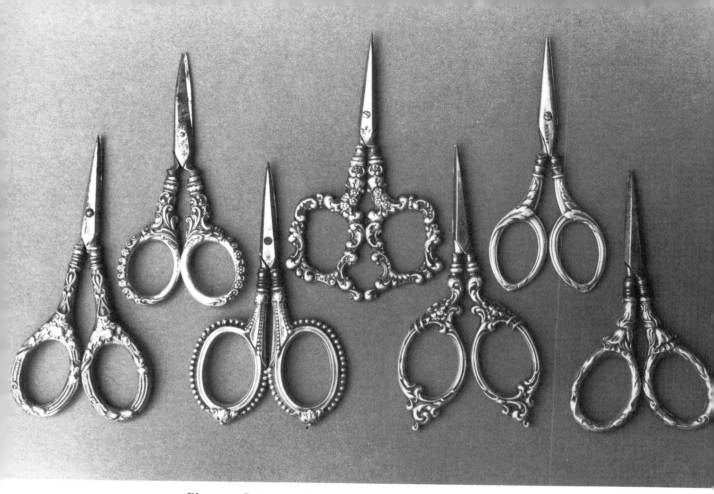

Plate 79: *Scissors with silver handles from left: 1 and 5: Blades marked 'Germany', and handles marked 'Sterling'. American. 10 cm. long. 2: Hallmarked Birmingham, 1912. 3, 4 and 7: Handles marked 'Sterling', American. 6: Blades marked 'Nogent'. French. All c. 1890–1920.*

scissors, such as the embroidery scissors illustrated here, were less likely to use the cheaper imported blades, reserving them for their more common scissors.

Although the advent of mechanization, with the use of dies and drop forging, reduced the variety of styles available in scissors, manufacturers tried within that narrower compass to reflect the fashions of their time. The scissors in plate 80 show the Art Nouveau and Art Deco styles. The scissors in hanging sheaths in plate 81 reflect the revival in popularity of the chatelaine toward the end of the nineteenth century.

All-steel scissors reveal, more than any others, the difficulty in distinguishing between scissors made largely by die-stamping and those made mostly by hand. In plate 82 are seven pairs of scissors, of which only the third pair from the left are known to be stamped out by machine. They were made by the J. Wiss Company of the United States in the early twentieth century. All the other pairs of scissors appear to be English. None dates from after 1890 when few English cutlery companies had yet introduced die-stamped scissors. The

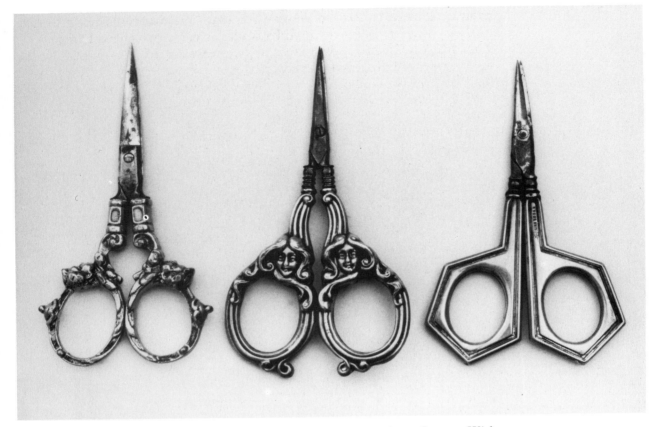

Plate 80: *Left: With silver plate handles. English, c. 1910. 11 cm. long. Centre: With silver Art Nouveau handles marked 'Sterling', American, c. 1900. Right: With silver Art Deco handles marked 'Sterling'. Made by Webster Co., c. 1930.*

finishing work, necessarily done by hand, could be of such high quality that it can be difficult to distinguish the well-designed die-stamped scissors from hand-forged ones.

Cheap and mass produced, die-stamped scissors were not necessarily inferior in strength or individual design to their hand-made predecessors. What suffered was the variety of decorative designs, since these reflected not the individual craftsman's expression of his art, but the demand of the machine for simple patterns in a few basic styles for easy mechanical replication. Nonetheless, the stamping method was always being improved because of the continuing search for a method to produce strong scissors with blades which would retain their cutting edges.

In the 1870s, scissors were often mass produced by steam-driven presses or stamping machines which compacted and shaped scissors blanks. These scissors were stronger than iron ones and cheaper than scissors forged and filed by hand. They had one major disadvantage compared to hand-made scissors: they could not hold a cutting edge as well as blades made from hammered steel. It was soon discovered that stamping could not give that elasticity and toughness required by blades as could prolonged hammering. This defect in die-stamped scissors was overcome by the introduction of the hot drop-forged process where a power-driven hammer drops repeatedly on hot metal resting on a die. This method produced relatively cheap but high quality blades with long-lasting sharp cutting edges.[10]

Plate 81: *Left: Scissors with silver handles and chatelaine sheath marked 'Sterling'. American, c. 1890. 13 cm. long. Right: Silver plate sheath. English, c. 1900.*

The effect of the general improvement in the manufacture of scissors can be seen in the differences in the advertisements for scissors in the Sears, Roebuck and Company catalogues from 1897 to 1908. In 1897 Sear's domestically produced embroidery sewing scissors were not guaranteed at all. Sears continued this policy until 1902 but that year changed from domestic to imported embroidery and sewing scissors.

In 1908 Sears announced that 'we are constantly improving and changing our line of cutlery'. Scissors of 'solid steel' imported from 'the best factory in Germany' were now guaranteed without qualification. This new confidence reflects the more substantial scissors with better cutting edges available. The cost increase was modest. In 1897, a pair of fancy, gilt-handled sewing scissors thirteen centimetres in length similar to those in plate 86 sold for thirty-five cents. In five years they rose one penny to thirty-six cents. By 1908 they sold for forty-two cents.

It is not surprising that Sears turned to Germany for reliable and cheap scissors. By the end of the nineteenth century, Germany was the leading exporter of scissors to the world, and it sold five times as many scissors to the United States as did the Sheffield cutlery companies. Despite increasing mechanization, Sheffield was unable to overcome Germany's lead in the production of scissors for the mass market. Sheffield scissors, plain and fancy, continued, however, to carry prestige and circulated throughout the world.

The German cutlery industry had been concentrated in the hillside town of

Plate 82: *All-steel scissors from left: 1, 2, 5 and 7: English, c. 1850–1880. Left pair 11 cm. long. 3: Marked 'J. Wiss'. American, c. 1920. 4: Marked 'Lund'. English, c. 1860. 6: With gilt handles marked 'F. West, St. James St'. English, c. 1880.*

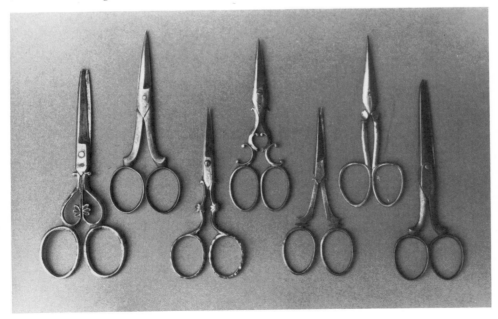

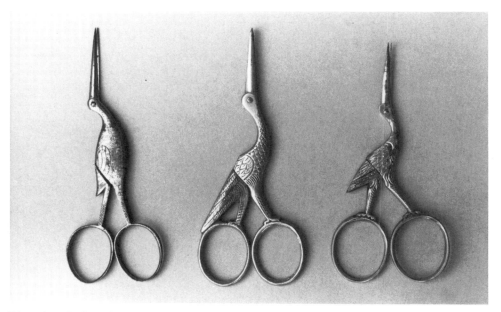

Plate 83: *Left and centre: English stork scissors, c. 1860–1890. Left pair 10 cm. long. Right: German, c. 1890–1930.*

Solingen since the fourteenth century. By the middle of the nineteenth century, Germany imported its steel from Sheffield and had mechanized as far as possible its scissors factories. By 1908 Solingen employed 3,200 workers in the scissors trade alone, and could undersell any other country in the world in the price of its common scissors.[11]

Thérèse de Dillmont suggested in her needlework encyclopaedia that two kinds of sewing scissors were indispensable: 'a pair of large ones for cutting out, with a rounded and a sharp point ... and a small pair with two sharp points, for cutting threads and removing small pieces of stuff....'[12] The latter embroidery type of scissors, as in the second pair from the left in plate 82 or in the stork shape in plate 83, were particularly popular from the nineteenth century to the present time. In 1895 Butterick sold English-made stork scissors for fifty cents which were very similar to the middle pair of stork scissors in plate 83. Butterick sold the larger sewing scissors recommended by Thérèse de Dillmont for twenty-five cents plain or fifty cents fancy.

These stork embroidery scissors as well as embroidery scissors with other animals on the shanks were first popularized by Joseph Rodgers and Sons, Thomas Wilkinson and Son, and others in Sheffield from the middle of the nineteenth century. By the end of that century, Germany had taken the lead in producing die-stamped animal figure scissors which it exported in ever greater quantities. Some examples of scissors with animal shanks, primarily of German origin, are in plate 84.

Although all-steel scissors were the strongest available, scissors with more fragile material for handles and shanks such as ivory, bone and horn were also

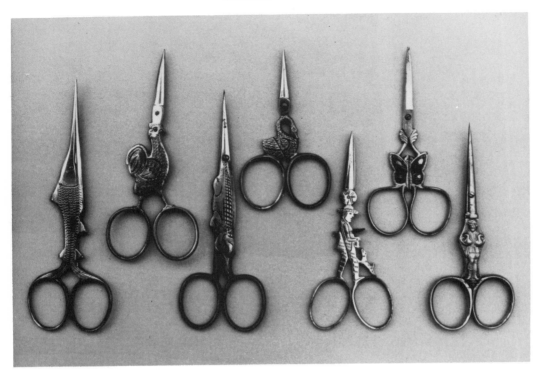

Plate 84: *Steel figural scissors from left: 1: Swordfish. British Reg. no. 154232. 12.5 cm. long. 2: Rooster marked 'Marshall Wells, Germany'. 3: Alligator marked 'Germany'. 4: Swan. 5: Hunter with dog. 6: Butterfly marked 'Asbro, Germany, Solid Steel'. 7: Farmer with two hens marked 'G. G. Leykauf', German. All c. 1890–1920.*

Plate 85: *From left: Two pairs of folding scissors. German and English. 9 cm. long. Dagger scissors with sheath from chatelaine. Two pairs of buttonhole scissors. German and English. Chinese scissors with green silk embroidered case. All c. 1890–1930.*

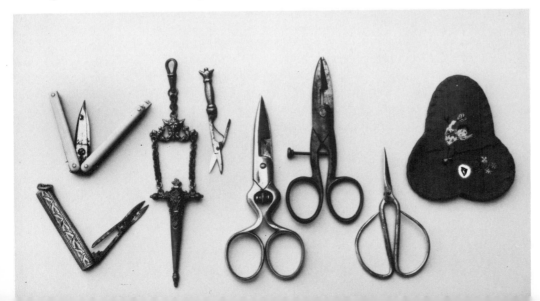

popular. Other scissors which might also be found in the workbox or on the chatelaine include folding scissors as in the two pairs on the left in plate 85 and the dagger scissors removed from their hanging sheath case. To their right are two pairs of buttonhole scissors. These were for plain sewing and were not usually ornamented. Manufacturers of such scissors competed on the basis of durability, price and the type of mechanism used to adjust the blades for cutting different size buttonholes. The buttonhole scissors on the left are German and have an interior mechanism for adjusting the blades. The English pair on the right use an exterior screw adjustment device which is more common. Montgomery Ward and Company sold a model similar to this English pair for thirty-nine cents in 1894.

Scissors were obviously not a European monopoly and were made in Asia as elsewhere. The picturesque Chinese scissors and case to the far right of plate 85 are not uncommonly found in Western markets and have always been

Plate 86: *Set of steel scissors in rose plush case. English, c. 1890. Case 16 cm. long.*

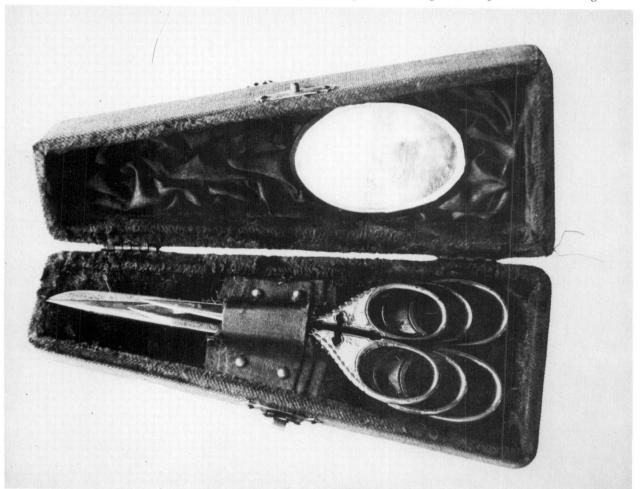

popular with collectors. Sewing scissors in different sizes were often sold in fancy cases in sets of three, sometimes with a mirror on the interior lid as in plate 86. Butterick sold similar English sewing scissors for fifty cents each under its Gloriana label at the end of the nineteenth century.

The collector will find that most of the interesting needlework scissors available in the market date from the last half of the nineteenth century and the first third of the twentieth. They come in a great variety of sizes and designs and many are still reasonable in cost. In the absence of marks, it is sometimes possible to date fancy sewing and embroidery scissors of this period by style alone. The Victorian scissors with silver handles are characterized up to the 1890s by somewhat elaborate designs and rather fine metal work. The traditional designs after the 1890s are heavier in concept and the metal work is less finely done than earlier. Because of the greater use of hand labour, English scissors have much better detail work than either German or American scissors during this entire period.

The marks usually found on scissors are those on the blade (often giving national origin) which may be different from those on the shank or handle which may identify either the manufacturer or the distributor. For example, Butterick marked its scissors, B.P. Co. Ltd, on the lower blade just below the screw and above the shank. Its scissors were usually of English manufacture but the blades were not infrequently of German origin and were sometimes so marked. Other marks which help date scissors are United States patent numbers or British registry marks. English scissors with silver handles will often have hallmarks which give both the place and date where the silver content was assayed in England.

The materials used in the construction of scissors are also of some help in determining the origin of scissors by date and occasionally by place. Scissors with mother-of-pearl handles, for example, were made primarily in the first two decades or so of the nineteenth century, and are usually of French origin. In the last quarter of the nineteenth century, celluloid and other plastics began to replace ivory, tortoise shell, horn and other natural materials previously used for shanks and handles. Nickel-plated scissors appeared only toward the end of the nineteenth century.

The method of manufacture is sometimes of help in separating hand-forged scissors from die-stamped scissors. A close study of the texture of the steel design may reveal the clear and individual marks of the hand-filed scissors by contrast with the more mechanical look of stamped or pressed scissors. In the absence of some other clue as to national origin, this may not establish any meaningful chronology since hand forging and filing of scissors continued in some Sheffield cutlery companies well into the twentieth century while this was the exception after 1870 in the United States, Germany and France.

Most of the collectable scissors in this period do not yet command a sufficiently high price to encourage reproductions or the alteration of scissors to make them appear older than they are. Where repairs or alterations have taken place, it is usually to make the scissors more functional. Major repairs which the collector should guard against are several: replaced handles which do not match one another exactly; replaced screws (to hold the blades together) which are not wholly functional; and points which have been filed down to make them meet once again in a single point. This last alteration is usually obvious if one compares the length of the blade to the shank of such scissors with another of the same type.

Perhaps the most common repair is the gluing together of non-metal handles or shanks which have been broken. What is most surprising is that it is not uncommon even in handles and shanks of silver or steel, particularly if they are delicate and relatively old. Collectors examining such scissors should be very cautious opening or closing them as the slightest strain may snap such handles or shanks and bring about an unwanted sale. It is prudent to ask the seller to test them.

6 Tape-measures, Emeries and Waxers

'Give him an inch and he will take a mile', is a saying we often hear, but how many of us know the original version of this proverb: 'give him an inch and he'll take an ell'? Before most European countries adopted the metric system in the early nineteenth century, Western Europe used the ell as a length of measure for fabric. The exact length of an ell, however, depended upon which country was using it.

Ell comes from the word for elbow, and originally meant the distance from the elbow to the fingertips or from the shoulder to the wrist. This may account for some of the differences in ell measurements. In earlier times, ell was such a common measure that it entered into our metaphorical language. Shakespeare has a character in *Romeo and Juliet* say: 'O, here's a wit ... that stretches from an inch narrow to an ell broad.'

A more direct predecessor of our contemporary foot and yard ruler is the folding ruler sometimes found in fitted needlework boxes such as the Palais Royal box in plate 1. This ruler is of mother-of-pearl and calibrated on one side in twelve divisions which each have twelve sub-divisions. It seems likely that this foot ruler was intended for the English market. It is, however, about a quarter of an inch too short for an English foot, and the divisions within each 'short' inch reflect this discrepancy. The reverse side has four markings: 1/6, 1/8, 1/12 and 1/16 which were common calibrations on fabric measures.

The sixteenth-century English yard was often subdivided into one-half, one-fourth, one-eighth and one-sixteenth of a yard. The last part was two and a quarter inches in length and was known as a nail, a measurement still found in early nineteenth-century tape-measures. The nail became obsolete as a measurement in the period 1824–55 when new standards for the measurement of a yard changed the older system.

The reality of measurement standards in England from the sixteenth century to 1824 was that while a more or less adequate legal standard did exist, it was the numerous local standards which took precedence because they were the most often used. These standards were usually embodied in the measuring stick of the local Guildhall.

In 1855 Parliament authorized the Imperial Standard Yard metal bar (sixteen parts of copper, two and a half parts of tin and one part of zinc) with the distance of one yard marked between two lines drawn on gold plugs set into the bar. The yard measurement was to be taken at 62 degrees Fahrenheit. The United States also accepted this standard the following year of 1856 but decided to take yard measurements at 68 degrees Fahrenheit.[1] This small deviation between the English and American yard was of no meaningful significance as local yard rulers, sometimes measured one against the other for accuracy, continued in both England and the United States to set the standard for approximate rather than precise measurement.

When the housewife or the tape-measure manufacturer in the early nineteenth century wanted to verify the length of the cloth tape, the tape was usually end-measured against a wood yard ruler or the measure at the local Guildhall which had been taken from the legally authorized standard. The housewife may have thought that in measuring her new, replacement cloth tape against the house yard ruler rather than against the tape being replaced that she was being more accurate. In fact, it did not matter which she measured as inaccuracy was built into the standards and the system of measurement itself. This is why collectors today may find discrepancies between tape measurements, whether in nails or inches, when comparing tapes that vary in age or origin.

Since no one handling fabric in the nineteenth century either expected or needed the kind of precise measurement taken for granted today, the slight variation in the yard rulers was not a source of great worry as long as a needlewoman could use her own ruler in a dispute with the pedlar or tradesman. Since these wood rulers were cumbersome to carry about, needlewomen welcomed the more portable cloth measuring tapes encased in decorative cylinders. If they were no more accurate than the wood yard rulers, they were probably no less accurate. In a world in which precise measurement was unknown, tape-measures were, indeed, much more convenient to use.

Many of the nineteenth-century tape-measures came from fitted needlework boxes. The carving on their tops matched the mother-of-pearl, ivory, bone or wood tops of the reels, emeries and waxers. They fitted into slots which left only the carved top visible on the surface. Their cloth tapes were usually the colour of the silk or velvet lining the interior of the workbox. Some representative mother-of-pearl tape-measures from workboxes are in plate 87. The yard-long tapes are stencilled in black or dark blue in inches or quarter yards or both. The tape is pulled through a slit in the side of the cylindrical case and rewound by turning the spindle protruding from the top or by turning the entire top. The bone and ivory tape-measures in plate 88 are also from workboxes and function in the same manner.

The Tunbridge tape-measures in plate 89 are another example of Tunbridge souvenir ware. This ware was also used in waxers, emeries, needlecases, workboxes, needlebooks, thimble cases, pincushions, thread containers, clamps, and many other domestic items. Tunbridgeware comes from the town of Tunbridge Wells which became a fashionable spa after the discovery of its chalybeate water springs in the seventeenth century. By the late eighteenth century, Tunbridgeware was famous for its high quality veneer and inlaid wood work. Tunbridge Wells had a well organized woodworking industry with skilled turners, cabinet makers, veneer and marquetry workers and painters. They specialized in the production of small and dec-

Plate 87: *Tape-measures with mother-of-pearl tops and silk ribbons from English workboxes, c. 1840–1880. Upper left tape-measure 4 cm. high.*

orative woodware for visitors to the spa, and they were quick to adapt to the changing fashions of the time.

Until the second decade of the nineteenth century, Tunbridge Wells made its reputation in high quality veneered and inlaid woodware, either in its natural state or painted black, green or red. One of the most popular patterns was a marquetry cube design applied in such a manner as to create a strong feeling of depth in perspective.

About the end of the second decade of the nineteenth century, Tunbridge Wells woodworkers began to experiment with end-grain mosaic which was quite different from the earlier and more expensive veneer mosaic of marquetry and inlay. End-grain mosaic was an attempt to lower the production cost of marquetry work. Painted woodware, made primarily between 1790 and 1830, was less expensive than end-grain mosaic or marquetry work but it did not command the popularity of either one. The problem with marquetry work was the laborious job of cutting individual pieces of veneer. For more

Plate 88: *Bone and ivory tape-measures with silk ribbons from English workboxes, c. 1800–1860. Upper left tape-measure 4 cm. high.*

stock patterns, workers could cut up to fifteen centimetres of a veneer piece and somewhat lower the cost of production, but the process remained expensive and time consuming.

End-grain mosaic not only solved the problem of the high cost of veneer work but it made far better patterns available. End-grain mosaic was a cheaper way of applying relatively large pieces of what looked like marquetry to plain wood surfaces. To make end-grain mosaic, the worker assembled and glued together narrow strips of various hardwoods of different colours. This made a rectangular or circular block about eight or ten centimetres in diametre and about twenty or twenty-six centimetres in length. The narrow sticks of wood were so assembled that when the end was held to view, it revealed a mosaic design made up of the assembled sticks. This mosaic design ran all the way through the length of the block.

The worker then sliced a thin veneer about one and a half millimetres deep off the end of the block and applied it to a wood object as the centrepiece or as a part of a band or as a complete surface veneer. The animal glue took about twelve hours to set. Then the worker sanded and either polished or varnished the end-grain mosaic and any exposed wood surface. Because end-grain mosaic became popular in the 1820s at the height of the fashion for rosewood, that wood often furnished the background for the end-grain mosaic centrepieces and borders.[2]

The economically applied end-grain mosaic proved extraordinarily fashionable in nineteenth-century England as well as abroad and consolidated the reputation of the Tunbridge woodworkers. A fitted needlework box exhibited at the Crystal Palace exhibition of 1851 had a mosaic design of the remains of Bayham Abbey and contained some 13,000 pieces of naturally coloured wood.

Many Tunbridge families claimed credit for the invention of end-grain mosaic, but the firm of G. & J. Burrows may have the strongest claim as the earliest users of the technique. It has been suggested that Tunbridge end-grain mosaic was an adaptation of Sorrento wood mosaic which began about the late 1820s in Italy. This claim seems unproveable because Tunbridge workers were already experimenting with end-grain mosaic at least by the 1820s. What has not been suggested before is the possible influence of Asian marquetry techniques which used an identical end-grain mosaic method. The difference was that the Asian sticks were not made of naturally coloured hardwoods but of silver and other metals, shell, ebony and exotic materials. Many of the Asian fitted needlework boxes have this type of end-grain veneer mosaic. England imported such Asian boxes long before Tunbridge workers began to experiment with end-grain mosaic.[3]

A variation on end-grain mosaic was stickware. This technique used the same type of glued block of sticks, but instead of slicing thin veneers off the end, the worker turned the block sideways on a lathe so that the various coloured sticks were exposed lengthways. In the upper row of plate 89, the middle tape-measure has its top section in stickware while the lower part is in end-grain mosaic. In the tray of a fitted needlework box, only the stickware top is visible.

The late Edward Pinto, who wrote the only monograph on Tunbridge ware, suggested that Tunbridge designs furnish a clue to the age of individual pieces. Marquetry cube designs date from the eighteenth century, but when combined with end-grain mosaic, they appear from the late 1820s into the twentieth century. The cube inlays are either the centre of the design with end-grain mosaic making up the border, or vice-versa. With regard to end-grain mosaic alone, as a general rule, the simpler the design, the earlier the work.[4]

Centrepieces of butterflies or birds were favoured from the late 1820s to the 1850s. Mosaic bandings were especially popular from the 1830s to the middle 1840s. At that time, floral designs began to imitate Berlin wool work patterns for embroidery. These appeared on graph paper, the pattern forming a geometric design in different colours.

Berlin patterns were an enormous rage among middle and upper class women and indeed, became so popular that by the 1840s embroidery was nearly synonymous with Berlin wool work. After the 1870s, Berlin work faced competition from 'art needlework', a movement away from the literal copying of representational paintings or scenes in needlework.

Berlin patterns influenced not only Tunbridge mosaic design but bead-work patterns on many needlework tools including needlecases, thimble cases and others. Though the influence of Berlin patterns was eventually diluted among the more sophisticated in taste by post-representational art and by the Arts and Crafts movement, it survived as a strong force in embroidery until the First World War brought about an aversion to everything Germanic in name. Berlin work patterns offered an excellent design source to the Tunbridge workers, who used them for the rest of the nineteenth century for banding and for centrepieces. In the second half of the century, however, Berlin work found strong competition from representations of castles, abbeys and diverse architectural ruins which, as items of souvenir interest, furnished another major source of design.[5]

Tunbridge mosaic ware or stickware used rosewood, mahogany and beech as its principal background woods. For the actual mosaic, it used these woods plus bird's-eye maple, sycamore, holly, walnut, oak, birch and satinwood. Sycamore wood turned grey when treated with chalybeate water from Tunbridge Wells while satinwood turned green.

Quality workmanship, such as the mitring of corners and the repeats of

Plate 89: *Tunbridge tape-measures with silk ribbons. Top row: Mosaic and stickware patterns with measurements in nails, c. 1825–1850. Left case 3.5 cm. high. Bottom row: Mosaic-pattern tops with measurements in inches, c. 1850–1880.*

designs is not a necessary indication of the age of Tunbridgeware. Much of the Tunbridgeware was varnished, especially in the later nineteenth century to meet the competition of other woodware, but this does not necessarily date it as much of the work originally polished was later refinished by varnishing.[6]

Of the six Tunbridge tape-measures in plate 89 the first from the left, upper row, is completely covered by end-grain mosaic, the second, as already mentioned, is half stickware and half mosaic, the third, as well as the entire bottom row, is mosaic only on the top of the cylinder while the bottom part is plain rosewood.

The three tape-measures on the upper row are older because their tapes are calibrated in nails rather than in inches. A nail is equivalent to two and a quarter inches or one-sixteenth of a yard. Such tapes were often marked: 1N, 2N, 3N, ¼YD, ½YD, 1YD. The practice of using nail measurements died out slowly rather than stopping at any specific time, but nail measurements are rarely found beyond the 1830s. Earlier tapes usually have somewhat irregular calibrations. The general rule is that the more regular the calibrated marks, the later the tape.

Silver was another popular cover for tape-measures. The first three tape-

Plate 90: *Silver tape-measures from top left: 1: American marked 'Sterling', c. 1890. 2 cm. diameter. 2: Hallmarked Birmingham, 1901. Bottom row: 3–5: From English sewing cases, c. 1850. 6: Silver filigree. English, c. 1820.*

Plate 91: *Left: Cowrie shell tape-measure. 5.5 cm. long. Right: Sea urchin tape-measure with rosewood mounts. Both English, c. 1850–1875.*

measures in plate 90 on the bottom row are from sewing cases and fitted into specific slots made to contain them. The shell tape-measures in plate 91 were usually bought as souvenirs. If they were added to a workbox, they would go into an open all-purpose compartment. The sea urchin tape-measure on the right is unusual because of its very small fragile shell and the careful work on its rosewood spindle top. Shell collecting was a widespread hobby in Victorian England, encouraged by the spread of cheap railway travel, the accessibility of numerous seaside resorts and the growing interest in geology and biology.

Vegetable ivory was a substance often used to make various needlework implements including tape-measures. Many of these vegetable ivory items are multiple needlework tools as in plates 92, 93. The Victorians accented the warm honey colour of vegetable ivory by adding the creamy white of ivory or bone. Vegetable ivory is the term sometimes mistakenly used for two vegetable products, the coquilla and corozo nut which, in common with ivory, are hard, lustrous and brittle. The term should be reserved for the corozo nut alone.

The coquilla nut comes from the Brazilian palm tree, *Attalea finifera*, known in Brazil as the *Piassaba*. It is about the size of a hen's egg and has been known and used in Europe by carvers since the Renaissance. Because of its rich burnt sienna colour and its hardness, the coquilla nut shell has always been popular with turners of small objects. It was an ideal material for snuff boxes in the eighteenth century because the oily nature of the kernel kept

Plate 92: *Vegetable ivory tape-measures from left: 1: With double-ended emery. 6 cm. long. 2: With needlecase and Stanhope viewer. 3–4: From workboxes. 5: With Stanhope viewer. All English, c. 1860–1890.*

Plate 93: *Vegetable ivory combination stands: Left: Emery, tape-measure and pincushion. 8 cm. high. Centre: Tape-measure and double-ended emery. Right: Emery and spool holder. All English, c. 1850–1890.*

snuff from drying out. This oily surface also made it difficult to glue one piece of coquilla shell to another. Large pieces are made up of smaller pieces pegged together.

The natural egg shape of the coquilla nut lent it to many purposes for needlework implements. Pierced all over and filled with a scented powder, it made a natural sachet. It could also be turned and carved for use as cotton barrels, pincushions, thimble holders and other small implements such as the two needlecases on the far right in plate 43 which resemble highly polished dark wood.[7]

Unlike the coquilla nut, where the artisan used the shell as the raw material for carving or turning, vegetable ivory was the hard albumen of the seed found in the nut of the South American palm, *Phytelephas macrocarpa*. Each nut, about the size of a human head, contains up to nine seeds. When cut open, the seeds resemble ivory in hardness, colour and texture. After exposure to light, the seeds take on an easily recognized honey colour.

Known to carvers and turners in Europe from the late eighteenth century, this nut was first called the corozo or ivory nut. It was sometimes also referred to as the tagua nut, which was the Colombian name for the palm tree from which it came. The term, vegetable ivory, has now become the conventional term for any work carved or turned from the seed of the corozo nut. It is still possible, however, to find dealers, especially in England, who refer to any non-animal 'ivory' as mutton-ivory.

The corozo nut was even more popular than the coquilla nut for the making of needlework implements. The collector will find nearly every article of the work table available in vegetable ivory including thimbles and their holders (often acorn-shaped), cotton reels, pincushions, waxers, emeries and needle cases. The designs on the corozo nut are generally more repetitive than those on the coquilla shell and make much use of piercing and ornamental turning of very standard motifs.

Souvenirs were very popular in Victorian England, and pictures of favourite resorts were among those most wanted by the public. Reverse glass painting was one novel way of preserving the scene of a memorable vacation. To paint on glass in reverse, the artist painted first the foreground details in the picture, and then worked back, step by step, to the background, such as the sky, which was painted last. This rather time-consuming method was soon replaced by the coloured print under glass, and then by the photograph under glass. Glass paperweights with coloured prints fixed to the bottom were a popular novelty at the Great Exhibition at the Crystal Palace in 1851.[8]

The use of a thinner glass made it possible to extend this pictorial souvenir to needlework implements such as needlebooks, pincushions and tape-measures. All three had the print (or later photo) set under glass on one side and on the reverse, a mirror or some inscription relevant to the picture. The area between the top and bottom of the disc allowed for space to store the rolled-up tape and for a small handle to pull it out. In plate 94 are examples of two such tape-measures, a disc pincushion and a needlebook with prints

Plate 94: *Souvenir prints under glass from top left: 1: Brass tape-measure with view of Alexandra Palace. Spring mechanism rewinds tape. 4 cm. diameter. 2: Brass tape-measure commemorating Prince Albert's death. Spring rewind mechanism. 3: Pincushion with view of Dartmouth from Mount Boone. 4: Needlebook with view of Beachy Head at Eastbourne. All English, c. 1850–1875.*

under glass. Both tape measures have a novel feature for the 1860s: a spring-activated retractor which automatically rewinds the tape into the disc case. This replaced the usual wind-up handle or spindle.

Improvements on this spring-activated retractor quickly followed. The most important was the addition of a button which allowed the tape to stay extended from the case until the pressing of the button activated the retractor. This more complex retractor became standard on some American and German tape-measures from the 1870s as seen in plate 95.

The tape-measure in plate 95, on the left of the bottom row, is made of gutta-percha. This is a substance like rubber but with more resin, and it is easily moulded by heating and pressing. Gutta-percha was introduced in 1845 and patented in 1846 by Alexander Parkes. It was commonly used on daguerrotype cases for early photographs.[9] The tape-measure here has a patent date of July, 1869.

From the 1870s to the 1930s, needlework tools in general, and tape-measures in particular, became much more whimsical in design. This may be partly the result of the cheapness of mass production which led to a never ending search for novelty. It may also be a result of the decline in hand sewing which made it less necessary to produce utilitarian tools of great durability or tools which would fit into a workbox.

Although England and the United States produced many of these toy-like tape-measures, Germany and Austria saturated the market with these novelties in the form of miniature grinders, coaches, irons, clocks, saucepans, tankards, violins, buildings and others as in plate 96. Most of these European tape-measures were calibrated in both inches and centimetres as they were aimed at domestic and foreign markets. The tape-measures had cotton tapes as did nearly all tape-measures made in the last quarter of the nineteenth

Plate 95: *Disc tape-measures from top left: 1–2: Silver marked 'Sterling'. Made by Webster Co. and by Gorham Co. American, c. 1900. 3.5 cm. diameter. 3: Brass perpetual calendar. American, patent date marked 'Jan 10, '82'. 4: Gutta-percha. American, marked 'Patd July 13th 1869, Reissue June 13th 1871'. 5–6: Brass plaques with owl and owl's face. Marked 'Germany', c. 1900. All have spring rewind mechanisms.*

century. The major exceptions were those tape-measures of silk destined for fitted needlework boxes or the luxury trade.

American tape-measures were made for a growing domestic market and were usually calibrated only in inches. Outside scientific and technical circles, the metric system was not well received in America. The majority of novelty tape-measures there were base metal, cheap and well suited to mass production. The inscriptions on the mass-produced tape-measures (plate 97) are typical of humour of the period.

Another substance which lent itself almost as well to mass production and

Plate 96: Tape-measures from top left: 1: Copper and brass coffee mill. 4.5 cm. high. 2: Gilt brass coach. 3: Book with tooled brown leather cover marked 'Made in Austria'. Second row: 4: Brass iron marked 'Germany'. 5: Yellow sheet metal clock marked 'Germany'. 6: Copper saucepan. Third row: 7: Brass stein with thimble in top. 8: Copper and brass ship's wheel. British Reg. no. 128885. 9: Brass cello. 10: Brass millhouse. All except no. 8 from Central Europe, c. 1889–1910. No. 3 and 5 have spring rewind mechanisms.

Plate 97: *Tape-measures. On left: Liberty Bell inscribed 'The Bell that got the Kaiser's Measure'. 5 cm. high. Shoe inscribed 'Three feet in one shoe'. Centre: Turtle inscribed 'Pull my head but not my leg'. On right: Whiskey flask inscribed 'I made Kentucky famous in a measure'. Hat inscribed 'Most hats cover the head. This covers the feet'. American, c. 1900–1920. All have spring rewind mechanisms.*

which simulated the more expensive look of ivory was celluloid. Invented in 1862, it at first failed in commercial applications. An improved form introduced in the 1870s succeeded commercially and soon established a wide market for producing die-moulded objects such as needlework implements.[10] Some celluloid tape-measures made in the United States and Germany are in plate 98.

Although England and Germany made the majority of souvenir tape-measures not only for their own countries but also for export, the United States also produced its own souvenir ware tape-measures. One type widely distributed in the 1930s was a disc-style tape-measure with a print under plastic applied on both sides of a thin metal case. The prints represented paintings of some salient feature of a major city or resort in the United States such as the beaches in San Diego, California or the Capitol Building in Washington, D.C. (plate 99).

In the middle of the nineteenth century, tape-measures were often associated with emeries and waxers. The three tools were sometimes arranged in three closely spaced slots in the tray of a fitted needlework box and were indistinguishable from each other if they had matching carved tops. A good

Plate 98: *Celluloid tape-measures from top left: 1: Sprig of currants. 5 cm. high. 2: Pansy marked 'Germany'. 3: Basket of fruit. 4: Three pansies. American, patent date 'July 19, 1917'. 5–6: Butterflies. All except no. 4 from Germany, c. 1900–1930. All have spring rewind mechanisms.*

Plate 99: *Souvenir disc tape-measures made in the United States, c. 1930. 4 cm. diameter. All have spring rewind mechanisms.*

example is in the coromandel box on the right in plate 10. It shows the three identical mother-of-pearl tops of the tape-measure, emery and waxer in the front centre of the box.

The word, emery, comes from France where such polishing powders were in wide use in the later middle ages. By the Renaissance, if not sooner, they had also made their appearance in England. The function of the emery was to remove rust from pins and needles. The emery, often in the shape of a small pincushion, was filled with a coarse variety of corundum powder or with sand. This polished the pin or needle as it was pushed into the emery and withdrawn. Because of its filling, the emery was heavier and stiffer than a pincushion of equal size. As a result, emeries usually came in small sizes, often in fanciful imitations of berries or of miniature fruit. They also came as discs which were similar to disc pincushions or as cylinders like tape-measures (plate 100).

Waxer is a term coined by needlework tool collectors for the wax holder, more accurately known as a thread-waxer. Before thread was machine twisted, a thread-waxer containing beeswax or white wax was necessary to

Plate 100: *Top row: Mother-of-pearl pincushion. 3.5 cm. diameter. Three mother-of-pearl emeries. Bottom row: Four mother-of-pearl waxers. All from English workboxes, c. 1830–1870.*

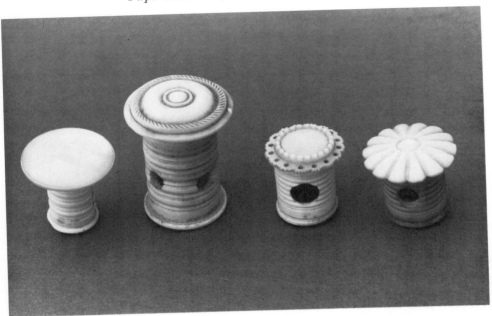

Plate 101: *Emeries with mother-of-pearl tops. Needles are inserted through holes covered with silk or velvet. All from English workboxes, c. 1840–1880. Left case 3 cm. high.*

Plate 102: *Waxers with mother-of-pearl tops which unscrew to fit cake of beeswax on bone shank. All from English workboxes, c. 1840–1880. Upper left case 3 cm. high.*

strengthen the thread, to keep it from tangling or to prepare thread when stringing beads. The most simple form of a thread-waxer was a cake of beeswax or a white candle cut to fit between two disc ends.

The collectable thread-waxers usually are in the form of a disc, like a small version of the disc pincushion, or in the form of an open cylinder about the size of a tape-measure. Waxers are often combined, when made of vegetable ivory, in the same multi-purpose implement with needlecases, tape-measures and pincushions. Other waxers are in fanciful shapes such as eggs, small barrels, acorn shapes, and most appropriate of all, small holders painted with flowers and beehives. The availability of wax was not a problem for those who carried a very small spoon in their étui although the way it was used is not very appealing: with its help, wax was extracted from the ear to put on the thread as needed.

The close resemblance of pincushions, emeries and waxers appears in plate 100. The first implement on the left, upper row, is a pincushion while the next three are emeries. The implements in the bottom row, in the same shape as the emeries, are all waxers.

A series of emeries in plate 101 and waxers in plate 102 have similar cylindrical shapes. The waxer on the top right of plate 102 without its wax looks almost like a reel.

Emeries and waxers not intended for a specific slot in a fitted needlework box are usually of more fanciful shape such as strawberry emeries with silver tops. Other types of emeries in plate 103 include small squares or circles of

Plate 103: *From left: 1 and 5: Silk and leather emeries. English, c. 1850. Left emery 2.5 cm. square. 2: Silver filigree emery. English, c. 1820. 3: 'Frozen Charlotte' doll set in green beeswax. American, c. 1920. 4: Strawberry emery with silver top marked 'Sterling'. American, c. 1900.*

Plate 104: *Tunbridgeware. Top row: Mosaic-pattern box with purple velvet pincushion. 8.5 cm. wide. Three stickware combination emeries and waxers. Middle row: Stickware emery, stickware waxer with slightly indented base for winding thread, and teapot-shaped stickware emery. Bottom row: Stickware container with mosaic-pattern top made to hold wax holder (to its right); double-ended mosaic-pattern emery. All English, c. 1820–1880.*

fabric, or silver filigree cylinders enclosing an emery. An unusual waxer in this plate is the so-called Frozen Charlotte doll mounted on a cylinder of green beeswax.

Emeries and waxers also came in Tunbridgeware, and often in combination in the same implement. In plate 104, the three cylinders on the upper right are both emeries and waxers. The top portion covered with velvet is an emery. The bottom portion unscrews to reveal a small cake of wax fitted over a small spindle. The very small stickware teapot has a lid which is a velvet covered emery.

At the turn of the century, tape-measures, emeries and waxers varied in price from a few pennies each to dollars or pounds depending upon the materials used to encase them. S. S. Kresge and Company sold in 1913, for example, strawberry fabric emeries for five cents, and celluloid or base metal tape-measures for ten cents each. Sterling silver-mounted emeries cost anywhere from thirty-eight cents up. Sterling silver tape-measures began at a little over a dollar although the more substantial ones started at two dollars. Today, of course, the price of these collectable implements has risen strongly, particularly for tape-measures where the demand is stronger than for emeries and waxers whose value seems to depend almost entirely on the shape and material of which they are made.

It is not difficult to vet tape-measures, emeries and waxers. There is little or no reproduction of tape-measures, but there is much repairing and replacing of missing parts. It is necessary first to check that the tape does exist, that it can be extracted and rewound, and if possible, that the top or bottom of the case comes apart so that a jammed tape can be taken out and rewound. A replaced tape is not necessarily a sign of fraud as many nineteenth-century owners of tape-measures replaced the tape when it broke or became worn. Tape-measures intended for fitted needlework boxes should have tapes of silk matching the silk lining of the box.

The two parts of tape-measures most often missing or replaced are the spindles or handles used to rewind the tape, and the very small handle at the end of the tape which is used to extract the tape, or in the case of spring-activated retractors, to prevent the tape from disappearing into the case. The handles and spindles should match the material and design of the case. It is important that they be functional and that spring-activated retractors work when the button controlling them is depressed. If such a mechanism suddenly breaks when the seller is demonstrating, ask that it be repaired. Malfunctioning tape-measures should bring a lower price on the market.

Emeries present few problems to the collector seeking authentic needlework implements. It is important that fabric emeries not be confused with small pincushions, but a comparison of the weight of each should solve that problem. Waxers also present no problem to the collector if the holder is in good condition. It is preferable to find a waxer that still retains some of its old wax. The collector will find, however, that many wax holders have been refitted with new beeswax, something that undoubtedly occurred many times in the past to any well used waxer.

7 Pins and Pincushions

Anyone surveying the vast domain of nineteenth-century pincushions is tempted to adapt *Ecclesiastes* to read: 'Of the making of pincushions there is no end.' The manufacturing of pincushions became a mania in the nineteenth century. It reflected not only the extraordinary interest in needlework of all kinds, but the need for an accessible place to put the mass-produced, cheap and well made pin.

The pin had once been a rare and expensive fastener for fabrics. Guilds and monasteries in Europe produced simple pins for use in household sewing and as fabric fasteners from at least the fourteenth century. Vast quantities of pins were needed because other fabric fasteners were rare. Women favoured French pins until the seventeenth century because they would not snag fine fabrics. By that time, the English began to produce equally high quality pins of tinned brass. These two countries remained the largest manufacturers of pins until the middle of the nineteenth century.

The United States imported its pins primarily from England until the middle of the nineteenth century when its own pin industry began to fill its needs. An attempt to manufacture pins in the American colony in the eighteenth century was not successful. Most American colonists, including George Washington, ordered their pins from England. There was an amazing variety available, and the names of some of these pins strike the modern ear as strange: corkins, middlings, shorts, whites and lillikins. Black mourning pins and lace pins were also available although none of these was cheap. In the late 1770s, the price for a dozen pins in the new United States was seven shillings and sixpence.[1]

In the eighteenth- and early nineteenth-century pin factory, it took some twenty operations to produce a single pin from brass wire to finished pin with its separate coiled wire head finally attached to its wire shaft. In the 1760s, Adam Smith described in his *Wealth of Nations* the division of labour in pin manufacturing which he so much admired for its efficiency. These factories were able to produce pins at the rate of several thousand pins per man per day. This brought down the previously high cost.

Pins became even cheaper after the invention of pin-making machines and the establishment of a mass-production pin industry in England and the United States. In 1824, the American, Lemuel Wellman Wright of Massachusetts, secured an English patent for a machine making one-piece pins. The company using his machine was not, however, successful. Daniel Foote-Taylor of Birmingham then acquired control of the factory and also an extension of Wright's patent for five years from 1838. His company was successful and became the first to carry out regular production of machine-made pins. The machine forced the warm brass wire into the shape of a head and shaft in a single operation so that it produced a strong, one-piece pin. Soon these machines were producing pins at a rate of up to two hundred pins per minute.[2]

The United States pin industry started at about the same time when the Howe Manufacturing Company of Connecticut began operations in 1836. The great advantage of the machine-made pin over the hand-crafted one was not only in the lower unit cost, but in the inability of the head of the pin to become separated from the shaft. The hand-crafted pin had its coiled wire head made separately and then clamped onto the wire shaft. Nothing guaranteed that the head would remain with the shaft. As the users of hand-crafted pins discovered, often to their discomfort, the coiled wire head had a marvellous capacity for jumping off the shaft and leaving the point of the pin to travel wherever gravity or other forces drove it.

The mass production of pins in the second half of the nineteenth century coincided with the advent of cheaper steel and more sophisticated power-driven machinery. The result was a dramatic increase in the rate of production of pins and an equally dramatic decrease in their unit cost. By the end of the nineteenth century, the English pin industry in Birmingham daily produced pins by the tens of millions and became the chief supplier to the world. There were approximately 16,000 pins to a pound, and the wholesale cost of a pound of pins varied from one shilling and three pence to three shillings.[3]

Pins required some sort of receptacle. From medieval times, closed containers for pins often showed in their elaborate decoration the high value placed on the pins themselves. Pincushions in their present form go back at least to the sixteenth century. These early pincushions were often large and highly decorated, and were sometimes as valued for their superb needlework as for the costly pins which they held. Other pincushions were smaller, and some were meant to be carried or worn. The pin-poppet was a combination pincushion and closed container which held needles as well as pins (plate 105). It was popular in the eighteenth and early nineteenth centuries.

By the end of the eighteenth century, the small pincushion worn suspended from the waist had evolved into two of the major types associated with nineteenth-century pincushions: the pinball and the disc. The pinball cushion was made of two fabric sections sewn together over a stuffed ball cushion. The fabric might be knitted silk, needlepoint embroidery or multi-colour patchwork as in plate 115, middle of the bottom row, and in plate 116, next to the extreme right of the bottom row.

A plaited cord of silk, often made on a lucet, hid the joining of the two halves of fabric of the pinball. A length of the same cord attached to the top and formed into a loop made it possible to suspend this pinball from the waist.

There is a story, perhaps apocryphal, that some of these old pinball cushions have been cut open and destroyed in the search for money or other treasures supposedly concealed inside. The story is ironic in view of the sentiments sometimes worked into the fabric covers of these pinballs such as

Plate 105: *Early painted Tunbridgeware. Left: Pin-poppet with blue silk pincushion. 3.5 cm. high. Centre: Tape-measure. Right: Pin-poppet with yellow silk pincushion. All English, c. 1800–1830.*

'Let virtue be your guide'.[4]

The more popular of the suspended pincushions was the flat disc pincushion which continued to gain adherents well into the twentieth century. Originally, it had been suspended from the waist by a long ribbon. But in the nineteenth century, the ribbon was shortened and nearly eliminated as the disc pincushion became a staple of the fitted needlework box.

The disc pincushion was like a sandwich, with the cushion placed between two flat discs sewn together to hold it in place. The discs could be of any material from mundane cardboard to precious and exotic materials. They were carved, pierced, painted, covered with decorative fabrics or treated in many different ways. Some examples in bone and ivory are in plate 106.

The late Georgian and Regency disc pincushions of bone and ivory came in many shapes: book, fan, wheelbarrow, bellows, fish, mandoline and other designs as in plate 107. Later in the century, when chatelaines came back in fashion, the disc pincushion again became suspended from the waist. Some silver chatelaine disc pincushions with their attached clasps are in plate 108. Other pincushions mass produced with stamped decorations, late in the nineteenth century, as in plate 109, also had fabric fasteners but were probably not meant for chatelaines.

Plate 106: *Disc pincushions clockwise from top left: Carved bone. English or French, c. 1850. 5 cm. diameter. Carved ivory. Bavarian, c. 1860. Turned and pierced bone. English, c. 1880. Two ivory disc pincushions, rectangular and circular. English, c. 1840.*

Plate 107: *Pierced bone pincushions made with two matching paper-lined pieces of bone and strip of silk filled with cotton wool to hold pins. All English, c. 1800–1840. Lower left cushion 4 cm. long.*

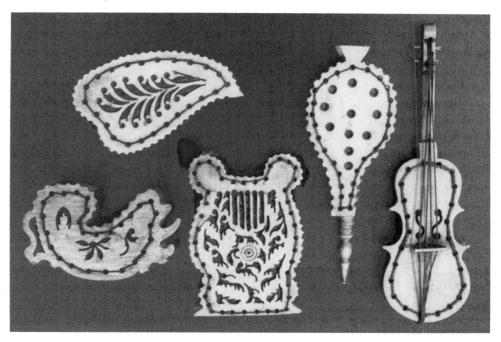

Plate 108: *Disc pincushions from chatelaines from left: Silver plate. English, c. 1900. 4 cm. diameter. Pierced silver. American, c. 1890. Steel. English, c. 1850. Pierced silver plate. English, c. 1900.*

Plate 109: *Metal disc pincushions. Left: Brass picture marked 'S. Georgius Eqvitum Patronus'. 5 cm. diameter. Centre: Gilded owl's face. Right: Pierced sheet metal with green glass stone. Reverse marked 'Paris Londres'. German and French, c. 1900.*

Plate 110: *English fabric pincushions from top left: 1: Green leather domino. 5 cm. high. 2–3: Designs from playing cards on silk. Bottom row from left: 4: Black silk faille with Prince of Wales feathers. 5: Heart-shaped paper with painted flowers. 6: White silk with painted ship. All c. 1830–1880.*

Other novelty pincushions of the disc type imitated playing cards or dominoes, or provided a surface for decoration of various types as in plate 110. In all disc pincushions, the pin heads can be seen round the edge where the pins are inserted into the cushion between the two discs.

The disc pincushion became the staple of the souvenir trade in pincushions in the nineteenth century. The flat discs furnished a convenient surface on which to paint pictures of places of historical interest. Even in the very late eighteenth century, such souvenirs, often with pictures transferred to silk, were sold at fashionable spas and resorts such as Bath. With the beginning of railway travel in the second quarter of the nineteenth century, these souvenirs became increasingly popular on both sides of the Atlantic. The international expositions, which became a regular feature in Western countries after the success of England's Great Exhibition of 1851, were often commemorated on these disc pincushions.

Pincushions were also souvenirs in the slightly different sense of remembrances of things past. Women often used the gold and silver work, or the fabric from uniforms or clothing of someone dear to them, to make a private commemorative pincushion. The popularity of home-made pincushions was not overlooked by publishers. The many embroidery books published for needlewomen in the nineteenth and early twentieth centuries devoted much of their space to descriptions of the art of making pincushions. Such questions as the best materials for stuffing pincushions were answered. They recommended among others down, wool, bran and sometimes sawdust for the reason that it 'is better than bran, for the mice do not like it'.[5]

Although sanitation, both personal and public, had improved in the nineteenth century, there was still room for further improvement or failing that, for further attempts to disguise its inadequacies. The author of an article on fancy pincushions advised the reader that 'in filling this cushion, it would be dainty to put in close to the top a layer of sachet powder, which, concealed in a sheet of cotton, can be separated from the other filling and made to concentrate its odour, and also to dispense it graciously'.[6]

The Victorians were particularly fond of pincushions made of fancy work such as bead or shell work or applied lace and crochet work. They also liked pincushions with sentimental messages spelled out in pins. These 'sticking pincushions' go back to the seventeenth century and originally commemorated private or public ceremonies by appropriate names or messages. The popularity of this type of pincushion and related 'message pincushions' continued into the twentieth century.

To preserve the message in 'sticking pincushions' permanent dummy pins called manikins often outlined the letters. Later the pins came to have glass, beaded, jet, wood and other unusual heads as the Victorians indulged their fondness for polychrome effects. The messages celebrated weddings with such greeting as 'May you be happy'; love and friendship with 'Remember me' or 'From a true friend'; and births with 'Welcome little stranger' (plate 111).

The poignancy of that curious word, stranger, reflects the high mortality rate of infants which continued to the First World War. Parents never had any certainty that their children would survive infancy. The conduct books of the eighteenth and nineteenth centuries advised parents to prepare children early for the possibility of their own death as well as that of their playmates. All collectors of samplers know the various morbid sentiments so popular as stitching exercises for young girls:

> Prepare my soul to meet the day
> When I shall quit this house of clay
> Leave all my dearest friends behind
> And share the fate of human kind.

Plate 111: *Layette sticking pincushion of white silk decorated with pins, beads and appliqué. English, c. 1850. 20 cm. wide.*

For the commemoration of death, there were mourning pincushions outlined in black with their sad messages picked out in black (japanned) iron pins. The only cheerful note in all this is that the collector will find that many of these 'sticking pincushions' include the date of the event as part of the message, and thereby tell us precisely when the pincushion was made.

Victorian beaded pincushions, many of them carrying sentimental messages, are often available on the market today. Some may be too large or flamboyant for contemporary tastes, but they have a certain *joie de vivre* even when the careful workmanship seems to have lost all control over proportion and style. Many are attributed to sailors and soldiers as in the examples in plate 112.

Soldiers in the Crimean War (1853–56) produced a number of such pincushions. They were probably not intended for their own use, and many of them cannot have functioned well as pincushions because their surfaces were tightly covered with beads, each one held in place by a pin. The workmanship on the more elaborate pincushions of this type suggests that they were probably made by army tailors or others equally skilled in working with fabrics. The diamond segments common to this kind are usually very well cut and

Plate 112: *Left and right: Pair of beaded pincushions with message 'Think of me' and name 'H.E. Green'. English, c. 1850–1880. 17 cm. diameter. Centre: Star-shaped pincushion made from soldier's uniform. English, c. 1850.*

Plate 113: *Left: Queen Victoria's Golden Jubilee souvenir silk pincushion. English. 8 cm. high. Centre: Beaded pincushion made by Tuscarora Indians. American c. 1900. Right: Souvenir silk pincushion from Dundee and Richmond. English, c. 1850–1880.*

fitted (plate 112). Moreover, the fabrics and colours used are precisely those that would be available to someone working in that branch of the armed services concerned with uniforms. These pincushions were probably made as a way of passing time and creating a souvenir for presentation on the return home.[7]

It is very easy to confuse Victorian beaded pincushions with bead work of the Tuscarora Indians of Niagara Falls as well as with other Indian tribes of the United States and Canada. An example of Indian beaded work in the form of a pincushion is in the centre of plate 113. The confusion is understandable since the Victorians and Indians copied from one another both in design and technique such as the use of overlaid or spot stitch and the lazy stitch or raised technique. It was recognized in the nineteenth century that the Indians adapted to their traditional designs the fancy work done by the Victorians. In return, the Victorians were equally indebted to the Indians for the inspiration for their bead designs. In 1859, for example, *Godey's Lady's Magazine* gave directions for a pattern in 'beautiful imitation of Indian beadwork' and then described the Indian 'raised technique' for applying the beads as though it were an invention from England.[8] Not all American Indian pincushions were of this beaded type. The pincushion and other needlework implements in plate 114 are quite different from Victorian styles in their extreme rustic simplicity.

In the nineteenth century, needlewomen made pincushions in every shape

Plate 114: *Indian sweetgrass sewing tools from left: Needlebook. 5.5 cm. diameter. Scissors sheath, pincushion basket and thimble case. American, c. 1920.*

Plate 115: *English pincushions from top left: Brown leather book with petit point insert. 4.5 cm. high. Three-dimensional beaded triangle. Gold-decorated blue paper book. From bottom left: Embroidered blue silk square. Pinball embroidered with spider-webs. Striped purple and gray silk square. c. 1820–1880.*

from stars, flowers, vegetables, and animals to domestic objects of every type. Some common shapes are in plates 115, 116. Looking at nineteenth-century pincushions, one begins to ask if there was any thing which could not become a padded receptacle for pins. The popular women's magazines in the last half of the nineteenth century recommended converting everything from silver wine coasters to beautiful eighteenth-century shuttles into pincushions.[9]

In the house there were smart box pincushions for the dressing table, large convenient ones for the work room, gigantic heart- or diamond-shaped pincushions for the kitchen covered with multi-coloured patchwork and edged with scarlet braid. Dainty ones appeared for pockets and small and elegant pincushions for the workbox.

The cult of pincushions was not necessarily functional. Many pincushions from the nineteenth century have no pin holes in them and were never used because they were made for no other purpose than to decorate walls and

Plate 116: *English pincushions from top left: Beaded. 2.5 cm. square. Gold-decorated white paper. Pink silk shoe with coil-head pins. Bottom row from left: Heart with wool French knots around shisha mirror. Silk patchwork pinball. Red leather disc. All c. 1830–1880.*

tables. Others were made as gifts or for the fancy work stalls in the charity bazaars.

Although it is easy to be overwhelmed by the sheer number of home-made pincushions in the nineteenth century, the majority probably came from commercial manufacturers. These fall into two overlapping categories. First are the pincushions designed as independent needlework implements or as parts of needlework tools such as clamps, waxers, cotton reel stands and multi-purpose tools. These could be plain or fancy depending upon the taste and the means of the purchaser. The second type were the souvenir pincushions which began to appear as early as the end of the eighteenth century.

Souvenir trade pincushions included those fashioned from seashells, reflecting the growing attraction and accessibility of seaside resorts. Taking advantage of the seemingly beneficent design of nature, the pincushion manufacturer placed the pincushion either in the cleft of such seashells as the

Plate 117: *Top: Turban shell pincushion mounted on silver stand hallmarked London, 1908. Bottom: Two scallop shell pincushions. Left shell 6 cm. wide. English, c. 1830–1860.*

Plate 118: *Top: Rosewood Tunbridge table pincushion with mosaic-pattern top. Bottom: Two Tunbridge mosaic-pattern disc pincushions. 4 cm. diameter. English, c. 1850.*

Plate 119: *Scottish Tartanware from left: Disc pincushion with fernware transfer print. c. 1900–1925. 5 cm. diameter. Disc pincushion with transfer 1863 wedding picture of Edward, Prince of Wales, and Alexandra. Double-ended emery, c. 1850–1890. Heart-shaped disc pincushion, c. 1880. Pin box, c. 1860.*

cowrie, or sandwiched it between the bivalves of scallops or similar shells of that type as in plate 117.

The most prolific and enduring souvenir pincushions of the nineteenth century were those known as Tunbridge and Scottish souvenir ware. The early Tunbridge pincushions were sometimes parts of needlework clamps. Before the 1820s they were often painted; later they had the distinctive Tunbridge mosaic end-grain veneer. These pincushions came in many shapes from the circular disc with its mosaic design to fanciful miniature representations of domestic objects such as the table in plate 118. What is unusual about the Tunbridge disc pincushions, aside from their distinctive mosaic design, is that the pins are not inserted at random into the sandwich cushion but are placed in holes evenly spaced in a wood rim which completely hides the sandwich pincushion from view.

Scottish souvenir pincushions had an entirely different surface treatment from those of Tunbridge. The earliest may have had painted tartan designs but it is more likely that these designs were applied by transferring a printed tartan design to the wood as in plate 119. A variation of tartan design was the fern motif which first made its appearance set within a tartan background late in the nineteenth century as shown on the extreme left of the same plate.

Another type of Scottish souvenir pincushion was the black and white transferware with designs transferred directly to the surface of the sycamore wood as in plate 120. The most popular Scottish souvenir pincushion was the disc whether in the shape of a circle, oval, trefoil, shield, heart, clover or whatever design would best frame a particular scene or portrait. The reverse side would often contain information about the picture and sometimes about the provenance of the sycamore wood of which the disc was made. These pincushions continued the tradition of the earlier painted souvenir disc pincushions.

The commemorative pincushion also appeared in the disc style and in embroidered pincushions, such as the one in the centre in plate 113 which commemorates the Golden Jubilee of Queen Victoria.

Towards the end of the nineteenth century, silver pincushions became very popular as they complemented the silver dressing-table sets of Edwardian bedrooms. They often came in various animal shapes such as swans, chickens and pigs with pincushions on their backs for pins, needles and hairpins as in plate 121. Figural silver pincushions were also often a part of sewing cases such as small silver basket pincushions. For those unable to afford silver, figural pincushions were also available in electroplate silver or gilded base metal as in the pair of shoe pincushions and the crown in plate 121. Some of the silver animal pincushions also pulled shell carts (plate 122)

Plate 120: *Scottish transferware clockwise from top left: Table pincushion with view 'Royal Hotel and Entrance to Pier, Clacton-on-Sea'. 7.5 cm. high. Shield pincushion with view 'The Art Gallery, Philadephia Exhibition' (1876). Double-ended emeries with view 'Abbotsford', and below, 'Enthroned among the clouds'. Disc pincushion with view of cottage on Mt McGregor. All c. 1850–1890.*

Plate 121: *English pincushions clockwise from left: Pair of base metal shoes, c. 1900. 10 cm. long. Two silver baskets, c. 1820. Silver swan hallmarked Birmingham, 1907. Silver newborn chick hallmarked Chester, 1907. Silver pig hallmarked Birmingham, 1906. (All three animals made by A & L Ltd.) Gilded brass crown, c. 1902.*

which made a convenient receptacle on the dressing-table for a watch fob.

Another popular material for figural pincushions and tools was bog wood which was carved into various shapes, often imitating domestic objects, such as the saucepan and top-hat in plate 123. Bog wood, as its name implies, was wood taken from peat bogs where it had blackened and hardened over the centuries. Bog wood is almost always referred to as bog oak but in fact it could just as well be alder, willow, birch, elm, hazel and others. The wood took carving very well and was highly prized by carvers, who often went to great lengths to secure bog wood from their fellow workers. This competition was the subject of a charming essay by Charles Dickens in an 1852 issue of his *Household Words* under the title 'Peatal Aggression'.

Plate 122: *English silver pincushion animals pulling mother-of-pearl carts to hold watch fobs. Hallmarked from left: Birmingham, 1925, 1911 and 1909. Left cart and elephant 10.5 cm. long. All made by A & L Ltd.*

It was the Germans, however, who took the lead in the production and distribution of novelty figural pincushions toward the end of the nineteenth and the beginning of the twentieth century. After the First World War, the Japanese flooded the market with even cheaper variations on the theme of figural pincushions made largely of ceramic, plastic or wood.

The contemporary collector will find available a wide variety of pincushions from the nineteenth and early twentieth centuries. Dating the commercially produced pincushions within that period presents some problems but is not necessarily impossible. The best, although not infallible, guide is style. The early pincushions tend to be small and fairly simple in design. The early nineteenth-century pinball and disc pincushions are easily recognized by shape, size and material. The pinballs are usually covered by knitted silk or patchwork while the early disc pincushions meant for workboxes are usually of mother-of-pearl, ivory or bone with silk-covered cushions.

The message pincushions become more gaudy as the nineteenth century progresses. The early ones are usually made of silk cushions and have the old two-piece pin with the coiled head. The Victorian ones introduced coloured fabrics and brightly coloured pins and beads. The precise distinction between Victorian and American Indian beaded pincushions is more difficult to resolve and is often a matter of opinion.

The home-made fabric pincushion is nearly impossible to vet because neither the style nor the fabric may be contemporary with the time it was actually made. In any event, this is counterbalanced by the low prices of such pincushions which are below reproduction cost. Shell pincushions also tend to be priced below reproduction cost.

Some of the more expensive pincushions are those from sewing cases or chatelaines because they are often of precious metals or exotic materials. If they are silver, they may be stamped or hallmarked. Otherwise, they have to be dated by their resemblance to the style of implements from known sewing sets or chatelaines. Style in the abstract is of little help here since the last half of the nineteenth century saw the revival and mixture of many styles of the past.

The situation is quite different for Tunbridge and Scottish souvenir pincushions. With the information that is now available on the evolution of design and technique in both these wares, it is possible to date pincushions of this type by the design, or how it is applied, or both.

The novelty pincushions date mostly from the last third of the nineteenth century and go well into the present century. The silver figural pincushions

Plate 123: *Bogwood thimble case and pincushion decorated with carved shamrocks. Irish, c. 1880. 3 cm. high.*

are usually stamped or hallmarked. Those of other materials can sometimes be identified by the subject matter if they are of the souvenir type. Novelty pincushions entering the United States were stamped by country of origin from 1890 because of a Federal requirement that from 1890 all goods exported to that country be marked with the name of the country of origin. In 1914 this requirement was amended to read that all articles must be identified not only by the country of origin but by a statement that the article was made in that country.

8 Thread Containers

The modern concept of a thread holder is something on which thread is wound. This concept dates from the era of machine twisted and finished thread which is stronger and more manageable than hand-spun thread. When thread was spun at home, or by hand elsewhere, it was more vulnerable to breaking, tangling and easy soiling. It often needed a container of some kind for safe storage.

Thread is made by spinning the fibres of cotton, flax, silk or other materials and combining the filaments. England began to manufacture white sewing thread, known as Ounce Thread, in the eighteenth century after the technique was introduced from Holland. Ounce Thread in Europe had earlier been known as Nun's Thread when it was spun by the nuns of Flanders and Italy. Scotland, rather than England, became a major centre for thread manufacturing.

Thread was sold by the skein or by the pound. At home it was often wound on spindles which fitted inside small containers known as cotton barrels. These barrels, usually of ivory, bone, horn or wood, were often a part of fitted needlework boxes until the middle of the nineteenth century. Typical of this type are the barrels and their protruding spindles visible in the front of the boxes in plate 4. Barrels, like those in plate 124 fitted into slots in workbox trays so that only the top was visible. The thread emerged from these barrels through small holes visible on the sides of the barrels.

Thread was also stored on reels. Nearly all fitted needlework boxes had some form of reel. In the Palais Royal box, it was usually a small mother-of-pearl reel on which to wind silk. In the Asian lacquer box, as well as the early English workbox, it was often a horizontal multiple winder of bone, ivory, mother-of-pearl, horn or wood which separated various kinds or colours of wound thread. Some workboxes, such as the horn box in plate 5 had all three thread containers: cotton barrels, multiple winders and reels.

By the 1840s, most fitted needlework boxes had matching sets of reels rather than cotton barrels or multiple winders. The reels, a number of which are in plate 125, had a base, a metal or bone shank, and a decorated top. Thread was often wound directly on the shank as seen in the example on the bottom row, far left of the same plate. But the major function of the reel was to enclose the commercially-produced spool of thread which became available in the second quarter of the nineteenth century. The top or base of the reel unscrewed, and the spool of thread dropped over the shank. In Ireland and the United States, reels were often called spools while in northern England they were known as bobbins. Although these reels were unnecessary for the functioning or protection of the commercially-produced spool of thread, they

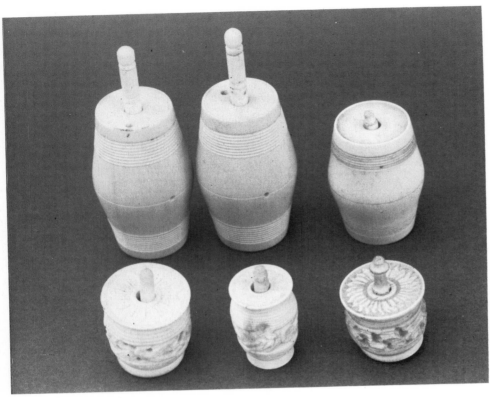

Plate 124: *Bone and ivory thread barrels from Asian workboxes made for export, c. 1800–1850. Upper left barrel 7 cm. high.*

continued to be manufactured as attractive accessories for use in fitted work-boxes up to the last quarter of the nineteenth century.[1]

The thread companies, such as I. W. Taylor, often sold carved bone reels marked with their label on the bottom as individual reels or as matching sets. Many of these bone reels had a knob on top which could be tightened over the thread end so that it would not unwind. Some examples of these commercial bone reels are in plate 126. The first reel on the left has a Clark label at each end.

This type of commercial bone reel was often sold in graduated sizes by the box. An example dating from about 1900 is in plate 127. Cox and Company advertised a similar type of box in the 1880s for one guinea and up, depending on the number of other supplies which came with the reels of thread. Their best seller was called the Guinea Haberdashery Cabinet and came in a fitted box of walnut with mother-of-pearl escutcheon and key.

Because silk thread was fine and delicate in texture, needleworkers often wound bits of it on paper, ceramic, wood, bone, ivory or mother-of-pearl silk winders where the silk was less likely to snag. The mother-of-pearl winders often came from Palais Royal boxes and sometimes resemble iridescent

Plate 125: *Reels with mother-of-pearl tops, bone bases and metal shanks from English workboxes, c. 1840–1880. Upper left reel 3.5 cm. high.*

Plate 126: *From left: Wood spool with bone ends. c. 1900. 4 cm. high. Two bone spools with knobs on top to hold thread end. c. 1860. Ivory reel, c. 1860. All English.*

snowflakes. Other bone or ivory winders came from China. Some of these winders are in plate 128.

The engraved Chinese silkwinders are easily confused with Chinese mother-of-pearl card counters which England imported by the hundreds of thousands in the eighteenth and nineteenth centuries. The counters are oval, round, rectangular and fish-shaped, and their edges are generally, but not always, smooth. Silkwinders, by contrast, nearly always have indented edges to catch and hold the thread in place. The confusion of winders and counters

Plate 127: *Clark and Co. ebonized wood box with two sets of spools with bone ends and wood shanks graduated in size from 4 to 6 cm. Made in Scotland, c. 1900. 34 cm. wide.*

arises when the winders have relatively smooth edges or the counters have indented ones.

In the absence of other clues, the engraving on the counters or winders is the best indication of their original function. The counters sometimes have numbers on the back indicating their value in a card game, or they bear a monogram or crest if they came boxed as a bespoke set of counters. Still other counters have engravings of men gambling which is sufficient evidence of their function. By contrast, the engraving on winders tends to be flowery.

Some gambling counters were used as silkwinders as the casual inspection of any museum collection of needlework boxes will show. There is no harm in this as long as the collector does not purchase a gambling counter at the price of a silkwinder. In general, counters cost less than winders although the gap is narrowing for the more elaborately engraved counters.[2]

Winders served a different function from the commercially produced spool of thread which was for storing sewing thread. By contrast, winders were convenient for storing fine embroidery silks and cottons that came in skeins. They continued to be made and used throughout the nineteenth and twentieth centuries. Tunbridgeware winders were in common use in the Victorian era as were other exotic wood winders (plate 129). Women often purchased

Plate 128: *Silkwinders. Top row: Mother-of-pearl winder. Chinese export, c. 1830–1880. 4 cm. wide. Three mother-of-pearl winders from English workboxes, c. 1840–1880. Second row: Mother-of-pearl winders from French workboxes, c. 1800–1825. Third row: Ivory and bone winders from English and Chinese workboxes, c. 1830–1880. Bottom row: Ivory and bone winders from English workboxes, c. 1840–1880.*

silk wound on paper winders which were, in effect, a part of the package. Otherwise, the paper winders were handmade as in plate 130, upper row and middle bottom. Sterling silver winders (plate 131) were especially popular in the United States at the turn of the century.

If the reels were a decorative way to store individual spools of thread, reel stands were even more convenient for storing and displaying many spools of coloured thread. Some of these stands, such as the American mahogany one in plate 132, were relatively plain and functional with a drawer built into the stand to hold other needlework implements. Others, like the unusually tall English reel stand in plate 134, had a striking resemblance to an ornate Christmas tree. The spools of thread for this stand were not commercially produced but individually made for each brass spindle on which they are

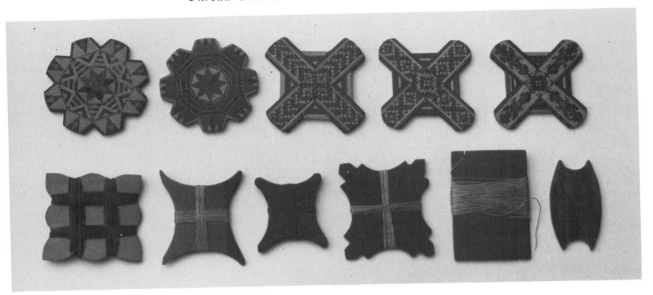

Plate 129: *Silkwinders. Top row: Tunbridge mosaic-pattern winders, c. 1850–1890. Left winder 4.5 cm. wide. Bottom row: Wood winders from English workboxes, c. 1840–1900, and a celluloid winder in imitation of tortoise shell marked 'Germany'. c. 1900.*

Plate 130: *English paper silkwinders: Centre Three: Hand-made paper stars edged with gold foil, c. 1870. Left winder 4.5 cm. wide. Bottom left and right: Commercially-made winders, c. 1850.*

Plate 131: *American silver silkwinders. Left: Marked 'Sterling'. 5 cm. wide. Centre: Marked 'Sterling'. Made by Unger Bros. Right: Unmarked silver, c. 1900.*

Plate 132: *Mahogany reel stand with pink velvet pincushion holds 24 spools. American, c. 1900. 18 cm. high.*

Plate 133: *Black iron reel stand holds 24 spools. American, patent date 'June 14, 1870'. 24 cm. high.*

Plate 134: *Brass reel stand with maroon velvet pincushion holds 24 spools. English, c. 1870. 51 cm. high.*

fixed. They decrease in size for each higher tier as do the historical and mythological figures which separate them. The spools have not been used which makes it likely that this was one of those Victorian parlour decorations intended for display alone. A more functional reel stand in plate 133 holds commercially produced spools of thread. The tray for sewing implements suggests that this was a convenient, work-a-day reel stand.

Like other needlework tools, novelty thread containers proliferated in the last part of the nineteenth century. Germany took the lead in making novelties for export such as the thread container in the shape of a miniature world globe in plate 135.

166

Plate 135: *Miniature tin world globe holds six wood spools and needlecase. Marked 'Made in Germany', c. 1914. 4 cm. high.*

Plate 136: *Clockwise from left: Tartan box with pincushion top, for Medlock clothing tape, c. 1900. 8.5 cm. high. Tartan cotton box with pegs for 6 spools of thread which is pulled out through holes in side of box. c. 1880–1900. Mahogany cotton box with pincushion top, c. 1880–1900. Fernware cotton box and disc pincushion, c. 1900–1930. Tartan egg-shaped sewing kit with thimble, needlecase and two spools. c. 1880–1900. Wood cotton box in shape of spool, c. 1900. All English or Scottish.*

Another form of thread container was a cross between the cotton barrel and the reel stand. This was the cotton box which had holes in the side from which the thread emerged as it did in the cotton barrels. The interior of these boxes held from three to six or more reels as did the reel stands. Cotton boxes came in many shapes. The majority were circular but there were also square, oblong, hexagonal and octagonal boxes.

Many of the cotton boxes were made of Scottish souvenirware as in the tartan and fernware cotton boxes in plate 136. Tartanware came from Ayrshire in Scotland and was first made on a wide scale in the 1820s, after George IV's visit to Edinburgh in 1822 had given tartan renewed prestige. Many firms from Mauchline, Cumnock, Auchinleck, Laurencekirk and other towns made these boxes as well as other tartan and Scottish souvenirware. The most enterprising firm was that of William and Andrew Smith of Mauchline who became Scottish snuff box makers to King William IV in 1832. Small factories turned out large quantities of tartan ware usually hand painted on sycamore wood. So many companies entered this once profitable trade that between 1825 and 1845 the market gradually became saturated. Prices soon dropped along with the wages of the workers and the profits of the companies.

By 1845 the Smiths of Mauchline were almost the only firm to have survived in the competitive manufacture of tartanware. They had a warehouse and showroom in Birmingham and agents in Paris selling their ware. The survival of the Smiths was due not only to their entrepreneurial skills, but also to the invention of a drawing machine which drew colour repeat patterns of tartanware on paper. It was much cheaper to glue this mass-produced tartan paper to wood than to paint it by hand although wrapping the paper around irregular shapes took no little skill.[3]

Needlework implements were nearly always covered with tartan paper. It is difficult to recognize the paper cover because the wood was first painted black to hide the paper joints. Moreover, the joints were often covered with a wavy, gold-tooled line. Examples of tartan needlework implements are in plates 119, 136, 137. The clan name of the tartan design is in small gold letters on each implement. Tartanware was produced throughout the nineteenth century but the later examples show some decline in quality.

Thread manufacturing was very competitive in Scotland until many of the companies joined together toward the end of the nineteenth century. Before then, the companies vied with one another to call attention to the unusual packaging of their spools of thread much as the needlemakers were doing at the same time with their novelty needlecases.

Clark and Company, whose major factory was Anchor Mills in Paisley, commissioned cotton boxes and other thread containers from the Scottish souvenirware makers, and in particular, from the Smiths of Mauchline during the last half of the nineteenth century. Some examples are the tartan cotton box in plate 136, the transferware cotton boxes in plate 138, and the black lacquer cotton box and barrel-top trunk-style box in plate 139. Each of

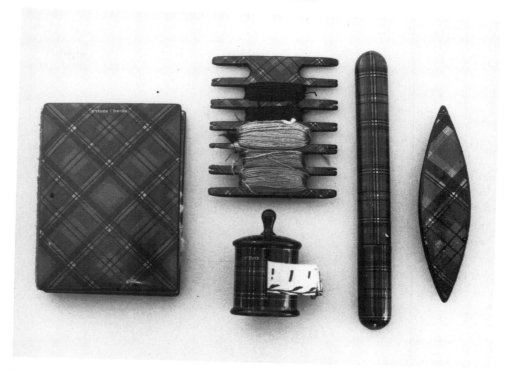

Plate 137: *Scottish Tartanware from left: Needlebook. 6.5 cm. high. Silkwinder, tape-measure, needlecase and tatting shuttle. All c. 1850–1890.*

these thread containers has a Clark and Co. label on the inside of the lid displaying one of Clark's trademarks: the anchor or the initials O.N.T.

The transferware cotton box was only one needlework implement of many made of transferware. Although the Smith brothers of Mauchline took the lead in transferware, as they had in tartan, they were not the only manufacturers of this distinctive ware. Other towns in Ayrshire such as Auchinleck also produced transferware.

The process of transferware was known as early as 1832, but regular production did not begin until 1845. It reached its height in terms of quantity in the period from 1860 to 1900, and unintentionally brought other companies from Great Britain as well as from France, Germany and Japan into the trade. The Smith brothers managed to overcome all domestic competition by 1865, but the competition from abroad increased up to 1900.

Transferware was a process intended to simulate pen and ink hand-drawn pictures. The Smith brothers had plates made of famous drawings of scenes from England and other countries. These plates were then printed on Japanese paper. Next the box or other wood utensil was prepared by several coats of shellac to receive the print. The Smith brothers preferred to use sycamore wood because it turned cream colour with age and exposure, seasoned well and was largely free from warping and knots. Shellacked or var-

Plate 138: *Scottish transferware top row from left: Two cotton boxes with sepia photograph on one and view of Swiss Cottage, Isle of Man on other. Left box 11 cm. diameter. Bottom row from left: Tatting shuttle and needlebook with views of Burns Monument. Two tape-measures with views of Marblehead, Massachusetts and of Saratoga, New York. All c. 1875–1900.*

nished, it made an ideal background for the transfer print. To transfer the print, the face of the print was varnished and placed face down on the box and left to dry. Careful sponging of the dried print and rubbing with a wet cloth removed the Japanese paper and left only the inked print on the box.[4]

The same thread companies which had ordered tartan thread containers to publicize their spools of cotton thread also ordered transferware boxes as in the two examples in plate 138. The needlework below the cotton boxes in the same plate has a print of Burns' monument with the comment: 'Made of wood which grew within the rail of Burns' monument.' If all the transferware items which claim this distinction did, in fact, come from within that rail, it is a marvel that the monument was visible at all through what must have been an enormous forest of sycamore trees.

The success of the Smith Company's transferware intensified foreign competition. In the late nineteenth century, competitors tried to cut the cost of transferware by using sepia or black and white photographs instead of transfer prints. The photographs were pasted directly on the box or object, varnished, and the raised edge somewhat concealed by applying a wavy, gold-tooled line over it. A typical example is the cotton box on the upper left in plate 138.

The Smith Company also tried to market in the decade from 1870 to 1880 woodware in imitation of lacquer or papier-mâché. It did not have any notable success. This souvenirware had a black lacquered ground with floral designs. Some had sayings commemorating a notable view or resort. Others had scenes in transferware set within the floral designs.[5] The cotton boxes on the left in plate 139 are two examples of this black lacquerware.

From about 1900 to 1930 the Smith Company also made a souvenirware

Plate 139: *Scottish black lacquerware clockwise from top left: Cotton box. 8 cm. diameter. Needlebook with verse. Disc pincushion from Isle of Man. Cotton box in shape of trunk. All c. 1870–1880.*

decorated with fern designs. At first, ferns collected from the Isle of Arran were placed over the wood object and varnished in place. Later, as cost-cutting took its toll, the ferns were only used for outlines which were subsequently filled in with various shades of brown paint. Finally, the extensive handwork which live ferns entailed gave way to printed ferns on paper, and then to varnished photographs of ferns pasted directly on the wood object.[6] A typical fernware cotton box is in plate 136 with a piece of thread emerging from one of the bone-lined holes in the side. Beneath these holes are numbers designating the gauge of the thread on the reel which each hole served.

As plain and fancy hand sewing declined and the Scottish thread manufacturers merged, it became unnecessary to package thread in novelty souvenirware containers. The Smith Company which had found it increasingly difficult to meet the stronger foreign competition also suffered a large fire in its factory in Mauchline in 1933. It never recovered from that disaster and ceased to operate in 1939.

Thread containers are fairly easy to identify and authenticate. Cotton barrels are usually from fitted needlework boxes but some individual ones are also occasionally found. It is important that the spindle which protrudes through the top not be broken off or missing which so often happens when they are not protected in a box. Cotton barrels should also have a hole in the side from which the thread can emerge. If they do not, they may not be cotton barrels, or they may be of Asian manufacture where the workman copied the design complete with spindle but did not understand the function of this Western implement.

Reels, which only a few years ago were plentiful and cheap, are now collected on their own with a consequent increase in price. The tops or the bottoms of the reels should unscrew, or the shank should separate in some way, so that the spool of thread can be fitted over the shank. Often the decorated reel tops are bent at an angle from the metal shaft. This cannot be easily repaired.

Bone spools of thread are collectable and are becoming relatively scarce. It is a bonus if they have the thread company label but that is not essential. It seems probable that within a decade even the wood spool, which was the common spool before the Second World War, will also become equally scarce. Those with thread company labels are the most collectable.

The difference between mother-of-pearl silkwinders and gambling counters has already been discussed. Other silkwinders of more accessible materials such as common woods should not command as high a price as those of exotic materials.

Reel stands are becoming expensive. Even the small base metal ones holding four spools which sold for ten cents in 1913 are no longer cheap. All reel stands should be examined carefully to make certain that the spindles or thin rods for holding the spools are not deformed in some way that prevents the easy changing of spools.

Cotton boxes are still relatively reasonable in price. Tartan ones should be checked to make certain that the paper has remained glued and that no joints have become visible. Inside, there should be a spindle for each reel, and a bone-lined hole for the thread from each reel. The bone lining not infrequently falls out of the holes.

The more desirable transferware cotton boxes have prints rather than photographs as decorations. Otherwise the interior is identical to the tartan box as is the interior of the black lacquer and fernware cotton boxes. The latter two types of cotton boxes are not as yet either recognized or collected to the same degree as tartan and transferware and are consequently far more reasonable in price. That situation undoubtedly will change.

9 Needlework Clamps

Needlework clamp has become the accepted generic term to describe the variety of fabric and thread holders which function as an extra hand to hold taut the fabric being stitched or the thread being wound. Nonetheless, needlework clamp is not an accurate description of these diverse holders. The stand of the needlework clamp is attached to the table edge not by a clamp but by a thumbscrew-operated slip-vice. Some of the mechanisms found on the top of stands may hold the fabric in a clamp such as the sewing bird or hemming clamp. Others, however, may use a pincushion to pin the fabric or reels and cages to wind thread. The name, clamp, will be used here as a generic term for these diverse holders but they will be described by function to illustrate their differences.

Early clamps of ivory, bone or wood were often carved or decorated. Some of the more elaborate ones were tokens of love and became part of the preparation of a trousseau. Some had attached holders to store thread, wax, needles and a thimble, as well as powdered alum to keep perspiring hands from staining fabric or rusting expensive needles. Many of these early clamps were hemming clamps and held large pieces of fabric such as bedclothes, household linens and wide skirts, providing the necessary tension so that straight seams or hems could be hand sewn by one person. The sewing birds, discussed below, were also hemming clamps. These hemming clamps were also known as 'third hands'.

The winding clamp is as old as the hemming clamp. The primary mechanism is a reel or cage revolving around a spindle fitted to the top of the clamp stand. The size of the winder depended upon the type of thread wound. Before commercially-produced spools of thread appeared in the second quarter of the nineteenth century, thread was sold by the skein or pound or spun at home. It then had to be wound onto spools, reels or into balls. A pair of winding clamps allowed one person rather than two to do the work. In the same way, many of us as children, have held out our arms to stretch tight a skein of wool. Someone could then take up one end of the thread and easily begin rolling a ball of wool while unrolling the skein stretched between our arms.

The winding clamps came in various sizes. The finer threads, such as cotton and silk, were wound on small reels or cages made of smooth materials such as ivory or bone as in plate 140. Winding clamps as pairs became unnecessary in the second quarter of the nineteenth century when commercially-wound thread appeared. They could still be found, however, in the fitted needlework boxes imported from Asia as late as the third quarter of the nineteenth century.

Plate 140: *Left: Pair of ivory winding clamps with spool tops and netting knobs. 12 cm. high. Centre: Carved bone winding clamp with cage top. Right: Pair of ivory winding clamps with spool tops and netting knobs. All from Asian workboxes after 1830.*

Winding clamps did not become entirely obsolete because they could still function as individual hemming clamps by gripping the fabric between the table and the clamp stand. Or they could function as netting clamps if they had knobs to which the foundation loop in netting could be attached, as do the pairs on the left and right in plate 140. There was, however, no point in keeping thread-winding clamps as pairs after the introduction of commerical spools of thread, and they were often distributed among different workboxes.[1] The collector will consequently value highly any such pairs which still exist.

Larger pairs of winding clamps intended for yarn or linen continued to function long after the thread-winding clamps became obsolete. A pair of rosewood clamps for winding fine yarns is in plate 141.

For more coarse yarns, a swift, as in plate 142, was preferable. This mahogany and holly swift revolves around a metal spindle fitted into a slip-vice stand which attaches to the table edge like any other winding clamp. The difference between the swift and a pair of winding clamps is that the larger swift has an expandable cage so that it can accommodate yarn skeins of various lengths. It would require two winding clamps separately set apart for the length of the skein to do the same task the single swift can do by simply expanding its cage.[2]

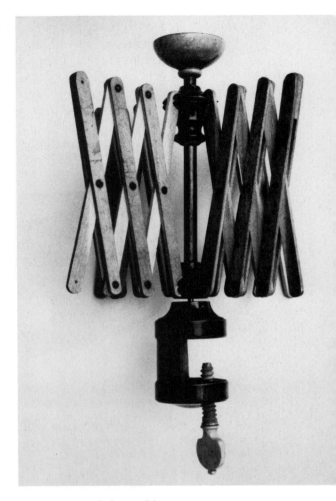

Plate 141: *Pair of turned rosewood winding clamps with cage tops. English, c. 1860. 14 cm. high.*

Plate 142: *Wood swift of mahogany and holly revolves on metal spindle fitted into clamp. Small wood bowl on top to hold yarn ball. English, c. 1860. 29 cm. high.*

At the top of the swift is a small wood bowl which looks as though it might once have held a pincushion but, in fact, it is a place to rest the ball of yarn when the swift is not in use. Just below the bowl is a turned piece of wood into which the tops of the four folding slats are fitted. As that turned piece is pushed downward, the folding slats decrease in height and increase in width. The extension of each of the four folding slats is like watching someone pull a folding wood gate across a garden path.

Another popular clamp was known as the lady's netting vice as in plate 143 on the extreme left and right. The craft of netting, which goes back to antiquity, does not require a netting clamp. Any kind of weighted base holding firmly the foundation loop of netting will allow the skilled artisan to produce

176

nets from the size of fishing nets to the finest of nets for household use. But the netting clamp was much more convenient than weighted cushions for most needleworkers. It could be combined with other aids as in the example in the centre of plate 143 which has both a pincushion and a winding cage in addition to a netting loop.

The netting clamp, on the left in plate 143, is similar to one advertised in the wholesale trade catalogue of R. Timmins & Sons of Birmingham in the 1840s. It sold wholesale for twenty-eight shillings a dozen. If the netting hook at the top were moved to the right and replaced by a spindle supporting a metal-enclosed pincushion, as in the clamp in the centre of plate 143, then the price rose to fifty-four shillings a dozen wholesale, or higher if the pincushion holder had elaborate decoration.[3]

By the late 1840s, netting produced by machine cost no more than the supplies alone needed to produce netting by hand. This brought an end to the cottage industry of hand-made commercial netting. But it had little effect on the art of netting for personal use. Many needlewomen continued to make netting for special items such as purses, handkerchiefs, and nightcaps, or for infant garments where they wanted to create a special design or effect not available commercially.[4]

To judge from the type of clamp that has survived in the largest number,

Plate 143: *Left and right: Steel netting clamps. Left clamp 9 cm. high. Centre: Steel pincushion clamp with winding cage and netting hook. English, c. 1850.*

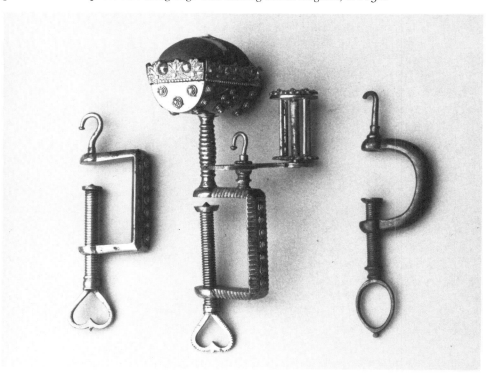

Plate 144: *Left and centre: Carved bone and ivory pincushion clamps from Chinese workboxes after 1830. Left clamp 6 cm. high. Right: Turned ivory pincushion clamp with netting knob. English, c. 1810–1850.*

Plate 145: *English ivory pincushion clamps, c. 1810–1850. Left clamp 13 cm. high.*

Plate 146: *Ivory clamp with pink silk pincushion. Probably Asian exportware, c. 1800. 20 cm. high.*

Plate 147: *Painted sycamore Tunbridge clamp with blue velvet pincushion. English, c. 1820. 10 cm. high.*

Plate 148: *Rosewood Tunbridge mosaic-pattern clamp with rose velvet pincushion. English, c. 1850. 10 cm. high.*

the most popular clamp in the nineteenth century must have been the pin-cushion clamp in its various forms. In a technical sense, the pincushion clamp is misnamed because the pincushion cannot grip heavy fabric. Such fabric, however, can be placed securely between the table and the clamp stand. In plates 144 and 145 are six pincushion clamps of bone and ivory. The clamp on the far right in plate 144 also has a netting knob of ivory. These pincushion clamps appeared in two basic types. The first is the box clamp which has the pincushion as the built-in top part of the box-like stand in plate 144 and in the middle clamp in plate 145. The second type has a pincushion cup mounted on spindles of various kinds attached to the top of the box-like or crescent-shaped stand of the clamp as in plate 145, extreme left and right, and in plate 149.

The tall pincushion clamp of ivory in plate 146 suggests the additional uses to which it might be put. Under the top is a small mirror. The pierced centre section conceals an ivory needlecase which also doubles as a spindle for tape or thread which can be pulled out through the pierced slots on the side.

Souvenirware from Tunbridge Wells and elsewhere also appeared in the form of pincushion clamps as in plate 147. This is a very early Tunbridge pincushion clamp of sycamore wood painted in red, yellow and black with the sentiment: 'Ever yours.' A similar pincushion clamp can be seen in the remains of a Spanish-grant villa in California called Adobe de Palomares with the true message of the souvenir gift: 'Remember the giver.' Two other examples of Tunbridge souvenir pincushion clamps are in plates 148 and 149. The first has a mosaic design; the second combines a stickware design for the pincushion holder with a mosaic design for the stand. A nineteenth-century Tyrolean souvenir pincushion clamp, in plate 150, has a small drawer beneath the cushion to hold other needlework implements.

Just as pincushions came in every conceivable type of holder, pincushion clamps also utilized those natural receptacles which could be attached to a stand, like the cowrie shell in plate 151.

The most elaborate pincushion clamps were those of metal, usually steel or brass. By the middle of the nineteenth century, the art of metalworking by machine was sufficiently advanced that ornamental variations on a common design could be turned out cheaply by the thousands without any appreciable sacrifice in quality. Wholesale trade catalogues of the period show numerous variations on a single sewing clamp design. In one, the thumbscrew of the clamp stand is faceted, in another bevelled, in another pierced, and still another both faceted and pierced, and so on. The same is true of the body of the clamp which might be plain, embossed, engraved, faceted or treated in many other ways.

The brass clamp in plate 152, for example, has the pincushion secured by an attractive cross stitch which creates a pattern across the metal holder. It also has a knob which unscrews to reveal a brass stiletto and beneath it, a hook for netting. The entire clamp is notable for its elegant simplicity and lack of decoration, similar to scientific instruments of the time such as brass micro-

Plate 149: *Rosewood and sycamore Tunbridge clamp with mosaic pattern on back and stickware pattern on cup. English, c. 1850. 14 cm. high.*

Plate 150: *Wood clamp with pink silk pincushion. Tyrolean souvenir, c. 1880. 15.5 cm. high.*

Plate 151: *Cowrie shell pincushion on metal clamp. English, c. 1800. 16.5 cm high.*

Plate 152: *Brass clamp with blue velvet pincushion, stiletto and netting hook. English, c. 1850. 17 cm. high.*

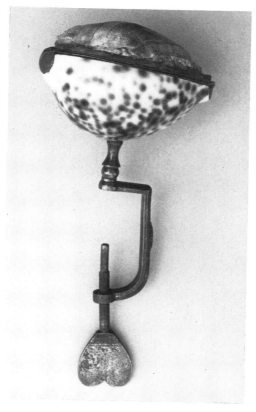

scopes. By contrast, the steel pincushion clamp in the centre of plate 143 is heavily ornamented from top to bottom. Even the attached winding cage and the thumbscrew at the bottom are without an unadorned surface.

If the pincushion clamp was the most popular type in the nineteenth century, the version of it that commanded the most attention in the United States was the hemming clamp in the shape of an animal with a pincushion. In England, these can be traced back to the eighteenth century, but they were most popular in the nineteenth century when whole kingdoms of natural and mythological animals found representation on these clamps. In England and on the Continent, the dolphin became the most popular. The dolphin clamps sometimes had one, two or no pincushions as in plate 153.

Most of the animal clamps gripped the fabric in their mouths. The needle-woman pressed down or squeezed together the tail of the animal to open the

Plate 153: *Metal dolphin clamp. English or American, c. 1870. 15 cm. high.*

Plate 154: *Gilded brass sewing bird with purple velvet pincushion. English, 1855. 16 cm. high.*

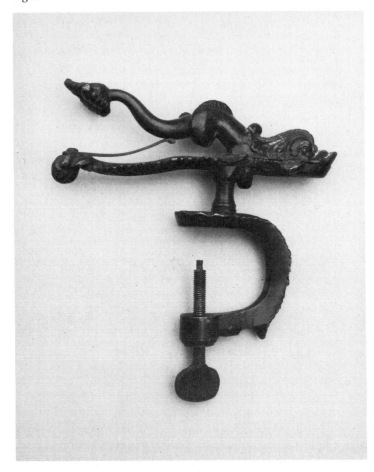

mouth which otherwise remained closed in a tight grip. A common English sewing bird clamp of the middle of the nineteenth century is the gilded brass bird with its high reaching pincushion as in plate 154. It sometimes has the date, 1855, impressed at the edge of the left wing.

If the sewing bird was popular in England, it found its true ecological niche in the United States. In the 1850s, thousands of these sewing birds were sold there. They appeared in a variety of metals: steel, iron, bronze, brass, silver, tin, pewter, base and plated metal. In the United States the sewing bird soon became synonymous with the hemming clamp itself.

In the 5 June 1852 edition of *The Hartford Times* of Connecticut, Elihu Geer of 10 State Street took out an advertisement purporting to demonstrate the difference in health between those women who used sewing birds and those who did not. The advertisement shows two women sitting at a table, one using a sewing bird to grasp her fabric while the other woman holds the fabric with some difficulty without a sewing bird. The latter droops listlessly over her sewing, weary and round-shouldered while the woman with the sewing bird sits with splendid posture, vigorous and happy.

Geer claimed that the sewing bird was 'the latest invented and most useful article for the use of ladies that can be found. The above engraving tells the whole story of its use and usefulness, and health preserving property. Look at the contrast of the human form where it is used and where it is not. . . .' Geer knew, of course, that he had not invented the sewing bird, but like other American manufacturers and distributors, he was quick to capitalize on the possibilities that minor variations in the design of the sewing bird offered for claims to the 'latest invented sewing bird'.

These claims were soon backed by American patents issued from 1853 for the innumerable design variations of the American sewing bird. The centre of their manufacture was Connecticut, and the first patent was taken out on 15 February 1853 by Charles Waterman of Meriden, Conn.[5] His sewing bird has upon its back what appears to be a small pincushion. Waterman made it clear in his application, however, that 'the burden borne upon the back of the bird is in fact the emery ball. . . .'

This first patented American sewing bird has certain specific characteristics shown in plate 155. First of all, the bird grasps the fabric in its bill which opens when the tail is pressed downward. Second, the bird has a feather pattern only on top of the bird; no such pattern appears on the lower part of the body. Third, there is an emery ball cup on the back of the bird, but there is no pincushion on the lower stand as in later variations. Finally, the entire body of the stand beneath the bird is without any decoration whatever. The thumbscrew may be pierced, as in the example illustrated, but the surface of the metal is not decorated.

Since the production of sewing birds involved both dies and moulds, changing only a single die or mould created variations on Waterman's basic sewing bird design. At least three different dies were used for variations of the feather pattern on the upper part of the bird, and four different dies to add

Plate 155: *Base metal sewing bird with red emery cushion. Patented by Charles Water-man 15 February 1853. American. 14 cm. high.*

Plate 156: *Metal sewing bird with coral velvet pincushion and emery. Most common variation on Waterman-type sewing bird and made well into the 20th century. American. 13 cm. high.*

feather patterns of various kinds to the lower part. The clamp stand had at least eight variations while the pincushion cup added later to the stand had five different versions. Finally, the thumbscrew eventually came in twelve different designs.

These thirty-two individual variations for the different parts of Waterman's basic sewing bird design could be combined to create an extraordinary number of different sewing birds, no one exactly like another, and yet no one requiring more than four dies or moulds.[6]

Other sewing birds beginning with a somewhat different concept from Waterman's also received patents. A. P. Bailey of Middletown, Connecticut, manufactured a cast iron bird of unusual simplicity without an emery cushion, pincushion or any decoration whatever. Allen Gerould and John H.

Ward, also of Middletown, patented later in 1853 a sewing bird which did not grasp fabric in its bill, but beneath the bill. When the tail was pressed downward, the bird tilted upwards to receive the fabric between its bill and the cup below. The spring mechanism concealed within the bird kept the bird's bill pressed firmly against the cup below when the tail was released.

Another bird gripped fabric beneath its entire body which tilted upward when the tail was pressed downward. This larger and stronger gripping surface suggests that it may have been used more for rug braiding than for needlework. Other sewing birds had figures of birds which had no relation to any clamping function. It has been suggested that this version of the sewing bird should be called a Bird of Paradise since it was ornamental in function and not part of the working class.[7]

Finally, there was a so-called sewing bird about four centimetres long which the needlewoman fastened to her clothes and then attached one end of

Plate 157: Silver sewing bird marked 'Marshall Field and Co. Sterling'. American, c. 1900. 12 cm. high.

Plate 158: Metal butterfly clamp marked 'Patented Nov. 8th 1853'. American. 13.5 cm. high.

the fabric on which she was working to a pin curving out from the back of the pinned sewing bird. This is, of course, not a true clamp, and it is not surprising that it was also advertised as a skein holder or sometimes even as a napkin holder for use in dining.

These more exotic sewing birds were never made in large numbers as they were not as popular as the variations of Waterman's basic design. The most popular variation of Waterman's design was the two-cushion sewing bird in plate 156. It has feather decorations on both the upper and lower body, as well as floral decorations on the cushion cup, the stand, and the quatrefoil-pierced thumbscrew. In the late 1890s, Marshall Field and Company of Chicago produced an even more decorated version of this sewing bird in sterling silver without an emery cup as in plate 157.

It has been estimated that more than one hundred and sixty distinct types of sewing birds were made in the last half of the nineteenth century in the United States. This does not include the other figural animal clamps which are often called sewing birds although they do not carry representations of birds. Butterflies, fish (plates 158, 159), and many other animals appeared on these hemming clamps. But it was the sewing bird which captured the fancy of needlewomen everywhere in America. Through nationwide distribution from stores, retail catalogues and itinerant pedlars, American manufacturers and distributors soon made the sewing bird native to all regions of the United States.

It has often been said that the decline of the needlework clamp, as well as other needlework implements, in the late nineteenth century was due to the widespread diffusion of the sewing machine popularized by Isaac Singer and others. This is not entirely accurate. The advent of the sewing machine was a boon primarily for those women who had borne the burden of hand sewing out of necessity rather than out of choice. Those women who had the leisure for the social art of handwork looked upon it as one of life's pleasures which they were not ready to forego. The plethora of embroidery books on needlework in the last decades of the nineteenth century bear this out.

Even the women who continued to sew out of necessity, and who bought the new sewing machine when they could afford it, discovered that some hand sewing was still necessary. Manufacturers and distributors found it still profitable to sell sewing birds at the very end of the nineteenth century and later. In London in 1898, *Weldon's Practical Netting* advertised Madame Bayard's workholder and pincushion clamp for one shilling, and another workholder (with pincushion, thimble holder and cotton reel) for two shillings. In the United States, variations on the sewing clamp continued to receive patents at the end of the century. On 23 January 1899, Gustaf Olin of Chicago obtained a patent for a pincushion clamp which had an internal spring mechanism that made it possible to tilt the bottom of the pincushion holder downward to grasp the fabric.

The sewing bird clamps also continued in production after 1900. Some of the original sewing bird patents were reissued before the First World War

Plate 159: *Steel fish clamp. American, nineteenth century. 15 cm. high.*

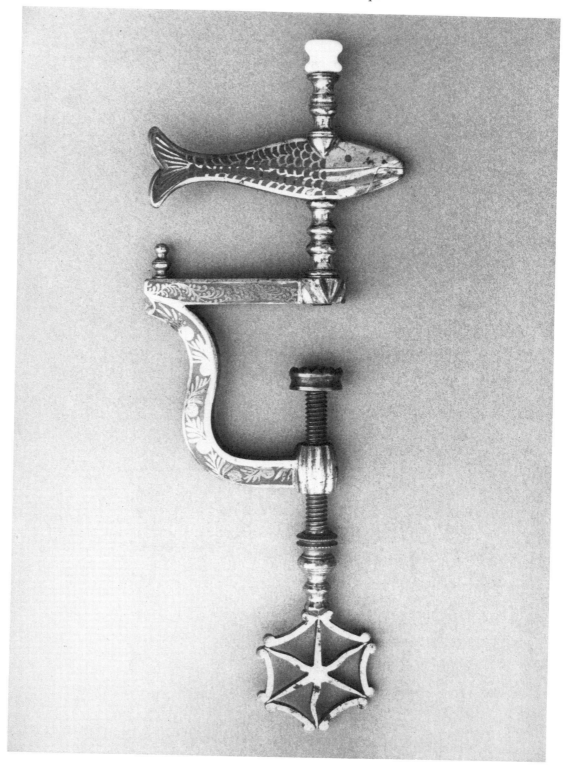

and again after the Second. A utilitarian sewing bird could still be purchased in the 'notions' department of many stores as late as the 1940s. Even the Singer Sewing Machine Company found it necessary in the twentieth century to devise a separate 'gripper' to function as an extra hand in the same way as had the more decorative sewing bird. This gripper only went out of production in the 1950s which suggests that the sewing clamp has had a longer and more viable history than has been generally recognized.

The collector will still find it possible to acquire a variety of needlework clamps at a wide range of prices although many prices are climbing rapidly. One of the most important things to look for in authenticating clamps is consistency of design over the entire surface of the clamp. The collector should look for accessory parts that have been replaced or added, such as pincushion cups. The telltale sign may be that the surface design, or the metal used, does not match the rest of the clamp. The same is true of clamps which have been 'simplified' to rid them of damaged accessories. Wherever a part has been removed, there will be a plain surface. Since many metal clamps have some design on the surface, careful examination will suggest whether it ought to have covered all surfaces of the clamp.

Replaced pincushions present a problem because very often the replacement is done with old material or fabric artificially aged. If there is any doubt about the authenticity of the pincushion, the collector should examine the entire clamp carefully, note its weight and the detailing on its surface and then compare it with dated clamps of the middle-to-late nineteenth century. If it compares unfavourably, it may well be a twentieth-century bird which is not without its charm, but is worth far less than the genuine clamp it imitates.

Sewing birds from the 1920s have acquired a certain collectability in their own right. They are not necessarily to be disdained as long as one knows them for what they are and pays accordingly. Most of these 1920s birds are from Japan. They are light in weight, usually of gilded and stamped base metal, and have a somewhat flimsy feel by comparison with the heavier and more solid clamps of the earlier period. The best way to date American sewing birds is by the patent date, if it is available. Failing that, heavier weight and finer detailing on the surface is usually a sign of the earlier sewing bird.

The problem of imitation of older sewing birds and other clamps arises primarily in clamps of cheaper metals which offer a considerable profit. Clamps of wood, ivory and bone, like those of silver and bronze, cost too much for the basic material or for the labour involved to encourage reproduction.

10 Handwork Tools

Handwork was not only a necessity in the pre-sewing machine era but also a way for a woman to display her skill and grace in movement. In *Mansfield Park*, Jane Austen describes the scene found by a young man visiting a parsonage: 'A young woman, pretty, lively, with a harp as elegant as herself ... was enough to catch any man's heart. The season, the scene, the air were all favourable to tenderness and sentiment. Mrs. Grant and her tambour frame were not without their use: it was all harmony....'

Tambour, meaning drum in French, was the name given to the round frames which tightly stretched white fabric like the top of a drum. The needlewoman embroidered the white fabric with white thread in the tambour stitch which required the use of both hands. It was believed for many years that the left hand manipulating the thread under the fabric must be visible to form the design correctly. Tambour work was thus done on relatively sheer fabrics such as crêpe, muslin and fine cambric.

The spool knave, suspended from one's belt, allowed the needlewoman to proceed with her tambour stitching without holding the thread. It let the thread flow effortlessly to her tambour frame, freeing both her hands to do the rapid tambour stitch. The spool knave was a freely revolving spool set within a metal holder, often of decorated silver as in plate 160.

Tambouring, as a cottage industry, furnished much employment until machine-made tambour stitching rendered hand tambouring unprofitable in the second quarter of the nineteenth century. But the idea of tambour work never went entirely out of fashion for domestic use. About this time, it came to be realized that the left hand need not be visible beneath the fabric to execute designs in the tambour stitch. This led to the use of heavier fabrics and different coloured threads as well as the use of gold thread.

The tambour stitch was made in the following way. After framing the material which had a line design traced on it, the thread was attached to the under side. With the right hand, the tambour hook was put through to the back of the frame at the commencement of one of the traced lines. Holding the thread in the left hand under the line, the needlewoman caught hold of the thread with the hook, and brought it through to the front of the work as a loop. She allowed only enough thread to come through to make the loop, which was retained on the hook. She then put the hook again through the material to the back of the frame, one-tenth of an inch beyond the first puncture. There, she took up the thread and pulled it up as a loop to the front, and let the first-made loop slide over the second and down upon the trace line.[1]

In the later part of the nineteenth century, with the revival of interest in

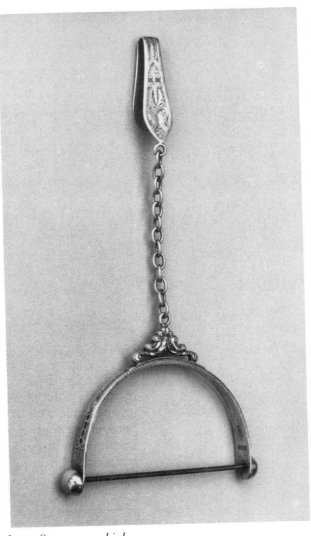

Plate 160: *Silver spool knave with ivory spool. Probably French, c. 1800. 25 cm. high.*

Plate 161: *Silver spool knave hallmarked Birmingham, 1876. Made by Mackay and Chisholm. 20 cm. high.*

sheer fabrics, tambouring was once again seen as a means of effective and rapid decoration. Using very sheer machine-made fabrics stretched on a round tambour frame, the needlewoman quickly worked her running chain stitch to decorate shawls, bridal veils, gowns and other articles of clothing.[2] With the new interest in tambour work came a revival of the eighteenth-century spool knave.

To a generation that had made the chatelaine once again fashionable, the hanging spool knave was one more example of a past way of life worthy of emulation. The late nineteenth-century spool knaves, as in plates 161, 162, were not quite as elaborate as their predecessors, but were admirably suited for their function. They appeared not only in silver but also in the new electro silver plate, and in brass and steel.

The collector will find that spool knaves, whether early or late nineteenth century, are quite expensive. At the prices they command, the clasp and the holder of the spool should match and not be a marriage of two different sets. In the earlier sets, the engraving, design motifs, and general ornamentation furnish valuable clues as to whether both the clasp and the holder are from the same set. On later sets, which may be quite plain, it may be necessary to check hallmarks, if made of English silver, which were usually stamped on both the clasp and the holder. Lacking hallmarks, it is necessary to rely on details of workmanship, finish, and any design elements present.

Tambour hook handles went through an evolution somewhat similar to that of spool knaves, changing from elegantly shaped tools to rather plain and functional ones. The late eighteenth- and early nineteenth-century tambour handles are easily recognizable by their graceful shape as in plate 163. The tambour handle always had a top to protect the hook. To use the hook, the top was unscrewed and threaded to the bottom of the handle. The hook fitted into a mounting on the handle and was tightened into place by the wing-nut. The bottom part of the tambour handle was always bulbous and served as a receptacle for extra hooks. These could be retrieved by unscrewing the bulbous section.

The small detachable tambour hook was always made of steel, and in shape was like the barb of a fish-hook by which the thread could be caught and drawn through the fabric. The tambour handle could be of turned ivory, mother-of-pearl, gold, silver or other materials while the mounting into which the hook fitted might be silver, gold, steel or gilt metal. By the middle of the nineteenth century, when crochet had come into fashion, tambour and crochet hooks and handles were often indistinguishable. An example of two of these hooks and handles, each in its own box, is in plate 164.

The only significant difference between the tambour and crochet hook was the smaller size of the steel tambour hook which was, in theory but not necessarily in practice, sharper than the crochet hook. In discussing crochet and tambour hooks in 1842, Miss Lambert observed: 'These instruments are to be procured of various sizes, but their excellence depends more on the proper fashioning of the hook, than on the material of which they are manufactured. The smaller sizes, and those used for tambour work, must necessarily be of steel; these are frequently made of the length of an ordinary sized sewing needle, that they may be fixed into a handle, which, by means of a small screw is capable of holding needles of various sizes.'[3] So interchangeable were crochet and tambour handles by the end of the century, that Thérèse de Dillmont, in the 1890 edition of her *Encyclopaedia of Needlework*, illustrated a contemporary tambour hook by showing what she described as a 'crochet hook for tambour work'.[4]

A minority of tambour handles did retain, however, a different shape from that of crochet handles well into the twentieth century. The tambour handle

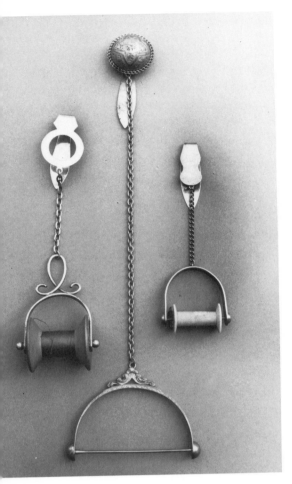
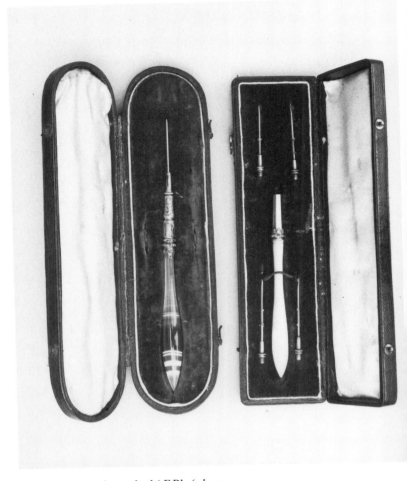

Plate 162: *Spool knaves. Left: Silver plate with wood spool marked 'EP' (electro plate). c. 1880. 22 cm. high. Centre: Brass with British Registry mark for 1876. Right: Steel, c. 1880. All English.*

Plate 164: *Left: Crochet hook with orange and white agate handle and engraved silver mount. 12.5 cm. high. Right: Crochet hook with mother-of-pearl handle, silver mount, and four hooks. Marked 'Made by Will. Lund'. English, c. 1850.*

on the left in plate 165 is a modified form of the early nineteenth century shape without the bulbous end for storing extra hooks and without the protective top. But it does still retain the distinctive wing-nut for tightening the hook into place. To the right of this handle in plate 165 is an early twentieth-century version of the tambour hook called an Art Needle. It consists of a steel holder, a sliding gauge to determine how deeply the needle will penetrate the cloth, and therefore what size loop it will leave on the other side, and needles of various sizes to fit into the holder.

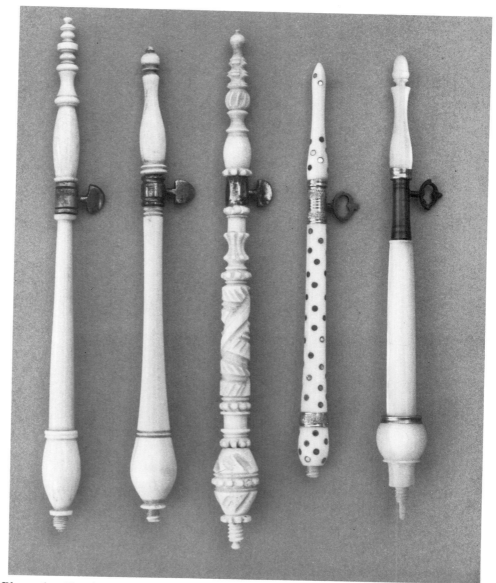

Plate 163: *Tambour hooks from left: 1–3: Ivory handle with steel mounts and wing-nuts. English, c. 1800–1820. Left hook 13.5 cm. high. 4: Ivory handle inlaid with steel studs. Gold mount and steel wing-nut. French, c. 1790. 5: Mother-of-pearl handle with gilt mount and steel wing-nut. French, c. 1800–1825.*

The Art Needle worked essentially the same effect as a tambour hook but instead of using the hook to pull the thread through from the reverse side to make a loop on the right side, the Art Needle worked from the reverse side and made loops automatically on the right side. The nearer the gauge was set to the holder, the longer the loop or nap produced on the right side.

The Art Needle was patented in February of 1922 and the directions for its

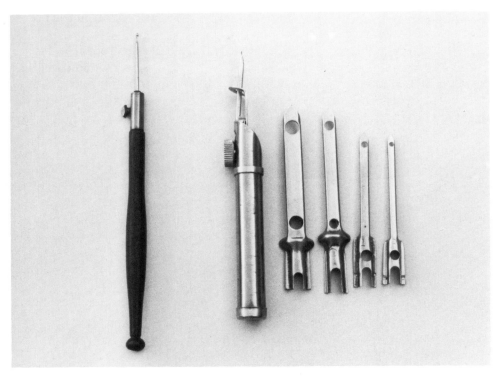

Plate 165: *Left: Tambour hook with wood handle and brass wing-nut and mount. English, c. 1890. 11.5 cm. high. Right: Punch needle with five interchangeable hooks. American, patented 21 February 1922.*

use were simple: 'Thread the needle by passing the thread through the large eye next to the thumb screw from the outside, then back through the eye of the needle from the groove side, and pull thread down through groove.... Pull the thread through the needle until there is about an inch of thread from the point. Do not hold thread at either end but simply push the needle through the cloth to the gauge. Then lift the point just high enough to scrape the surface of the cloth. Never lift the needle from the cloth. For the second stitch push the needle back through the goods as close to the first stitch as possible. Continue in this manner.... Always work on the wrong side.... Keep your cloth well stretched ... on embroidery hoops....' Thus a variation of tambour work continued in the 1920s long after its supposed demise in the 1840s.

The tambour handles which are most collectable are the early ones with the bulbous ends. It is necessary to check them carefully to ascertain that neither the top nor the wing-nut is missing or loose. The tambour handle should have one hook in place in the mounting receptacle, and the wing-nut should function both to hold it securely in place and to loosen it. The top should fit over the hook in place if both the hook and the top are original to the handle. The top should also be tested to see that it rethreads to the bottom of the handle, and that the threads are not stripped. It is a lucky bonus if the bottom receptacle contains extra tambour hooks.

Crochet comes from the French word for little hook but crochet hooks vary in size from small to large. Although crochet as a form of handwork was practiced in Europe as early as the Renaissance, it did not become popular in the Atlantic states until the second quarter of the nineteenth century. Then special patterns became widely available to meet the demand for this form of handwork requiring varying degrees of skill but only a trifling amount of money for the materials involved.

The foundation of all crochet work is the chain stitch and all other crochet stitches have their beginning in their relation to it. The crochet hook, some-

Plate 166: *Scottish transferware crochet case with 'View of Wimborne Minster'. 10.5 cm. high. Inside case are seven slots for bone crochet handle with collar mount and six hooks. c. 1860.*

Plate 167: *Brass crochet case marked 'Exhibition of all Nations, 1851' depicting Crystal Palace. 8.5 cm. wide. Case holds two bone crochet handles with collar mounts and six steel hooks. Example shown by side of case. English.*

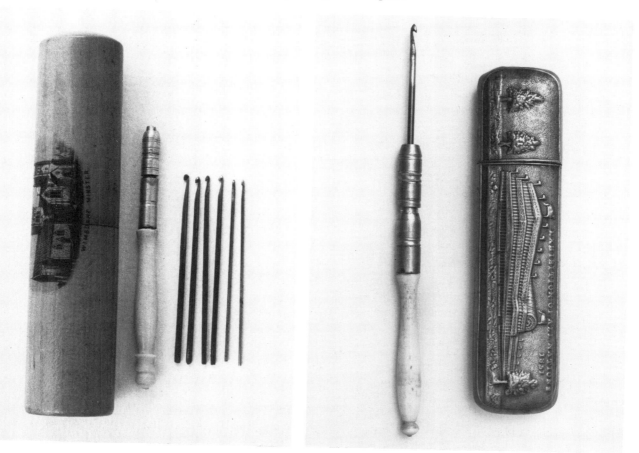

times called shepherds' hook, is usually larger than the tambour hook and is not necessarily made of steel. It has a hook at one end similar in shape to the barb of a fish-hook, and may come in materials as diverse as bone, ivory, gutta-percha and others, including steel. What is important is that the hook is the proper size for the thread, and that it is firmly made and smooth. Many needlewomen prefer used crochet hooks rather than new ones because use confers a smoothness rarely attained by other means.

Crochet hooks often came in boxed sets containing a holder and an assortment of crochet hooks of various sizes. Crochet as a form of handwork became popular at about the same time as Scottish souvenirware. The two were soon put together in cylindrical cases such as the transferware case in plate 166. The case serves as a receptacle for the crochet holder and six hooks.

Many of the crochet hooks attach to the holder by a threaded mount. In others, such as the transferware case mentioned above, or in the souvenir case of the Great Exhibition at the Crystal Palace in 1851 (plate 167), the shank of the crochet hook attaches to the holder by a collar mount which, when turned, tightens the mount around the base of the shank.

Plate 168: *Crochet hooks from left: 1–2: Bone and silver handles with collar mounts. Left handle with hook 10 cm. long. 3–6: With mother-of-pearl and bone handles from English workboxes. 7: Steel hook with bone handle also recommended for tambour work. 8: With handle marked 'Sterling'. American, c. 1890. 9: With brass handle. 10: One-piece bone. American, c. 1900–1930. 11: One-piece steel marked: 'Queen's Own 4½' with British Reg. no. 457654. All except no. 8 and 10 are English, c. 1860–1905.*

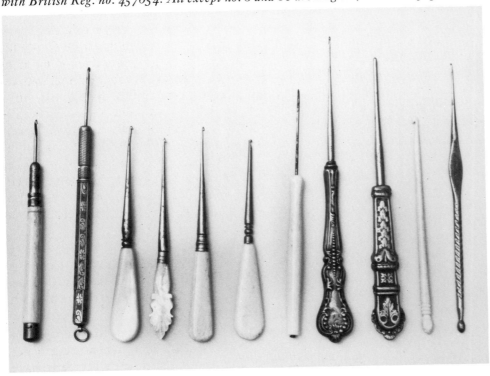

The range of crochet handles in plate 168 are typical (with the exception of the two on the extreme right) of those commonly found in the last half of the nineteenth century in everyday use. Mostly mass-produced by stamping and embossing machines, the metal handles of brass or silver still show some individuality where they have been engraved or finished. The bone and mother-of-pearl handles required more hand work for carving and shaping at the lathe. All the crochet hooks are of steel or brass.

The two crochet hooks, without separate handles, in the extreme right of the same plate, are from the early twentieth century. They represent the triumph of the machine in producing a one-piece crochet hook and handle over the older process which required hand labour to join together the machine-made hook and handle. They are not, unfortunately, as attractive or as interesting as the hooks with handles attached separately. But the one-piece crochet hooks were cheap and found a wide market.

In the early twentieth century, Campbell, Metzger & Jacobson of New York City advertised their own and imported crochet hooks of wood, steel, bone and ivory. Most were of one piece without separate handles. At wholesale the wood crochet hooks sold per gross (144 pieces) from $6.75 to $13.50. The steel hooks sold from two to four dollars per gross or about .013 to .028 cents each. Kresge's retail price about this time for a nickel-plated steel crochet hook was five cents and for bone, half that price. By contrast, highly decorated silver crochet hooks with handles could be relatively expensive. Marshall Field and Co. advertised in 1896 a silver crochet set of two hooks and embroidery scissors for four dollars and fifty cents.

Many of the advertisements of this period suggested the purchase of some type of cover to protect the carrier of sharp crochet hooks. The Canfield Rubber Co. advertised in 1887, for example, a plain pocket crochet hook with a cylindrical metal cap selling for ten cents. This was a rather unimaginative solution to the problem of sharp crochet hooks compared to the three ingenious devices on the left in plate 169. On the left is an incised brass handle in a trefoil design with a sliding embossed flower button which slides the crochet hook down into the handle when it is not in use. The crochet hook to its right has a handle cover which slides off to allow one of three crochet hooks of different sizes to rotate upward, and then to be held firmly by the replaced cover. When in place, the cover could also shield the points of all three hooks. The third crochet hook to its right works on a principle similar to the one on the far left.

The three metal crochet hooks with black glass ends in the middle of plate 169 have hooks of different sizes. The cork handle on the one to the left is removable and can be transferred to the other crochet handles for a better grip. To the far right of plate 169 is a gilt metal crochet handle from a French workbox which has six interchangeable hooks.

Crochet handles should be checked for any parts which may have been chipped off and then smoothed over. This is most likely when the crochet handle comes to a point at the bottom. This may, because of an accident, have

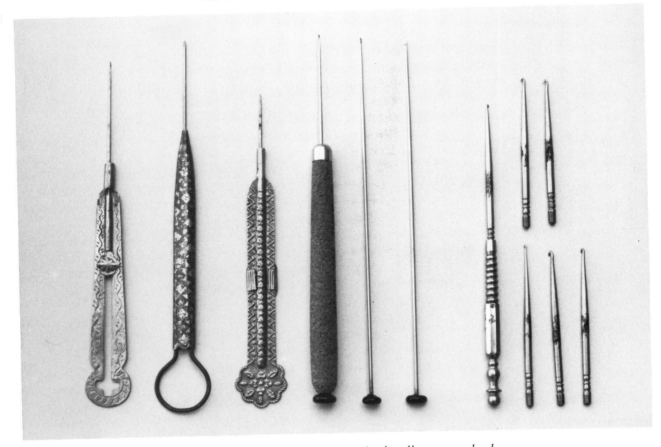

Plate 169: *Crochet hooks. Left: Three metal hooks with protective handles to cover hooks when not in use. English and American, c. 1870. Left handle with hook 11 cm. long. Centre: Three metal hooks with black glass ends and interchangeable cork handle. Right: Gilt metal crochet handle with six interchangeable hooks. French, c. 1860.*

been made into a rounded terminus. The mounting device used to hold the crochet hook in place should be examined carefully to make certain that it does function. If the handle has a protective cover, that should also be checked. Crochet sets usually have separate compartments or places for each hook. The set loses some of its value if any of the hooks is missing. The individual all-steel or all-bone one-piece crochet hook still sells for so little that it requires less attention.

Knitting needle sheaths are rather curious implements whose primary purpose is not apparent at first sight. Their function is not to act as a case for knitting needles but to make knitting more efficient. The sheath is usually tucked into one's belt on the right side so that the top inch or two forms a support for the bottom of the right knitting needle. By resting the right needle firmly in the hole at the top of the sheath, the knitter is able to free the right

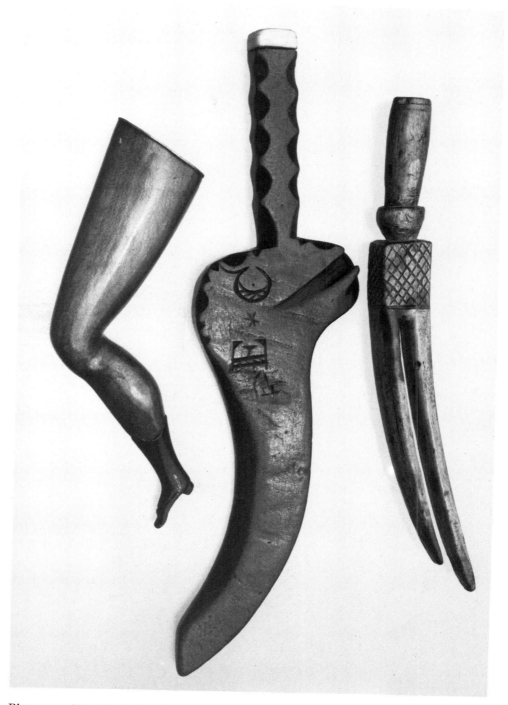

Plate 170: *Wood knitting sheaths. Left: Leg-shaped with black boot and brass plate at top. 14 cm. high. Centre: Goose wing style with square bone plate at top. Right: With two prongs to fit over belt or pocket. All English, c. 1810–1880.*

Plate 171: *Wood knitting sheaths from left: 1, 3, 5 and 8: Variations on goose wing style. Left sheath 25.5 cm. high. 2: Violin scroll style. 4: Possible goose wing style variation. All English, nineteenth century. 6–7: South Pennine style known as knitting sticks. c. 1800.*

hand to throw the thread without interruption to steady the right needle. In addition, the sheath keeps the stitches from sliding off the bottom of a double-ended needle.

Knitting sheaths go back at least to the seventeenth century, but the collector will probably not find any earlier than the nineteenth century. In northern Europe, knitting sheaths were usually a product of folk crafts and some are quite crudely made. Most were of wood although a few were of bone or ivory and even fewer of tin, brass or other materials. The hole inside the top of the sheath sometimes had a lining of metal, ivory or bone to keep the needle points from wearing the wood. The hole was occasionally capped with the lining material through which a smaller hole was cut to offer more support to the shank of the needle.

Knitting came to England from Italy through Scotland, and most sheaths found in England are from the Lake District, Yorkshire or Scotland. Many of

Plate 172: *Bone knitting needle guards with black elastic bands fit over needle ends to keep knitting from slipping off needles. Probably Asian export, c. 1850–1890. 3 cm. high.*

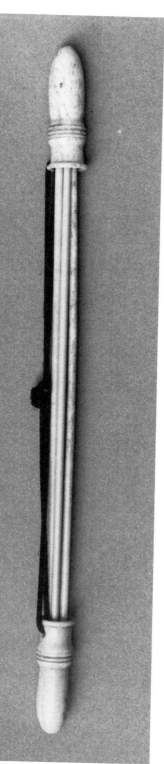

the knitting sheaths were made as love tokens which accounts for the hearts so often found on the surface decoration. A date on the surface identifies when a given sheath was made but is of little help in identifying other sheaths of similar shape. A conservatism in design led the carvers to continue to reproduce similar designs over decades and even centuries.[5]

The knitting sheath in the shape of a woman's leg, on the left in plate 170, is a typical figural sheath of the early part of the nineteenth century. It has a brass cap with a small hole over the top hole of the sheath. In the centre of the plate is another variation of the goose wing type of sheath. On the right is a knitting sheath usually made by sailors. It is a well known type, with a knob, sometimes faceted, below the handle, and below that, the sheath separates into two slightly curved blades. This type of sheath usually came from the north-east coast of England.

The crudeness of the carving or of the design is no indication of the age of knitting sheaths as the Victorian ones are often quite primitive in style and execution. By contrast, the simple, turned knitting sheaths of the South Pennine type, in plate 171, second and third from the right, date from the eighteenth century and are quite rare. Except for the violin-scroll type (second from the left) and the South Pennine types mentioned above which are also known as knitting sticks, all the rest of the sheaths in this plate are the fairly common goose wing types.

Knitting sheaths are relatively expensive, and difficult to date. It is not impossible although unlikely that some are still made for personal use, and may eventually make their way to the market. Since many of the sheaths are crudely carved, it is not difficult to imitate them. If the top of the sheath is not lined in metal, bone or ivory, then marks from the insertion of the ends of the knitting needles should be very visible and should not look newly made. The safest course is to compare knitting sheaths for sale with those known to be old.

Knitting needle guards had quite a different function from knitting sheaths. The guards, which always came in pairs connected by a ribbon, cord, chain or elastic, were placed at each end of a pair of knitting needles to keep them together as in plate 172. This was particularly important if one of the needles held knitting in progress. The connecting band kept the two needle guards pulling toward each other and prevented the stitches from slipping off either end.

The design of knitting needle guards reflected the whimsy of their makers and buyers. The guards came in many designs but boots, shoes and animal feet were particularly popular, followed by representations of fish. Other designs are more abstract, but many reflect in their careful workmanship the skills of the turner, carver or metal worker. Knitting guards were made of ivory, bone, horn, mother-of-pearl, wood, gilt metal, brass, silver and gold among other materials. They were often highly decorated as in plates 173, 174. All guards had to have either a hole drilled near the top of the guard or a metal loop attached there to which the connecting band could be tied.

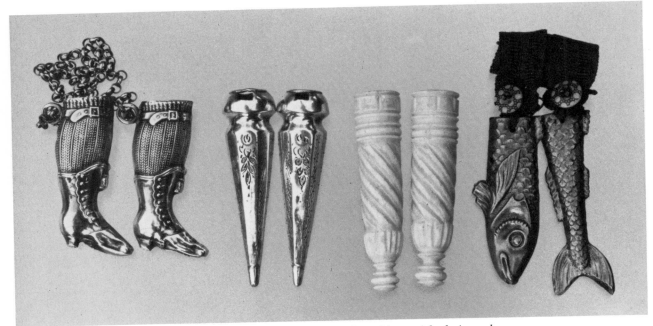

Plate 173: *Knitting needle guards from left: Silver shoes and stockings with chain and hook to adjust for needle length. Probably German, c. 1900–1920. 3.5 cm. high. Silver. European, c. 1880. Turned bone. Probably Asian, c. 1850–1890. Brass fish. European, c. 1880.*

Plate 174: *Knitting needle guards from left: 1–2: Mother-of-pearl boots and fish. 4 cm. high. 3: Silver slippers. German, c. 1900–1920. 4: Black boots with bone tops. 5: Bone pig's trotters. 6: Stamped gilt metal. 7: Turned bone. All except no. 3 are English, c. 1850–1900.*

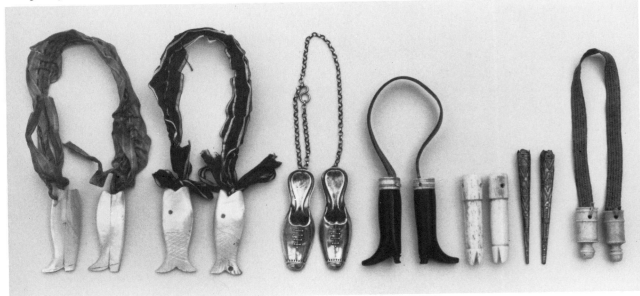

Knitting guards are not as yet as expensive as knitting sheaths, but like so many other needlework tools, they are rapidly climbing in price. Obviously a pair of knitting guards should match. It is a pleasant bonus, but not a necessity, for the guards to have their original band which attaches them one to the other. The holes or loops to which the band attaches should be visible and in good shape. The most common fault found in knitting guards is missing parts, such as chips off boots, shoes, or knobs from ornamental turning.

Knitting and crochet are methods of creating fabric 'in air', as it is sometimes expressed. The art of netting is another such method. This ancient art goes back to antiquity where it was used for fish-nets, bird-nets and clothing of various types. By the Middle Ages, netting also served ecclesiastical purposes. It was known as *Opus Filatorium* and considered as lace. By the Renaissance, netting was made into curtains and bedhangings, and continued to be used for this purpose until the new popularity of crochet in the second quarter of the nineteenth century.

The advantage of netting is its strength. Each loop is made independently, and if properly knotted, remains firmly in place regardless of what happens to the loops around it. The beauty of netting for domestic apparel consists of the regular size of the loops and the tightness of each knot which produce an overall pattern of great regularity, delicacy and strength. The Victorian embroidery manuals gave much space to detailed descriptions of how to make from various netting patterns such things as antimacassars, purses, curtains, edging and fringes of various kinds, hair-nets, hammocks, tennis nets, mittens and many other domestic articles.

The tools necessary for netting are basically two: the netting needle and the mesh. They are made of bone, ivory, wood, steel or celluloid. The netting needle comes in several forms, but the most basic one is in plate 175, third object from the left and second from the right. Although it is not visible without close inspection, the long netting needle is split at each end of the oval loop to admit the thread which is wound length-wise around the needle. The thread is secured to the needle through the small hole drilled near one end of the needle. The size of the needle used depends on the size of the mesh to which it must be exactly matched. The netting needle in plate 175, next to the right case, matches the mesh next to it, third from the right.

The mesh is the implement on which the loops are made, and it may be either round or flat as in plate 176 (first, third, fifth and seventh objects from left) depending on the size of the loops wanted. For long loops, a flat mesh is preferable. Most important, the mesh should be the same thickness throughout so that the loops made upon it may all be of the same size and easily slipped off. It is also important that the needle and the mesh match each other not only in size, but that they are appropriate to the thread used and to the size of loop required. The thread wound on the needle, for example, must not make the needle so thick that it cannot pass through the loops as the netting is made.

Other implements used in netting include a netting case. Two examples are in plate 175, on the extreme left and right. These cases hold netting needles of various sorts. Some other types of netting needles are also illustrated in the same plate. The shorter and wider needle, fourth from the right object, has the thread wound around the inside needle.

The art of netting requires that a foundation loop be attached to a netting clamp or hook on a sewing or pincushion clamp, or to a leaded cushion which will not move, or to a stirrup held by the left foot, or to a reel in a box fitted for the purpose so that it is possible to control the tension of the net as the process proceeds. After the foundation loop has been established, as Thérèse de Dillmont explained in the nineteenth century, 'take the mesh in the left hand, holding it between the thumb and forefinger stiffening the other fingers extended beneath. Take the netting needle . . . in the right hand and pass the thread downwards over the mesh and over the 2nd, 3rd and 4th fingers of the left hand, carry it upwards behind these three fingers and lay it to the left, where it is held fast by the thumb.

'Carry the thread downwards again behind the four fingers, put the needle upwards from below through the loop on the fingers and through the loop at the back of the mesh or through the one to which the thread is fastened; a second loop is thus formed on the left hand, which loop is held open by the little finger.

'Gradually tightening the thread, disengage the fingers from the loop held by the thumb, and tighten the loop that is round the fingers. Keep the last loop upon the little finger until the first has been entirely closed. Then, only, draw the little finger out of the loop and tighten the knot, thus completing the stitch.

'The next stitches are made in the same way, whether for casting on or for the actual netting.'[6]

More collectors are interested in netting cases than in netting needles. The needles are relatively cheap while the cases are more expensive, especially if they are good examples of Asian carving in bone, ivory, horn and wood. The carving can sometimes be crude; it can also be so fine that it approaches a filigree effect.

Netting cases are occasionally confused with bodkin and needle cases although both of the latter are much smaller in size. Netting cases may also appear similar to those general all-purpose cylindrical cases of the late eighteenth and early nineteenth century. The eighteenth-century cases were often of enamel, porcelain or precious metal while nineteenth-century netting cases were often of bone or ivory carved in Asia for export to Europe.

Men sometimes did netting since nets were of use not only to fishermen but also to gentlemen amateurs of various sports. Many women preferred, at least in public, to do knotting rather than netting since the art of knotting displayed their hands to greater advantage, and the decoration of the knotting shuttle complimented their appearance.

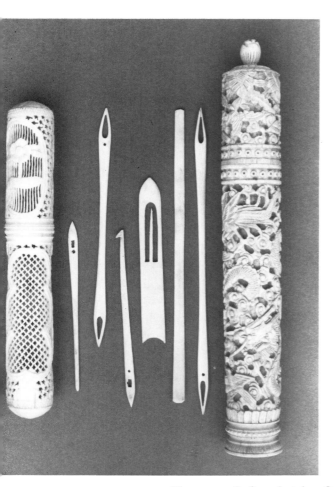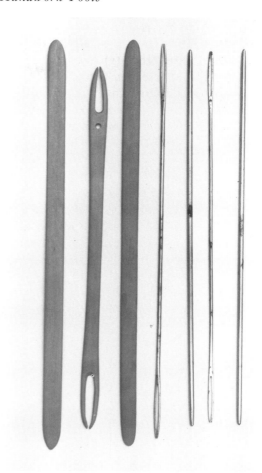

Plate 175: *Left and right: Carved ivory and bone netting cases. Left case 13 cm. high. Third object from right is bone netting mesh. Others are bone netting needles. Chinese, c. 1830–1880.*

Plate 176: *From left: 1–3: Two sandalwood netting meshes on either side of sandalwood netting needle. Mesh 18.5 cm. long. 4–8: Alternating steel netting needles and meshes. All English, c. 1850.*

Another way of making fabric 'in air' and in this case without the use of needles is by the lucet as in plate 177. The lucet was also known as a lyre, a lutal or most appropriately, as a chain fork which describes its major function in the nineteenth century: making chains or braids. A very fine silk produced an imitation of a small French hair chain very popular as a neck chain. Coarse black silk produced, by contrast, a very sturdy watch chain.[7]

Holding the lucet between her thumb and forefinger of her left hand, the needlewoman brought the thread end through the lucet hole from the back to the front and held the thread tail against the lucet with her left thumb. She then brought the working thread from the back through the horns of the lucet and wrapped the thread around the right horn from front to back and then around the left horn from front to back forming a figure eight. She now held the working thread across the front of the right horn in a position above the loop. Then with her right thumb and forefinger she loosened the loop and slipped it over the working thread and off the horn, pulling slightly to tighten threads. She was careful to leave the working thread in position around the right horn to form a new loop. She then turned the lucet around so that the right horn now became the left horn. She now held the working thread across the front of the 'new' right horn above the loop. She then loosened the loop and slipped it over the working thread and off the right horn and tightened the threads to form a knot. Again, she was careful to leave the working thread around the horn to form a new loop. She then reversed the lucet once more and repeated the process. As the cord or chain formed, she pulled it through the lucet hole.

Lucets were usually of ivory, bone, mother-of-pearl, tortoise shell or wood. Some lucets were flat as on the left in plate 177. Others were more rounded as in the one on the right. The steel points inlaid in an early nineteenth-century ivory lucet reflect the influence of the eighteenth-century respect for steel as an expensive metal not at all inappropriate for inlay work.

Lucets command a high price in the market because of their rarity. The

Plate 177: *Left: Ivory lucet with steel inlay. 11 cm. high. Right: Shaped ivory lucet. English, c. 1800.*

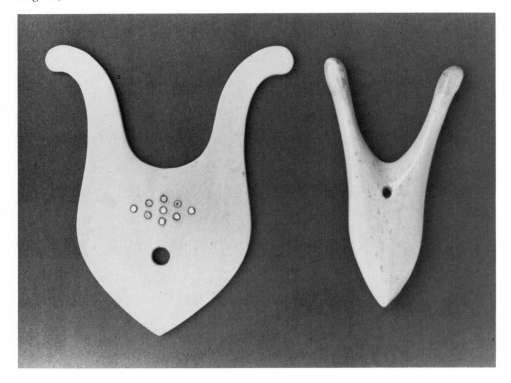

more desirable ones have metal inlay. It is fairly easy to inspect lucets for any obvious damage by chipping. The difficulty arises with wood lucets which may well be genuine but which, because of the high price they attract, could also be of more recent origin. If the lucet is skillfully shaped and if it has any kind of metal point inlay, the likelihood of its authenticity increases because this reflects a more difficult process of manufacture. The prospective purchaser of plain wood lucets should try to obtain some proof of their authenticity.

The lucet had been a popular and valuable implement in the eighteenth century when fancy chains were sometimes used as clothes fasteners for better clothing. For ordinary clothing, the holes for utilitarian cords were made by stilettos, sometimes called piercers or punches. Many elegant stilettos were an integral part of the fitted needlework box. The advantage of the stiletto was that unlike a knife or scissors, it could make holes in fabric without the risk of tearing the material. In the nineteenth century, needlewomen used stilettos primarily for whitework. They were also used to make eyelet holes in dressmaking and for embroidery of various kinds.

The stiletto is a sharply pointed implement with a round tapering blade graduating down to a sharp point. It may be of one material such as steel, silver, bone, ivory, mother-of-pearl or other substantial substances such as wood. It was more common in the nineteenth century, however, to make the stiletto in two parts: a steel point set in a solid material such as mother-of-pearl, bone, ivory or metal.

Many stiletto handles were elaborately carved as in plate 178. The first and third stilettos from the left are from early nineteenth-century French workboxes. They have steel points set in mother-of-pearl and banded with gilt metal at the junction. The fourth, fifth and sixth from the left are from English workboxes in the latter half of the nineteenth century and have similar handles. The elaborately carved bone handle depicting feathers and fruit (fourth from the right) is probably mid-nineteenth-century English or French. The two stilettos to the right of it are two-piece carvings so that the points can be inverted and threaded into the handle for a closed position as shown in plate 178. The last stiletto on the right is a common variety of bone stiletto made in the United States and elsewhere in enormous quantities.

Other stilettos were commonly made of wood and metal. The two-piece rosewood stiletto in plate 179 shows that type of stiletto as it appears just before it is closed. To its right is the recognizable Tunbridge end-grain mosaic pattern handle. The next three stilettos with silver or silver gilt handles are from French workboxes. The similar stiletto, sixth from the left, is from an English workbox of about the same time, c. 1850. The three stilettos to its right are probably from sewing cases. The lyre-shaped handle of the stiletto, fifth from the right, is French. It is early nineteenth century as is the English stiletto to its right with imitation filigree work on the handle.

The stiletto, third from the right, is of interest because of its adjustable stopping device visible on the steel point above the sterling silver handle. This device will determine how deeply the point will penetrate the fabric, and therefore how large a hole it will make. It has an American patent date of 1909. To its right are two other sterling silver handle stilettos also of American manufacture.

Between these relatively fancy stilettos and the plain steel or bone stiletto, there was a wide discrepancy in price. At the end of the nineteenth century, the fancy silver stiletto cost at retail anywhere from a dollar up while the steel stiletto cost about ten cents and the bone stiletto five cents.

Unless stilettos have fancy, carved or precious metal handles, they are less expensive than most needlework tools. Aside from checking the handle for possible damage, and making certain that the point is not wobbly in the mounting, the collector should check the length of the point. Its proportion to the handle and to its own diameter should be such that there is little possibility that it has been cut down and resharpened either to repair a broken point, or to make it fit into a recessed compartment of a fitted needlework box or sewing case. If the stiletto is part of a set, the handle should match the design of the other implements.

Plate 178: *Stilettos from left: 1–6: Steel points with mother-of-pearl handles. From French and English workboxes, c. 1820–1870. Left stiletto 9.5 cm. long. 7–8: With bone handles. From English and French workboxes, c. 1850. 9–10: Ivory and bone points with protectors. English, c. 1850. 11: Common bone point. American, c. 1900–1930.*

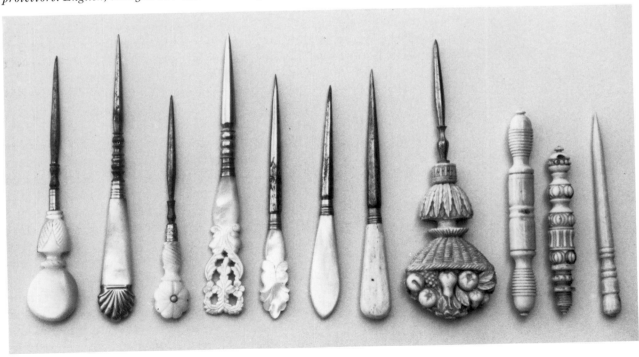

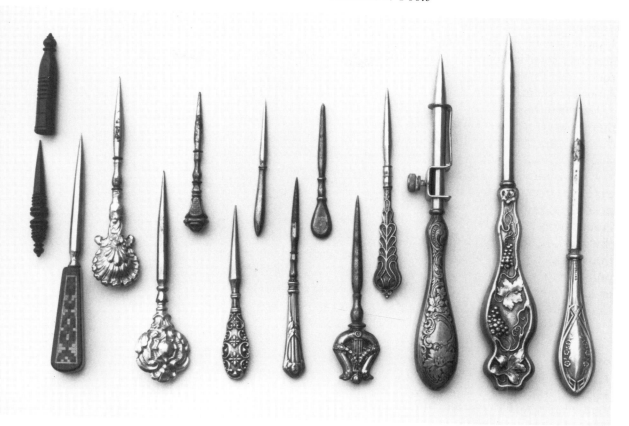

Plate 179: *Stilettos from left: 1: Rosewood point and protector. English, c. 1850. 2: Steel point with Tunbridge mosaic-pattern handle. English, c. 1860. 10 cm. long. 3–6 and 8–11: Steel points with silver handles from French and English workboxes, c. 1820–1880. 7: Steel point with gold handle. European, c. 1900–1920. 12–14: Steel points with silver handles marked 'Sterling'. American, c. 1890–1910. No. 12 has stopping device marked 'Pat'd Apr 6, '09'.*

Another handwork technique which also produced fabric 'in air' was tatting which by means of shuttles produced a type of lace. Tatting is a very old art but it became prominent in Europe in the nineteenth century among leisured women because it was easily mastered, eminently portable and showed off a woman's hands to advantage. It thus filled the same social function as had knotting in the eighteenth and early nineteenth centuries. Moreover, tatting had the inestimable advantage of losing nothing by interruption. Tatting could be put down for a few minutes, without in any way becoming disarranged, and then picked up later and continued.

The English name of tatting comes from tatters and indicates its fragile appearance, as does the French word for it, *frivolité*. In fact, tatting, unlike knitting and crochet, produces very strong stitches which are independent knots. Tatting originally was made of a succession of knots over a loop of its own thread. This was then drawn up and the stitches or knots on it formed into an oval which had the appearance of a buttonhole. An example of tatting with a series of knots on thread where only one oval has been made is in plate 180.

To make any kind of design, these ovals had to be connected by needle and thread, a tedious and unsatisfactory arrangement. In the middle of the nineteenth century, needlewomen began to join these tatted ovals by means of decorative lace loops called purls or picots. The advantage of this method was that the tatted ovals were joined by their own thread and knotted securely without interrupting the tatting to have recourse to needle and thread. This innovation gave body to tatted lace and allowed the use of finer threads as well as smaller shuttles which now often had a pointed pick or hook to facilitate the joining of the tatted ovals. These picks can be seen on some of the shuttles in plate 181.

The basic stitch or knot in tatting is the simple half hitch which is made around a loop of thread drawn from the shuttle. The loop of the thread is held in the left hand between the thumb and forefinger. The shuttle with the trailing thread is held in the right hand and it now makes a second half hitch from the other direction. This results in a double half hitch.

Another innovation in tatting in the nineteenth century was the introduction of a second shuttle with a second thread. 'Two shuttles are used in tatting when the little [loops] are not intended to be connected at their base by a single thread, or when it is desired to conceal the passage of the thread to another group of stitches, or else when different coloured threads are used.

'In working with two shuttles, the ends of the two threads are tied together. One of the threads is passed over the middle finger of the left hand, wound twice round the little finger and the shuttle allowed to fall free.

'The second shuttle is then taken up with the right hand and the same movements are made with it as when a single shuttle only is used.'[8] The addition of the second shuttle made the work not only more ornamental but also facilitated the making of larger and wider designs.

The shuttle used in tatting is made in three pieces: the top and bottom which are convex in shape with their points nearly touching, and the centre section which joins them together and through which a hole is often drilled to secure the thread around it. Shuttles can be roughly categorized as: small for very fine work; medium for ordinary work; and large for coarse work.

Large tatting shuttles should not be confused with knotting shuttles which may be the same size, or if French, much larger. The knotting shuttle uses a larger thread to produce a cord for appliqué in surface embroidery, while the tatting shuttle creates its own fabric. Moreover, the tools themselves are somewhat different. The tatting shuttle has pointed ends nearly touching because of its convex top and bottom. The knotting shuttle has a nearly flat top and bottom and considerable space between its rounder ends. The knotting shuttle was often made of costly materials and was a prized possession of eighteenth-century women. It was used at social gatherings as much for

Plate 180: *Left: Four bone tatting shuttles. Asian and English, c. 1830–1870. Top shuttle 8 cm. long. Right: Knotting shuttle and two tatting shuttles of mother-of-pearl. French and English, c. 1800–1870.*

Plate 181: *Knotting and tatting shuttles: Left: Horn inlaid with mother-of-pearl and abalone, 8 cm. long, and two tortoise-shell. English, c. 1850–1870. Centre: Gold marked '14 kt'. Two silver marked 'Sterling', made by Webster Co., c. 1900–1910. Right: Abalone. American, c. 1900–1920; wood marquetry, Indian, c. 1850; and base metal, American, patented April 17, 1923.*

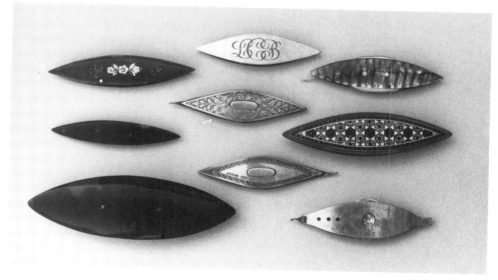

Handwork Tools

display as for anything else. The dramatic difference between a large knotting shuttle of ivory and gold and a tatting shuttle of bone is apparent in plate 182.

Because shuttles played such an important social role, many are well made, elegantly proportioned and some are ornamented on the top and bottom. They are made of almost every precious and exotic material as well as of more common ones. The top and bottom of some shuttles are attached to the centre section by several studs. Sometimes these studs show as inlay points on the surface. It is important that they do not extrude above the surface which would be unpleasant to see and feel and would also risk catching the thread and tangling the tatting.

Although tatting continued until the First World War as not uncommon handwork, the shuttles made after the Second World War were more utilitarian and less decorative than earlier ones. In New York City, for example, Campbell, Metzger & Jacobson advertised celluloid shuttles in the 1920s in ivory, black or shell colours, with or without picks. The company also sold metal shuttles with detachable centre sections which were now called spools or bobbins. Retail stores sold celluloid shuttles for ten cents and metal ones for twenty cents.

The collector of shuttles will quickly become aware of the common problems encountered. Because of their shape, shuttles are easily cracked or chipped at the points. The risk is increased when picks are added to the points. Shuttles are often sold with the thread still wrapped around the internal bobbin or centre section. It is prudent to unwrap the thread to find out the condition of the centre.

All the needlework tools discussed above which produce openwork weaves are making, in effect, a type of lace. We usually think of lace, however, as something more delicate, as gossamer as cobwebs. Like the Venetians, we want to describe it as *punto in aria*, a stitch in the air. Lace is, in fact, simply

Plate 183: Lacemaker's box holds dressed lace pillow, additional wood bobbins, glass-head pins, other tools and patterns. Made by Cartier-Bresson, French, c. 1900. 33 cm. wide.

Plate 182: *Top: Bone tatting shuttle. English, c. 1870. 6.5 cm. long. Bottom: Ivory and gold knotting shuttle. French, c. 1760. 14.5 cm. long.*

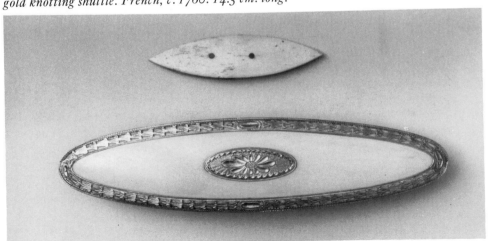

212

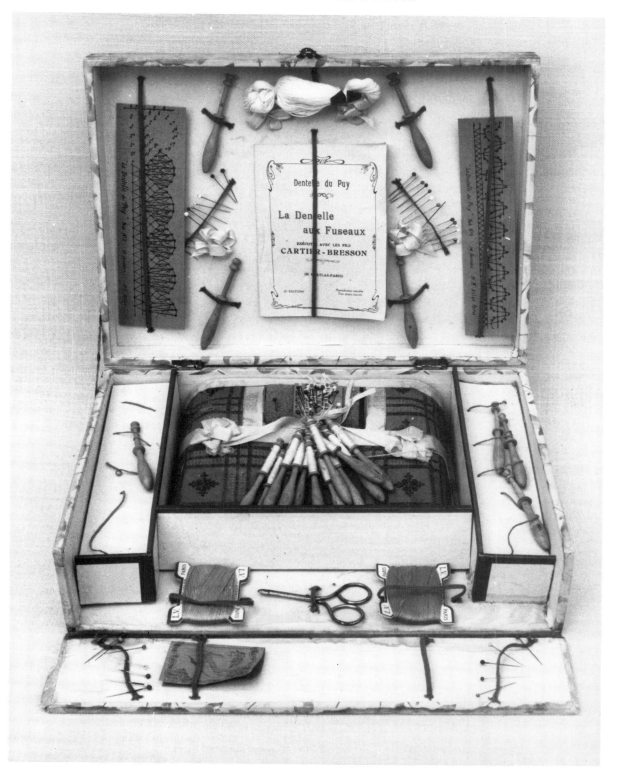

made of open mesh-work interchanges. It is made either by needle and called needlepoint lace, or by bobbins and called pillow or bobbin lace. Because our interest here is in the lace bobbins, we are concerned only with the lace produced by them.

The French lacemaker's box in plate 183 shows the essential tools needed to make bobbin lace, or as the French call it, *dentelle aux fuseaux*. First, a pattern is placed on a roller fitted in the top centre of the pillow, and pins are stuck into the pattern as a guide for the thread. The bobbins are wound with white thread and attached to the pattern, hanging downward. Half of the bobbins are called 'Hangers' or 'Passive Bobbins' and half 'Workers' or 'Active Bobbins'. The 'Workers' guided by the pattern and pins, work from side to side of the pattern, over and under the 'Hangers', to make the lace.[9] Although machine-produced lace had made lace-making as a cottage industry unprofitable by the middle of the nineteenth century, certain fine laces still found a small market.

The lace bobbin is divided into several sections which an examination of the bone lace bobbin, on the left in plate 184, will make clear. The top part, turned in the form of a double knob is the head. The thinner space between the two knobs is sometimes called the short neck. The thin spindle connecting the double knob and the carved shank is known as the long neck around which thread is wound. The centre section with its incised turning and spiralling message picked into the bone is the shank. The ring of beads at the bottom is the spangle which came into existence at the end of the eighteenth century to compensate for the lighter weight of bobbins then introduced. The function of the spangle is thus to give extra weight to the bobbin to keep it steady against the pillow. The spangle wire is usually brass or copper. In most cases, the spangle wire loops directly through the bottom of the shank. Sometimes, as here, the spangle wire is attached to another small loop, known as a shackle, which in turn threads through the bottom of the shank.

The beads strung on the spangle follow a certain pattern or variations on it. They may number from seven to nine although more or less is not unusual. The top bead on each side of the spangle is called simply that. The next two beads on each side are called square cut because of their shape. To obtain that shape, the bead is heated and then squared with the help of a file. Square cut beads are often red or white but they may also be dark blue, turquoise, amber, brown or green. The bottom bead, if it is a single bead, is usually much larger than the rest and decorated in some special way, as in the bobbin third from the right. If there are two bottom beads, as in this first bobbin on the left, then they are usually only slightly larger than the other beads.

Bobbins are generally made of bone or wood. If the latter, a close-grained hardwood such as fruitwood is preferred. Bone bobbins are less common than wood ones because of their cost. They last longer and have been so associated with bobbin lace from the Renaissance that this form of lace was known as bone lace in the sixteenth century. Shakespeare writes, for example, in *Twelfth Night* of 'the spinsters and the knitters in the sun and the free maids

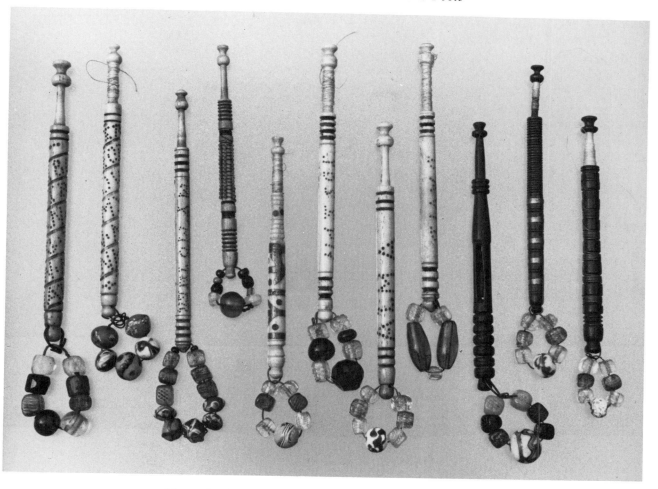

Plate 184: *Lace bobbins from left: 1–3: Bone with messages. Left bobbin 14 cm. long. 4: Bone 'Beaded Birdcage'. 5 and 10: Butterfly and Tiger bobbins. 6–8: Bone with names. 9: Wood church window bobbin called 'Mother-and-babe'. 11: Wood with brass wire bands. English, c. 1840–1900.*

that weave their threads with bone'.

Bobbins have also been made of brass, pewter, iron and silver although their weight was a disadvantage unless they were very thin. Bobbins of glass and agate were usually too fragile to survive while bobbins of ivory were too expensive to make in any quantity. Many bone bobbins worn very smooth are sometimes described as ivory.

The collector will find that most bobbins available today are either of wood or bone, and if English, usually from the East Midlands. The most collectable bobbins are the carved or decorated ones. Some examples are in plates 184, 185. The first three from the left in plate 184 are commemorative bobbins. The first gives a name and birthdate, the next two have messages. The fourth is unusual because it is bound with wire over bone in a pattern known as a beaded birdcage. The fifth from the left, a butterfly bobbin, belongs to a type made in Bedford in which the shape of the pewter inlay determines its name. Bobbins with pewter wings are called butterfly, with pewter studs, leopard, and with pewter bands alone, as in the second from the right, tiger bobbins.

In the same plate, the third bobbin from the right is the most valuable of the lot because of its carved windows with a bobbin inside, which looks like an abstract representation of a woman. As a type, this bobbin is known as a church-window bobbin, and this specific version of it is called a mother-in-babe bobbin. All carved bobbins with pierced windows, and there may be several tiers of windows in a given bobbin, are quite rare.

The other bobbin in demand has hand decoration on the shank. Bobbins were usually turned on a lathe, but the shanks were sometimes left blank to be

Plate 185: *Rosewood Tunbridge lace bobbin box. English, c. 1830. 14 cm. wide. Three bone name bobbins. English, c. 1840–1900.*

decorated by the giver. These bobbins are more valuable if the name or message was added by the purchaser and was not simply a readymade name or message put in coloured drilled dots on the shank by the manufacturer. The more valuable commemorative bobbins refer to specific individuals by family name or birthdate or both as in the example of the first bobbin on the left in plate 184 which reads: 'Hallen King born Octr 2 1863.' Other valuable commemorative bobbins refer to some particular personal, local or national event, sometimes even a hanging, which makes a very collectable bobbin. It was not unusual in the East Midlands to make commemorative wedding bobbins from bones left after the wedding feast.[10]

Lace bobbins have risen dramatically in price in the last few years, appearing even in the best auction houses. Since commemorative bobbins began to command unusually high prices, they have appeared in unusually large quantities. Plain bone bobbins, by comparison, are relatively plentiful and cheap. This raises the question as to when some of these names and messages were added to the bone bobbins. When the collector purchases a nineteenth century 'name' or 'message' bobbin, he or she wants the name or message to have been added either by the nineteenth-century maker or purchaser and not by a twentieth-century craftsman. The prudent course is to ask the seller when the name or message was added, and then to compare it with a dated one.

The other problem with lace bobbins is the spangle. The beads may have been replaced, altered, added to or subtracted from the original number. This is not necessarily a sufficient reason for rejecting a lace bobbin, but it does lower its value. Modern cheap beads are no substitute for the decorative nineteenth-century beads which often included Venetian beads and others of that quality.

Bobbins were sometimes stored in bobbin boxes about thirteen to eighteen centimetres wide. These are more rare than the bobbins themselves. Usually made in oak, the rarer ones came in souvenir ware like the one from Tunbridge Wells in plate 185. This box has a wire hinge which was typical of bobbin boxes. It is lined with paper and the outside has the Tunbridge cube marquetry as the centrepiece, set in rosewood, while the border is an early example of end-grain mosaic. It probably dates from the second quarter of the nineteenth century. Three 'name' bobbins which fit inside are shown next to the box.

11 Plain Sewing and Handwork Gadgets

The nineteenth century saw the introduction of a number of sewing and handwork aids which while not essential, were, sometimes, useful. These gadgets often received patents for trifling variations in design or innovation. The very process of industrialization in England and the United States encouraged a mechanical turn of mind. It is doubtful if any of these gadgets for plain sewing and handwork made any fortunes, but they reflect in their curious forms the attempt to adapt the mechanical knowledge of the time to problems encountered in the domestic arts, and particularly, in sewing and handwork.

The users of the knitting needles discussed in the chapter on handwork, for example, needed an easy way to measure the diameter of the needles so that both the seller and the buyer would know that they were handling pairs of matching needles. The idea of a needle gauge came from the industry most intimately connected with the manufacturing of all kinds of needles, the wire industry. The needle gauge for handworkers was nothing more than an adaptation of the wire-gauge of the wire-drawers.

The needle gauge at first had no universal standard to which it could apply. The numbers of one needle gauge had no necessary correlation to the numbers of another needle gauge. This was not, however, a problem for the shopkeeper, who sold knitting needles or for the woman who used them. Each only wanted to be sure that the needles sold or used matched one another, or matched some other needle which they wanted to duplicate. Later the needle sizes were standardized to correspond to the sizes required by patterns.

The gauge for knitting needles could be in almost any shape although bell-shaped and circular forms were most common. They were usually of metal and had on their outer edge a series of graduated circular cuts, each with its own number to distinguish it from the others. Some also had one or more circles in the centre to give additional measurements as well as to furnish a convenient hole by which to hang the gauge. Other needle gauges were oblong with similar arrangements for the notches. More than two dozen varieties of needle gauge have been recorded.[1]

The bell-shaped needle gauge, manufactured by H. Walker of London, in plate 186, has large holes in the centre numbered from one to five. Circular notches around the edge are numbered from six to twenty-four which is the smallest. Most needle gauges, like this one, are of steel. The Colonial Williamsburg Foundation of Virginia has, however, a tapered, rectangular gauge of ivory with holes numbered from one through nineteen.

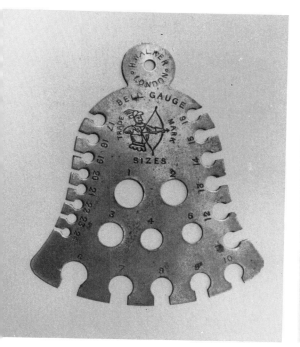

Plate 186: *Steel bell gauge to measure diameter of knitting needles. English, c. 1880–1900. 7 cm. long.*

Plate 187: *Top left: Oval 'Kenberry Scissors Sharpener'. 6 cm. wide. Bottom left: Triangle 'Middy's Scissor Sharpener'. Right: Original cardboard packaging for Kenberry, patented 1943. American.*

Needle gauges, like most of the handwork gadgets, do not as yet command much attention. The collector should make certain that the device in question is a needle gauge by following the criteria suggested above. The needle gauge for knitting needles should not be confused with the needle gauge for sewing needles which is quite different in appearance as in plate 42.

For those who wanted to sharpen their own scissors, there were patented scissors sharpeners as in plate 187. These metal sharpeners had a slot bisected by a sharpening rod attached above and below the slot. By holding the scissors by their handles, and then inserting the open blades into the slot, one on each side of the sharpening rod, it was theoretically possible to sharpen the scissors by pushing the blades back and forth against the sharpening rod. It does not seem an easy task, and one wonders if the cutlers' shops sold this scissors sharpener to convince their customers that a better sharpening job could be done by the old method where the cutler held the blade to a revolving wheel.

Another aid to plain sewing was the hem measure. Hemming was at best a tiresome task and the hem measure was handier than a ruler or tape measure, being only three inches in length. Hems were rarely that wide. It could be

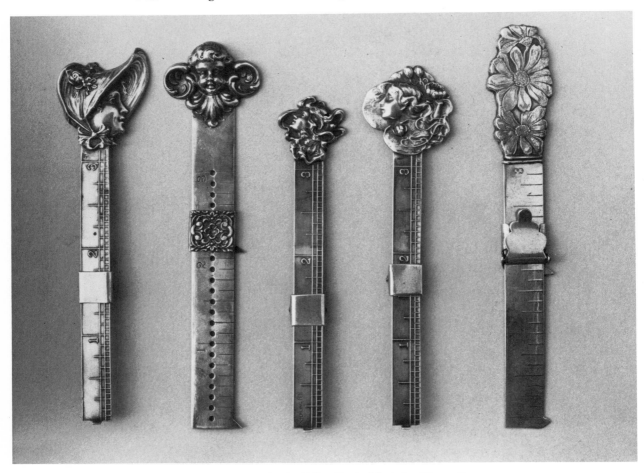

Plate 188: *Hem measures from left: 1, 3–4: Marked 'Sterling'. Made by Unger Bros.,*
1900–1904. Left measure 11 cm. high. 2: Marked 'Sterling, Pat Oct 2, '94'.
5: Marked 'Sterling'. Made by Webster Co., c. 1900. All are American.

easily moved, as the needlewoman pinned the hem, with its mark set at the
hem depth, thereby guiding her work.

Needlewomen found these silver hem measures as in plate 188 very attractive. The Unger Brothers of New Jersey advertised in their catalogue of 1904
sixteen quite different hem measures. Most of these had at the top of the
measure a striking representation of a woman's head in the Art Nouveau
style.[2] These hem measures, like other Unger Bros. silver needlework tools,
are avidly sought by collectors today and are priced at high levels.

In the 29 August 1868 issue of *Harper's Bazaar* was a sketch of a tracing wheel
which appeared to have a wood handle with a metal shank and revolving
notched wheel. The advertisement referred to the device as a copying wheel:
'By the means of the newly-invented Copying Wheel, patterns may be trans-

ferred from the Supplement with the greater ease. This Wheel is equally useful for cutting patterns of all sorts, whether from other patterns or from the garments themselves. For sale by News-dealers generally; or will be sent by mail on receipt of 25 cents.'

Thirty years later, Sears, Roebuck and Co. sold similar tracing wheels for five cents each. For ten cents it was possible to buy a double adjustable tracing wheel which could be adjusted along the axis of the wheels by a set screw to obtain the desired distance between the wheels. Some of the different types of tracing wheels are in plate 189. The black enamel handle with single wheel was one of the more common American types at the end of the nineteenth century. Next to it is a more interesting variation sold by Montgomery, Ward and Company. It has a nickel handle which comes off the wood handle to protect the wheel when not in use. The middle tracing wheel with the embossed silver handle has a small thumb rest allowing the exertion of greater pressure on the cutting edge of the revolving wheel. The two tracing wheels on the right have double revolving wheels. The one on the far right can be adjusted to change the distance between the two wheels.

Plate 189: Tracing wheels from left: 1–3: Single spoke wheels with black handle, wood handle and nickel cover, and silver handle hallmarked Birmingham, 1904. Left tracer 15.5 cm. long. 4: Double spoke wheels with wood handle. 5: Double adjustable spoke wheels with black handle. All except no. 3 are American, c. 1890–1910.

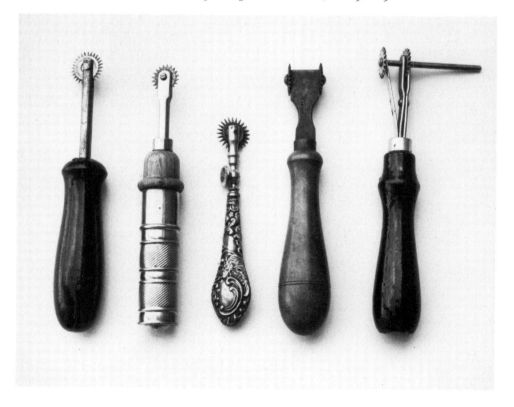

Brass gadgets were also popular in the later nineteenth century like the brass tracing wheel or the brass Barry Button Gauge shown on the left and right in plate 190. The button gauge served two functions. By measuring the buttonhole, it set the gauge at the size to be repeated for all the other button holes. Second, by measuring the distance between the button holes the button gauge made certain that this was also kept constant.

The implement between the brass button gauge and tracing wheel is a button remover which works like the fork of a hammer removing nails. This uncomplicated tool has an attractive silver handle of far better design and workmanship than would be expected of a tool so eminently dispensable, since either the scissors or the penknife from the workbox could equally well remove buttons.

When the Barry Button Gauge had measured the size of a button hole, the hole could then be cut out by a special button hole cutter patented in 1872 by D. M. Co. The cutter has a brass handle and steel blade (plate 191). A sliding tab attached to the back end of the blade moved up and down on top of a groove set in the handle. Alongside the groove were calibrated marks from one to ten to guide the needlewoman in setting the tab (and therefore the blade) at that mark corresponding to the size of the buttonhole needed.

Plate 190: *Left: Brass tracing wheel. 8 cm. long. Centre: Button remover with silver handle. Right: Brass buttonhole gauge. All American, c. 1900.*

Plate 191: *Brass buttonhole cutter marked 'D.M. Co., Pat. Sept 3, 1872'. American.*

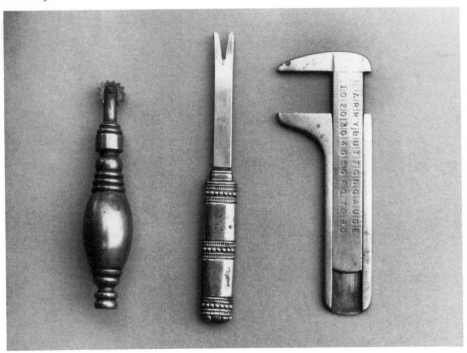
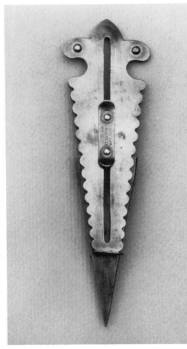

Plate 192: *Darners from left: 1: Wood mushroom marked 'Hungary'. 13 cm. high. 2: Black with cloisonné handle. 3: White milk glass. 4: Clear glass. 5: Maroon with handle marked 'Sterling'. 6: Silver with oval opening at top. 7: Silver marked 'Sterling', for gloves. Below: Ivory with wood handle. All made for American market, c. 1850–1900.*

One of the most familiar aids to plain sewing and handwork is the darner. When socks, gloves and other clothing were made of materials not easily or cheaply replaced, the darner was a necessity for nearly every house. The majority of darners came in the shape of a large egg on a stem and were made of wood. How long they have been in use is unknown. Mushroom shape darners probably date from the nineteenth century. Needlewomen preferred darners of close-grained hardwoods because they were cheap and wore well against the pressure of the needle.

Darners for mending gloves came in different shapes. Some had round balls at each end of a stem of wood, metal, bone or ivory. Others had a single ball. The French made sets of miniature darning eggs in graduated finger sizes called appropriately *oeufs à gants*.

Needlewomen also saw the possibility of using darners as small receptacles. The darners sometimes came in two pieces; the handle might unscrew from the egg or the egg itself would separate into two parts. Often the egg was used to store needles and thimble or the stem also functioned as a needlecase. In

223

the nineteenth century, eggs of glass or china filled with water often served as hand coolers for needlewomen in the summer. In winter, women sometimes put metal eggs filled with hot water into their muffs to keep their hands warm.[3]

Some examples of decorated darners are in plate 192. The mushroom darner at the extreme left was painted in Hungary in a flowery folk design. To its right is a black egg with an interesting blue, white and rose cloisonné handle. The third darner is of hand-blown glass with an inner lining of milk glass on which is painted, Home Sweet Home, with a picture of a house in a natural setting. Quite striking, although not as valuable, is the clear glass darner in the middle of the plate. The more common darning egg at the end of the century was the painted or enamelled egg with a silver handle as in the example third from the right.

Not all darners worked on the principle of placing the fabric to be repaired directly on the curved surface of the darner. Some darners, as in the silver one, second from the right, had a hole at the top over which the fabric was placed for repair. This allowed the needlewoman to weave in and out of the damaged fabric without coming into contact with the darner's surface, at the same time that the darner supported the fabric. The usual shape for glove darners appears in the silver darner at the extreme right. These sometimes served a double function as darner and needlecase. This particular example has a silver loop so that it can hang from a chatelaine or a ribbon around the neck.

Not all darners were so highly decorated. Indeed, the majority were probably of wood, either plain or enamel-painted with shaping and turning by the lathe adding the major decorative touch. The plain wood darner was in widespread use in the United States and is valued today as folk art for its clean lines and simplicity of design. The enamel-painted darner was equally popular, and examples of both are in plate 193.

The enamel-painted darner on the left with its multi-colour swirling design and the darner to its right, painted green enamel, are more common than the shaped wood darner to the right. The small, white enamel-painted darner, fourth from the left, was probably for a child.

The plastic darner in the centre of plate 193 adds an amusing touch in its attempt to be a darner for all occasions. Half the darner is blue with the note: 'for light material'. The other half is white 'for dark material'. The handle has a note saying 'for glove fingers' with an arrow pointing toward the end.

The darner on the extreme right is a typical plain wood darner common in the United States in the late nineteenth and early twentieth centuries. The three mushroom darners to its left are somewhat interesting. The one without the metal clamp is German and stores needles in its handle. The two with metal clamps are intended to hold the fabric securely in place as would an embroidery hoop.

Darners were comparatively cheap in the nineteenth and early twentieth centuries. In plain wood, japanned or in white enamel, darners cost about five

Plate 193: *Darners from left: 1, 2 and 4: Enamel-painted wood. Left darner 15 cm. high. 3: White-washed wood. 5: Blue and white plastic marked 'Hungerford Darn Aid' for light and dark fabric. 6: Wood mushroom. Handle holds needles. Marked 'Asbro, Germany'. 7–8: Wood mushrooms with metal clips to hold fabric. 9: Natural wood. All made for American market, c. 1900–1940.*

cents each. They are still in plentiful supply and are relatively cheap. The decorated darners bring a higher price, and those with precious metal parts even more. The most expensive are the art glass darners. One can only hope that they will not go the way of other glass objects which became so expensive that they brought a flood of reproductions on the market. The very mellow tone of old glass is, fortunately, difficult to reproduce, and a comparison of the old and new will often show the difference.

Not all darners were cheap even at the end of the nineteenth century. Sears, Roebuck and Co. advertised in 1897, for example, a darner with a white enamelled ball and a highly ornamented solid silver handle for one dollar and seventy-five cents. The detachable handle also served as a needlecase. Sears suggested that the darner was 'a very desirable present for an elderly lady or anyone who has such work to do'.

The decline of interest in plain sewing by younger women at the end of the nineteenth century could not have been more clearly stated. How different is this attitude of 1897 from that of the late twentieth century, when it seems to be the young, who seek out the best in the utilitarian domestic tools and objects of the past.

Notes

Introduction (pp. 15–17)

1 David Pye, *The Nature and Art of Workmanship*: 4.
2 Eric H. Robinson, 'Problems in the Mechanization and Organization of the Birmingham Jewelry and Silver Trades, 1760–1800', in Ian M. G. Quimby, ed., *Technological Innovation and the Decorative Arts*: 76–77.
3 Robinson, 'Problems in the Mechanization': 78.
4 Kenneth Roberts, *Tools for the Trades and Crafts*: 7–12.
5 Plate No. 87 in *R. Timmins & Sons Pattern Book* as reprinted in Roberts, *Tools for the Trades and Crafts*: 144.
6 Susan Burrows Swan, *Plain & Fancy: American Women and Their Needlework 1700–1850*: 12.

1 Fitted Needlework Boxes (pp. 19–43)

1 For an excellent discussion of the distinction between plain and fancy sewing as well as a penetrating social history of the needleworkers themselves, see Susan Burrows Swan, *Plain & Fancy: American Women and Their Needlework 1700–1850*: 18–41.
2 Lucretia P. Hale and Margaret E. White, *Three Hundred Decorative and Fancy Articles for Presents, Fairs, etc.*
3 As quoted in Geoffrey Warren, *A Stitch in Time: Victorian and Edwardian Needlecraft*: 3.
4 For a discussion of lever locks and their markings, see F. Lewis Hinckley, *A Directory of Antique Furniture*: 31.
5 Instructions on how to make workboxes out of old cigar boxes and the like are given in Mrs C. S. Jones and Henry T. Williams, *Household Elegancies*: 160–76.
6 Ralph Palmer, Chief Justice of Madras, ordered a nearly identical box made in ivory in 1828 as an engagement gift for his niece, Elizabeth Biddulph. See Mary Andere, *Old Needlework Boxes and Tools*: 31.
7 This description of Indian 'end-grain' mosaic technique is from George Watt, *Indian Art at Delhi*: 157.
8 Edward H. Pinto, *Treen and Other Wooden Bygones; an Encyclopaedia and Social History*: 300.
9 Honour Lumsden, 'Lord Byron's Friend', Letter to *Country Life* (June 7, 1979): 1814.
10 Yvonne Heckenbroch, *English and other Needlework: Tapestries and Textiles in the Irwin Untermyer Collection*: 39 and plate 74.

11 Polly Anne Earl, 'Craftsmen and Machines: The Nineteenth-Century Furniture Industry', in Ian M. G. Quimby, ed., *Technological Innovation and the Decorative Arts*: 307–329.

12 Shirley Spaulding Devoe, *English Papier-Mâché of the Georgian and Victorian Periods*: 81–88.

13 Richard B. Prosser, *Birmingham Inventors and Inventions*: 38–48.

14 Plate 148 of *R. Timmins & Sons Pattern Book* as reprinted in Kenneth C. Roberts, *Tools for the Trades and Crafts*.

15 'Decorative brasswork also appeared on . . . ladies' workboxes . . . and represents a vigorous branch of the Victorian vernacular style . . . that owed nothing to the handicraft revival or to the contemporary fashion for imitating antique prototypes.' John Gloag, 'Victorian Desk Furniture', *Connoisseur* (April, 1975): 276.

16 Nina Fletcher Little, *Neat and Tidy, Boxes and Their Contents Used in Early American Households*: 150–57.

2 *Sewing Cases and Chatelaines (pp. 44–57)*

1 Howard Ricketts, *Objects of Vertu*: 36–56.

2 Ricketts, *Objects of Vertu*, 19: 'The exact mixture of the metals needed to achieve these colours is given in *Secrets concernant les arts et métiers*, published in 1790.'

3 Camille Pagé, *La coutellerie depuis l'origine jusqu'a nos jours*: IV, 280.

4 Gabrielle Walker, 'The Sewing Companion', *Spinning Wheel* (Jan.–Feb., 1979): 9.

5 The Birmingham Directory of 1770 observed that toymakers 'are divided into several Branches, as the Gold and Silver Toy Maker. . . . The Tortoise Toy Maker makes a beautiful variety . . . as does also the Steel Toy Maker . . .' as quoted in Kenneth C. Roberts, *Tools for the Trades and Crafts*: 17.

6 Plate 148 of *R. Timmins & Sons Pattern Book* as reprinted in Roberts, *Tools for the Trades and Crafts*.

7 See the plate, 'Sewing Articles' in the 1904 Unger Brothers catalogue as reprinted in Dorothy T. Rainwater, ed., *Sterling Silver Holloware*.

8 See the expensive silver chatelaine novelties in the Marshall Field & Co., *1896 Illustrated Catalogue of Jewelry & European Fashions*: 262–71.

3 *Needles and Needlecases (pp. 58–79)*

1 *Prospectus of the Canfield Competitive Art-Needle-Work Exhibit*: 59.

2 Charles Singer *et al.*, eds., *The Late Nineteenth Century 1850–1900* in *A History of Technology* 5 vols.: V, 624.

3 *Clark's O.N.T. Book of Needlework*: 97.

4 From the description inside the wrapper.

5 Barbara and G. W. R. Ward, eds., *Silver in American Life*: 4.

6 Molly G. Proctor, *Victorian Canvas Work, Berlin Wool Work*: 7–17.

7 Jane Toller, *Prisoners-of-War Work 1756–1815*: 1–8.

8 Denis Szeszler, 'Is It Ivory?' *Antique Collecting* (Jan., 1980): 5–7.

9 Ian M. G. Quimby, ed., *Technological Innovation and the Decorative Arts*: 21–23.
10 Robert S. Woodbury, *Studies in the History of Machine Tools*: IV, 13–39.
11 H. Lee Pratt, 'Stanhopes: Miniature Peep-Eye Viewers', *The Antiques Journal* (April, 1980): 12–13.

4 *Thimbles and Thimble Cases (pp. 80–104)*

1 The discussion purposely omits porcelain thimbles because there is a question whether they were ever genuinely functional. For an excellent discussion of the porcelain thimble, see Edwin F. Holmes, *Thimbles*: 30–37.
2 The construction of metal thimbles could be a complex process. It varied by time and place as well as by the type of metal used.
3 Louis Carré, *A Guide to Old French Plate*: 190–91.
4 'The Origin of the Thimble', *The Dorcas Magazine* (Aug., 1884): 222.
5 See the illustration in Holmes, *Thimbles*: 87.
6 Rosa L. Goldenberg, *Antique Jewelry*: 54. *Trade Marks of the Jewelry and Kindred Trades*: 268–80.
7 Hugh McDougall of Brooklyn, for example, took out Letters Patent No. 247,384 on 20 September 1881 for a novel method of rolling the thimble blank which could also emboss the ornamentation in one operation.
8 Holmes, *Thimbles*: 85.
9 Horner's illustrations of his three-part thimble for his United States patent application are reproduced in Bertha Betensley, *52 Thimble Patents*: 55.
10 Sears was still selling these cheap solid silver thimbles as late as 1897 by which time they had dropped to twenty cents each. Sears, Roebuck and Co., *Consumers Guide No. 104*: 435.
11 'Origins of the Thimble', *The Dorcas Magazine* (Aug., 1884): 222.
12 American-manufactured thimbles of the late seventeenth and early eighteenth century were exceptions because American manufacturers could not compete with the enormous installed capacity for manufacturing thimbles in the Netherlands and in England at this time. From a communication from Mr. Holmes to the author.
13 Quoted in Elizabeth Galbraith Sickels, 'Thimblemakers in America', *Antiques* (Sept., 1967): 373.
14 Dorothy T. Rainwater, ed., *Sterling Silver Holloware*: 6–7. The individual states began to regulate the use of the sterling mark in 1894. *Trade Marks of the Jewelry and Kindred Trades*: 280.
15 The author is grateful to Mary Keyser for correcting the above text written on Simons Bros. Co. See the *Bulletin Thimble Collectors International* (July, 1979) and the *Trade Marks of the Jewelry and Kindred Trades*: 71 for illustrations of the Waite Thresher Co. thimble trademarks discussed above.
16 Letters Patent No. 247,384 dated 20 September 1881.
17 Apparently not all the large square trademarks were S in shape. Some were G in shape and had a smaller S instead of G for the smaller initials inside. See the different versions illustrated in *Collectors Circle Gazette* (Summer, 1977): 10.
18 The Webster trademark and a picture of some of the thimbles from the 1921–22

Webster catalogue are illustrated in the *Collectors Circle Gazette* (Summer, 1977): 10–11.

19 Betensley, *52 Thimble Patents*: 15.
20 The most complete account of 'thimble-rigging' is found in the chapter under that title in Holmes, *Thimbles*: 135–40.

5 *Scissors (pp. 105–119)*

1 G. I. H. Lloyd, *The Cutlery Trades*: 37–57.
2 For illustrations of the different types of blades and handles, see Joseph B. Himsworth, *The Story of Cutlery*: 154–7.
3 J. Robert Wiss, *A Story of Shears and Scissors 1848–1948*.
4 Lloyd, *The Cutlery Trades,*: 354–65.
5 Lloyd, *The Cutlery Trades*: 359.
6 Himsworth, *The Story of Cutlery*: 57–82.
7 Himsworth, *The Story of Cutlery*: 189–91.
8 Lloyd, *The Cutlery Trades*: 392–5.
9 'Shears and Scissors Ninety Percent Hand-Made', *Scientific American* (June, 1927): 393.
10 Lloyd, *The Cutlery Trades*: 38–9; 186.
11 Himsworth, *The Story of Cutlery*: 182–4.
12 Thérèse de Dillmont, *Encyclopedia of Needlework*. New ed., rev. and enlarged: 2.

6 *Tape-measures, Emeries and Waxers (pp. 120–139)*

1 P. H. Sydenham, *Measuring Instruments: Tools of Knowledge and Control*: 180–95.
2 Edward H. and Eva R. Pinto, *Tunbridge and Scottish Souvenir Woodware*: 47–50.
3 See the discussion of Indian marquetry workboxes in Chapter One.
4 Pinto, *Tunbridge Woodware*: 28–9; 51.
5 Molly G. Proctor, *Victorian Canvas Work, Berlin Wool Work*: 7–26.
6 Pinto, *Tunbridge Woodware*: 51–2.
7 Edward Pinto, *Treen and Other Wooden Bygones; an Encyclopedia and Social History*: 194–6.
8 Ian T. Henderson, *Pictorial Souvenirs of Britain*: 147–54.
9 Carl W. Dreppard, *The Primer of American Antiques*: 172.
10 Ian M. G. Quimby, *Technological Innovation and the Decorative Arts*: 21–3.

7 *Pins and Pincushions (pp. 140–158)*

1 Richardson Wright, *Hawkers and Walkers in Early America*: 45–6.
2 Eleanor D. Longman and Sophia Loch, *Pins and Pincushions*: 21.

3 Charles T. Singer *et al.*, eds., *The Late Nineteenth Century, 1850–1900*; Vol. V in *A History of Technology.* 5 vols.: V, 624.

4 Mrs R. E. Head, 'The Work Table: Some Old-Fashioned Pincushions', *The Queen, the Lady's Newspaper* (March 7, 1903): 368–9.

5 John Q. Reed and Eliza M. Lavin, *Needle and Brush: Useful and Decorative*: 198.

6 Reed and Lavin, *Needle and Brush*: 200.

7 Longman, *Pins and Pincushions*: 185.

8 Lillian Baker Carlisle, 'Beadwork Whimsies', *Spinning Wheel* (Sept., 1964): 8–9; Georgiana Brown Harbeson, *American Needlework*: 10–19.

9 Elizabeth Aldridge, 'Nineteenth-Century Pincushions', *Antique Collecting* (Nov., 1975): 15–17.

8 *Thread Containers (pp. 159–173)*

1 Edward Pinto, *Treen and Other Wooden Bygones; an Encyclopedia and Social History*: 300–301.

2 Graham Shearing, 'Chinese Mother-of-Pearl Card Counters', *Antique Collector* (May, 1977): 90–91.

3 Edward H. and Eva R. Pinto, *Tunbridge and Scottish Souvenir Woodware*: 90–107.

4 Pinto, *Tunbridge Woodware*: 108–16.

5 Pinto, *Tunbridge Woodware*: 117.

6 Pinto, *Tunbridge Woodware*: 119.

9 *Needlework Clamps (pp. 174–188)*

1 Gabrielle Walker, 'Needlewoman's Clamp', *Art & Antiques Weekly* (June 5, 1976): 26–8.

2 Edward Pinto, *Treen and Other Wooden Bygones; an Encyclopedia and Social History*: 324.

3 Plate 87 of *R. Timmins & Sons Pattern Book* as reprinted in Kenneth C. Roberts, *Tools for the Trades and Crafts*: 144.

4 *Home Decorative Work* (complied from *The Housekeeper*): 319–23.

5 *Annual Report of the Commissioner of Patents*: 69.

6 Manton Copeland, 'Sewing Birds Viewed by a Naturalist', *Old-Time New England. The Bulletin of the Society for the Preservation of New England Antiquities* (April, 1950): 191–7.

7 Copeland, 'Sewing Birds': 196.

10 *Handwork Tools (pp. 189–217)*

1 Sophia Frances A. Caulfeild and Blanche C. Saward, *The Dictionary of Needlework; An Encyclopaedia of Artistic, Plain and Fancy Needlework*, 2 vols.: I, 470–71.

2 Lewis F. Day and Mary Buckle, *Art in Needlework; a Book about Embroidery*: 38–46.

3 Miss A. Lampert, *The Hand-Book of Needlework*: 93.

4 Thérèse de Dillmont, *Encyclopedia of Needlework*, new ed., rev. and enlarged: 152.

5 Owen Evan-Thomas, *Domestic Utensils of Wood, XVI to XIX Centuries*: 130–3; Edward Pinto, *Treen and Other Wooden Bygones; an Encyclopaedia and Social History*: 305–8.

6 Dillmont, *Encyclopedia of Needlework*: 486–7.

7 Arlene Zeger Wiczyk, ed., *Godey's Lady's Book*: 114.

8 Dillmont, *Encyclopedia of Needlework*: 410.

9 Caulfeild, *Dictionary of Needlework*: 316.

10 Jeffery Hopewell, *Pillow Lace and Bobbins*: 15–32; Pinto, *Treen*: 310–12.

11 Plain Sewing and Handwork Gadgets (pp. 218–225)

1 Miss Florence Hartley, *The Ladies' Hand Book of Fancy Ornamental Work*: 155.

2 Dorothy T. Rainwater, ed., *Sterling Silver Holloware*: Plate on 'Sewing Articles' in the reprinted 1904 Unger Brothers catalogue.

3 Edward Pinto, *Treen and Other Wooden Bygones; an Encyclopedia and Social History*: 301.

Bibliography

Aldridge, Elizabeth, 'Nineteenth-Century Pincushions'. *Antique Collecting* (Nov., 1975): 15–17.

D'Allemagne, Henry René, *Les Accessoires du Costume et du Mobilier*. Paris: J. Schemit, 1928. Reprinted New York: Hacker Art Books, 1970.

D'Allemagne, Henry René, *Decorative Antique Ironwork*. Paris: J. Schemit, 1924. Reprinted New York: Dover Pub., 1968.

Andere, Mary, *Old Needlework Boxes and Tools*. Newton Abbot: David and Charles, 1971.

Annual Report of the Commissioner of Patents. Washington, D.C., 1854.

Betensley, Bertha, *52 Thimble Patents*. Westville, Indiana: B. Betensley, 1980.

Bhavnani, Enakshi, *Decorative Designs and Craftsmanship of India*. Bombay: D. B. Taraporevala and Sons, 1969.

Bond, Sylvia, *History of Sewing Tools*. London: Embroiderers' Guild, 1967.

Buist, J. S., 'Mauchline Ware'. *Connoisseur* (Aug., 1973): 269–73.

Bulletin Thimble Collectors International (July, 1979).

Campbell, Metzger & Jacobson, *Catalogue Art Needlework Materials and Accessories*. New York: Campbell, Metzger & Jacobson, 1921.

Carlisle, Lillian Baker, 'Beadwork Whimsies'. *Spinning Wheel* (Sept., 1964): 8–9.

Carré, Louis, *A Guide to Old French Plate*. London: Chapman & Hall Ltd, 1931.

Caulfeild, Sophia Frances A. and Blanche C. Saward, *The Dictionary of Needlework; An Encyclopaedia of Artistic, Plain and Fancy Needlework*. 2 vols. London: L. Upcott Gill, 1882. Reprinted New York: Dover Pub., 1972.

Clark's O.N.T. Book of Needlework. Newark, New Jersey: Clark Thread Company, 1916.

Colby, Averil, *Pincushion*. New York: Charles Scribner's Sons, 1975.

Collectors Circle Gazette (Summer, 1977).

Copeland, Manton, 'Sewing Birds Viewed by a Naturalist'. *Old-Time New England. The Bulletin of the Society for the Preservation of New England Antiquities* (April, 1950): 191–9.

Day, Lewis F. and Mary Buckle, *Art in Needlework; a Book about Embroidery*. London: B. T. Batsford, 1900.

Devoe, Shirley Spaulding, *English Papier-Mâché of the Georgian and Victorian Periods*. Middleton, Conn.: Wesleyan University Press, 1971.

de Dillmont, Thérèse, *Encyclopedia of Needlework*. New ed., rev. and enlarged. Mulhouse, France: DMC Library, 1890.

Dreppard, Carl W. *The Primer of American Antiques*. New York: Doubleday, Doran & Co., Inc., 1945.

Earl, Polly Anne, 'Craftsmen and Machines: The Nineteenth-Century Furniture Industry', in Ian M. G. Quimby, ed., *Technological Innovation and the Decorative Arts*. Charlottesville, Va.: University of Virginia Press, 1974.

Evan-Thomas, Owen, *Domestic Utensils of Wood, XVI to XIX Centuries*. London: Owen Evan-Thomas Ltd, 1932.

Field, June, *Collecting Georgian and Victorian Crafts*. New York: Charles Scribner's Sons, 1973.

Fresco-Corbu, Roger, 'An Eye for Needle-Cases'. *Art & Antiques Weekly* (Jan. 28, 1978): 14–17.

Fresco-Corbu, Roger, 'Pincushions of the Past'. *Art & Antiques Weekly* (July 2, 1977): 22–5.

Gloag, John, 'Victorian Desk Furniture'. *Connoisseur* (April, 1975): 276.

Goldenberg, Rosa L., *Antique Jewelry*. New York: Crown Pubs., Inc., 1976.

Groves, Sylvia, *The History of Needlework Tools and Accessories*. Newton Abbot: David and Charles, 1973.

Hale, Lucretia P. and Margaret E. White, *Three Hundred Decorative and Fancy Articles for Presents, Fairs, etc.* Boston: S. W. Tilton & Co., 1885.

Hanley, Hope, *Needlepoint in America*. New York: Weathervane Books, 1979.

Harbeson, Georgiana Brown, *American Needlework; the History of Decorative Stitchery and Embroidery from the Late 16th to the 20th Century*. New York: Bonanza Books, 1938.

Hartley, Miss Florence, *The Ladies' Hand Book of Fancy Ornamental Work*. Philadelphia: G. G. Evans, Pub., 1859.

Head, Mrs R. E., 'The Work Table: Some Old-Fashioned Pincushions'. *The Queen, The Lady's Newspaper* (March 7, 1903): 368–9.

Heckenbroch, Yvonne, *English and other Needlework: Tapestries and Textiles in the Irwin Untermyer Collection*. Cambridge, Mass.: Harvard University Press, 1960.

Henderson, Ian T., *Pictorial Souvenirs of Britain*. Newton Abbot: David and Charles, 1974.

Himsworth, Joseph Beeston, *The Story of Cutlery*. London: Ernest Benn, 1953.

Hinckley, F. Lewis, *A Directory of Antique Furniture*. New York: Bonanza Books, 1953.

Holmes, Edwin F., *Thimbles*. Dublin: Gill and Macmillan Ltd, 1976.

Home Decorative Work (Compiled from *The Housekeeper*). Minneapolis: Buckeye Pub. Co., 1891.

Hopewell, Jeffery, *Pillow Lace and Bobbins*. Aylesbury, Bucks: Shire Pubs., Ltd, 1977.

Hughes, Therle, *Edwardiana for Collectors*. London: G. Bell and Sons, 1977.

Hughes, Therle, *English Domestic Needlework 1660–1860*. New York: The Macmillan Co., 1961.

Jewell, Brian, *Veteran Sewing Machines: A Collector's Guide*. Newton Abbot: David and Charles, 1975.

Johnson, Eleanor, *Needlework Tools*. Aylesbury, Bucks: Shire Pubs., Ltd, 1978.

Jones, Mrs C. S. and Henry T. Williams, *Household Elegancies*. New York: Henry T. Williams, Pub., 1875.

Klamkin, Marian, *The Collector's Book of Boxes*. Newton Abbot: David and Charles, 1972.

Kresge's Katalog of 5c & 10c Merchandise. Detroit: S. S. Kresge Co., 1913. Reprinted New York: Random House, 1975.

Lampert, Miss A., *The Hand-Book of Needlework*. New York: Wiley & Putnam, 1842.

Little, Nina Fletcher, *Neat and Tidy, Boxes and Their Contents Used in Early American Households*. New York: E. P. Dutton, 1980.

Lloyd, Godfrey Isaac Howard, *The Cutlery Trades. An Historical Essay in the*

Economics of Small-Scale Production. London: Longman's Green, and Co., 1913.

Longman, Eleanor D. and Sophia Loch, *Pins and Pincushions*. London: Longmans, Green, and Co., 1911.

Lumsden, Honour, 'Lord Byron's Friend'. Letter to *Country Life* (June 7, 1979): 1814.

Lundquist, Myrtle, *The Book of a Thousand Thimbles*. Des Moines, Iowa: Wallace-Homestead Co., 1970.

Lundquist, Myrtle, *Thimble Americana and Contemporary Collectibles*. Des Moines, Iowa: Wallace-Homestead Co., 1981.

Lundquist, Myrtle, *Thimble Treasury*. Des Moines, Iowa: Wallace-Homestead Co., 1975.

Maines, Rachel, *The Tools of the Workbasket: Needlework Technology Since 1850*. Pittsburg: Center for the History of American Needlework, 1977.

Marshall Field & Co., *1896 Illustrated Catalogue of Jewelry & European Fashions*. Chicago: Marshall Field & Co., 1896. Reprinted Chicago: Follett Pub. Co., 1970.

McClinton, Katharine M., *The Complete Book of Small Antiques Collecting*. New York: Coward-McCann, Inc., 1965.

Montgomery Ward and Co., *Catalogue and Buyers Guide, Fall & Winter, 1894–95, no. 56*. Chicago: Montgomery Ward and Co., 1894. Reprinted Chicago: Follett Pub. Co., 1970.

Morris, Barbara, *Victorian Embroidery*. New York: T. Nelson & Sons, 1962.

Needlework and Allied Crafts in Guildford Museum. Guildford: Guildford Corp., 1972.

'The Origin of the Thimble'. *The Dorcas Magazine* (Aug., 1884).

Pagé, Camille, *La coutellerie depuis l'origine jusqu'a nos jours*. 6 vols. Chatellerault: H. Rivière, 1896.

Pearce, Molly, 'Needlework Tools Made by Joseph Rodgers & Sons'. *Antique Collecting* (May, 1979): 25–7.

Pinto, Edward H., *Treen and Other Wooden Bygones; an Encyclopedia and Social History*. London: G. Bell and Sons, 1969.

Pinto, Edward H., *Treen or Small Woodware Through the Ages*. London: B. T. Batsford Ltd, 1949.

Pinto, Edward H. and Eva R., *Tunbridge and Scottish Souvenir Woodware*. London: G. Bell and Sons, 1970.

Pratt, H. Lee, 'Stanhopes: Miniature Peep-Eye Viewers'. *The Antiques Journal* (April, 1980): 12–13.

Proctor, Molly G., *Victorian Canvas Work, Berlin Wool Work*. London: B. T. Batsford Ltd, 1972.

Prospectus of the Canfield Competitive Art-Needle-Work Exhibit. New York: Canfield Rubber Co., 1887.

Prosser, Richard B., *Birmingham Inventors and Inventions*. Birmingham: The *Journal* printing works, 1881. Reprinted London: Redwood Press Ltd, 1970.

Pye, David, *The Nature and Art of Workmanship*. Cambridge: At the University Press, 1968.

Quimby, Ian M. G., ed., *Material Culture and the Study of American Life*. New York: W. W. Norton & Co., 1978.

Quimby, Ian M. G., ed., *Technological Innovation and the Decorative Arts*. Charlottesville, Va.: University of Virginia Press, 1974.

Rainwater, Dorothy T., *Encyclopedia of American Silver Manufacturers*. New York: Crown Pubs., Inc., 1975.

Rainwater, Dorothy T., ed., *Sterling Silver Holloware: Gorham Manufacturing Co., 1888; Gorham Martelé, 1900; and Unger Brothers, 1904*. Des Moines, Iowa: Wallace-Homestead Co., 1973.

Rath, Jo Anne, *Antique and Unusual Thimbles*. New York: A. S. Barnes and Co., 1979.

Reed, John Q. and Eliza M. Lavin, *Needle and Brush: Useful and Decorative*. New York: Butterick Pub. Co., 1889.

Ricketts, Howard, *Objects of Vertu*. London: Barrie and Jenkins Ltd, 1971.

Roberts, Kenneth C., *Tools for the Trades and Crafts: An Eighteenth-Century Pattern Book, R. Timmins & Sons, Birmingham*. Fitzwilliam, New Hampshire: Old Time Printing, 1976.

Robinson, Eric H., 'Problems in the Mechanization and Organization of the Birmingham Jewelry and Silver Trades, 1760–1800', in Ian M. G. Quimby, ed., *Technological Innovation and the Decorative Arts*. Charlottesville, Va.: University of Virginia Press, 1974.

Romaine, Lawrence, *A Guide to American Trade Catalogs 1744–1900*. New York: R. R. Bowker Co., 1960.

Schiffer, Margaret, 'Needlework Accessories'. *Antiques* (Sept., 1962): 282–3.

Sears, Roebuck and Co., *Consumers Guide No. 104*. Chicago: Sears, Roebuck and Co., 1897. Reprinted New York: Chelsea House Pubs., 1968.

Shaffer, Sandra C., 'Sewing Tools in the Collection of Colonial Williamsburg'. *Antiques* (Aug., 1973): 233–40.

Shearing, Graham, 'Chinese Mother-of-Pearl Card Counters'. *Antique Collector* (May, 1977): 90–91.

'Shears and Scissors Ninety Percent Hand-Made'. *Scientific American* (June, 1927): 393.

Sickels, Elizabeth Galbraith, 'Thimblemakers in America'. *Antiques* (Sept., 1967): 372–3.

Singer, Charles T., *et al.*, eds., *The Industrial Revolution, 1750–1850*. Vol. IV; *The Late Nineteenth Century, 1850–1900*. Vol. V in *A History of Technology*. 5 vols. Oxford: Clarendon Press, 1954–8.

Swan, Susan Burrows, 'Collecting Sewing Implements'. *Early American Life* (June, 1979): 26–30.

Swan, Susan Burrows, *Plain & Fancy: American Women and Their Needlework 1700–1850*. New York: Holt, Rinehart and Winston, 1977.

Sydenham, P. H., *Measuring Instruments: Tools of Knowledge and Control*. Stevenage, U.K.: Peter Peregrinus Ltd, 1979.

Szeszler, Denis, 'Is It Ivory?' *Antique Collecting* (Jan., 1980): 5–7.

Toller, Jane, *Prisoners-of-War Work 1756–1815*. Cambridge: Golden Head Press, 1965.

Trade Marks of the Jewelry and Kindred Trades. New York: The Jewelers Circular Publishing Co., 3rd ed., 1915.

Walker, Gabrielle, 'Needlewoman's Clamp'. *Art & Antiques Weekly* (June 5, 1976): 26–8.

Walker, Gabrielle, 'The Sewing Companion'. *Spinning Wheel* (Jan.–Feb., 1979): 8–10.

Ward, Barbara and G. W. R., eds., *Silver in American Life*. Boston: D. R. Godine, Pub., 1979.

Warren, Geoffrey, *A Stitch in Time: Victorian and Edwardian Needlecraft*. Newton Abbot: David and Charles, 1976.

Watt, George, *Indian Art at Delhi*. Calcutta: Superintendent of Government Printing, n.d.

Whiting, Gertrude, *Tools and Toys of Stitchery*. New York: Columbia University Press, 1928. Reprinted New York: Dover Pub., 1971.

Wiczyk, Arlene Zeger, ed., *Godey's Lady's Book*. New York: Arco Pub. Co., Inc., 1972.

Wiss, J. Robert, *A Story of Shears and Scissors 1848–1948*. Newark, New Jersey: Wiss, 1948.

Woodbury, Robert S., *Studies in the History of Machine Tools*. Cambridge, Mass.: Massachusetts Institute of Technology Press, 1972.

Wright, Richardson, *Hawkers and Walkers in Early America*. Philadephia: J. B. Lippincott Co., 1927.

Zupko, Ronald Edward, *British Weights & Measures*. Madison, Wisconsin: The University of Wisconsin Press, 1977.

Index